THE
CAKE AND
THE RAIN

Jimmy Webb with his Shelby Cobra 427 Super Snake. *(Courtesy of Henry Diltz)*

THE
CAKE AND
THE RAIN

JIMMY
WEBB

ST. MARTIN'S PRESS ❧ NEW YORK

To Laura

THE CAKE AND THE RAIN. Copyright 2017 by Jimmy Webb. All rights reserved. Printed in the United States of America. For information, address St. Martin's Press, 175 Fifth Avenue, New York, N.Y. 10010.

www.stmartins.com

Designed by Steven Seighman

The Library of Congress Cataloging-in-Publication Data is available upon request.

ISBN 978-1-250-05841-6 (hardcover)
ISBN 978-1-250-15094-3 (signed edition)
ISBN 978-1-4668-6257-9 (e-book)

Our books may be purchased in bulk for promotional, educational, or business use. Please contact your local bookseller or the Macmillan Corporate and Premium Sales Department at 1-800-221-7945, extension 5442, or by e-mail at MacmillanSpecial-Markets@macmillan.com.

First Edition: April 2017

10 9 8 7 6 5 4 3 2 1

My face looks like a wedding-cake left out in the rain.

—W. H. AUDEN

Marquee at Desert Inn, Las Vegas. *(Courtesy of Janice Linnens)*

CHAPTER ONE

They say a man can't love a material thing
With aluminum skin and a cast iron soul
But they never heard your engine sing
Ah, there's peace in losing control . . .
—JLW, "Too Young to Die," 1993

1969

"So let me get this straight," I said into the telephone. "You have a new Corvette for me?"

"That's right, Mr. Webb. We owe you three brand-new Corvettes for the work you did with Mr. Campbell."

"So this would be my second Corvette and . . ."

"And, we would owe you one more. You could get the four-hundred-fifty cubic-inch option next year. That's a lot of car."

"Wow, that's far out!"

I had done some work with Glen Campbell on a commercial earlier in the year. We had already collaborated on a top-twenty record, "By the Time I Get to Phoenix," but had met only once, when we shook hands at the Grammys. When I had walked into Armin Steiner's Sound Recorders in Hollywood, Glen looked up from tuning his guitar and I extended my hand.

"Hi, Glen! I'm Jimmy!" I blurted as I approached television's familiar coiffed and blue-jeaned figure. He scanned my skin-and-bones frame, my leather jacket, and my hair hanging down to my shoulders.

"When ya gonna get a haircut?" he asked.

Writing hit songs was so damn easy I fantasized I could write one whenever I wanted or needed to. My songs dominated easy-listening pop radio. My manager was Sandy Gallin, who also handled Cher and the Osmond Brothers. I was one of the first guys since Burt Bacharach and Hal David to be famous for writing songs. I wasn't a Beatle. I wasn't a bandleader or an arranger. And I was definitely not a performer. I used to joke around with other songwriters that they had to be very careful and not sing a demo too well. Great singers loved to have a terrible demo that needed their particular brand of refinement.

I lived in a vintage "Valleywood" mansion that movie star Phil Harris had built for his screen darling, Alice Faye, in the 1930s. It housed two grand pianos and a handmade billiard table with my name inscribed on it. On my front porch, I stood at the top of a hill that crowned six acres of pools, gardens, and waterfalls rambling down to the bottom of a wooded hill to a quaintly wrought stable and corral. Huge, century-old white oak trees intertwined their canopies on the hillside, inspiring a pet name for the estate: Campo de Encino (Fort of the White Oaks).

In my living room I erected a temple to the idols of my profession. Artist Jeffrey Speeth, who was known to ride with the Hells Angels, had delicately torched two stained glass panels, each twenty feet wide by eight and a half feet high. On the right panel were Joni Mitchell, Art Garfunkel, Paul Simon, and Bob Dylan. To the left was George Harrison, John Lennon, and Elvis Presley, each traced with thousands of intricately shaped stained glass ellipses. Elvis stood tall—a colossus in antique purple and red glass. Joni, a golden angel, rendered in sunny yellow and clear. In the same room was a pipe organ that stretched floor to ceiling, much bigger than the one Captain Nemo played in *20,000 Leagues Under the Sea*. Much bigger. In addition to my two grand pianos, there was a two-manual German harpsichord. My whole house was wired as a recording studio.

The glowing room was a glimpse of rock 'n' roll heaven . . . would I ever get there? Perhaps not. And perhaps that's the reason I went for the fast cars instead of fast money. I was twenty-three years old. Life beyond the age of thirty was unimaginable.

By writing songs for Glen Campbell, Mr. Sinatra, Liza Minnelli, and others, I had opened myself up to a left cross from snobby journalists and other elitists. Some said I was "middle of the road," "represented the establishment," and all that left-wing folkie exclusivity that doesn't buy a stick of gum in the world of music today.

The truth is I was a heavy pot smoker, a sexual adventurer, and a hopelessly liberal Democrat who hated the war in Vietnam. I had some redeeming qualities: Aside from the occasional beer, I didn't drink or smoke tobacco. I was lauded as "The Cole Porter of the Sixties" or—even worse—as "Pop Music's Mozart!" in a critical press more than slightly intimidated by the proliferation of loud rock bands. Journalists and mature people all over the country were encouraged by the fact that I was a young man who saw things their way. I wrote 'em the way they used to write 'em. Meanwhile, just like every other kid, my favorite bands were The Beatles and the Stones.

That summer, I threw my suitcase into the trunk of my brand-new, sleek, sharklike silver Corvette 427 and drove out through San Bernardino and the Inland Empire to Route 390 going north. I opened her up at close to one hundred miles an hour, heading for Las Vegas, where I was appearing with "the hardest-working little girl in show business," Connie Stevens. After a sudden divorce from crooner Eddie Fisher, she was remounting her career with a show at Wilbur Clark's Desert Inn, which had just recently been purchased by Howard Hughes. He bought the hotel and casino after arguing with a manager over extending his reservation. He now occupied the blacked-out top two of the tower's nine floors.

On the drive, I was steaming over an item I had read in the *New Musical Express* on my last trip to London: "Jim Webb is back in town, with his orchestra or whatever," the paper sneered. Who was I? Percy Faith? And who was "Jim Webb" anyway? The same London publication groused that whoever had "changed" my name to "Jimmy" was an asshole. My name is Jimmy Webb on my birth certificate. Upon moving to Hollywood and being informed that "Jimmy" was not an especially cool name and would have to be changed, I had fired that particular manager.

Perhaps someone who was more concerned about dropping their left for a bunch of Donny Osmond and John Denver haters might have thought twice about baiting the bear with an appearance at a casino, but I met Connie and she charmed me without any particular effort. I knew her mostly from 1963's *Palm Springs Weekend*, in which she played the good girl. It was no act. With my guitarist Fred Tackett—a true hippie—I worked up a few songs for Connie and me to perform.

I idled through the gate of the Desert Inn, one of Vegas's original five casinos. In five-foot-tall letters, the marquee said CONNIE STEVENS. Underneath, it said JIMMY WEBB. Connie had insisted on me having equal billing.

There was a message from Connie at the front desk to meet her in the Crystal Room to rehearse our duet of a song called "Didn't We?"

The Crystal Room was a modest venue; our capacity was 450 for dinner and the stage itself. Frank Sinatra, Tony Bennett, Noël Coward, Bobby Darin, and thousands of others had performed on that stage. I was one large nerve as I hesitantly touched the keys on the grand piano with Connie sitting beside me on the bench, relaxed and graceful, the pretty girl known in the business as "Dollface." We parted with a pact to meet again later at the pool so I could meet her and Eddie Fisher's two little girls: Joely, two years, and Tricia, one.

The next day Freddy and his very pregnant lady Patricia checked in after their drive from L.A., and the three of us went out to the hotel's trademark figure-eight-shaped pool. Freddy and I detuned a couple of gut-string acoustic guitars to an open D, or what we called a "Joni Mitchell tuning." The hardened gambler crowd sat under umbrellas, drinking and smoking their cigars, waiting for it to get dark, as the two long-haired kids beat the crap out of guitars and harmonized to the heavens, "And he cries and he cries, there's an ocean in his eyes . . ." All the while, Patricia, pretty and burstingly pregnant in a flowing white dress, danced improvisational free-form on the grass.

When Connie came down with her girls, she took us in stride. We pitched camp beside the large pool: water bottles, beers, babies, guitars, long hair, cassette players, and all. Connie took both of her children into the water to teach them to swim. Every eye at the pool was on Connie. Folks asked for her autograph or a photo; there were no private pools at the Desert Inn. The stars were expected to entertain.

That night I took Connie out for a ride in my Corvette. We went out to the highway, Nevada's autobahn, and I let it fly. We laughed like hell as the warm summer wind caught in our hair and the mile markers rushed past. I got to know her a little at the hotel bar after; I had a beer and she had a glass of water. It had been quite a rough time for her during the divorce and she paled a little talking about it. She said she was doing a very physical show with a lot of dancing so she had to get to bed early. We said our good-nights. A hallmark of a lady, she had two little girls and a broken marriage and she was hitting the boards and hoofing to get her life on track. "The hardest-working little girl in show business" wasn't just a release from some press agent.

On opening night, Freddy and I went out and joined Ray Noble and His Orchestra. We performed for twenty minutes with Connie, then she invited me back on stage as part of her finale. We sang

"Didn't We?" to exceptional howls of approval from the packed audience. After our third curtain call, I said to Connie in amazement, "What are these people making such a fuss about?"

"People love a fresh face!" She laughed.

We were poolside virtually every day after that and performing at night, though I still got around some. I met Paul Anka at his condo one afternoon and we talked about songwriting and Vegas. He looked at me with the knowing smirk of a seasoned pro surveying a helpless greenhorn.

"Hey, listen," he said. "After your second show tonight come over and meet me and some of the guys at the Sands Health Club."

I raised an eyebrow. A health club that stayed open until one in the morning?

After my show, I went over to the venerable Sands in my silver shark and parked in the back as I had been instructed. Nothing. Pitch black. Suddenly a crack of light as a door opened directly on the parking lot.

"Pssst. Hey Jim!" It was Anka, silhouetted in the doorway.

I locked up my ride and went into the light. I was inside the Men's Health Club at the Sands. All the heavies were in there—the Righteous Brothers, Vic Damone, Redd Foxx. Some were leaving, some arriving, some were in towels, some even had ladies. This was the ex-officio men's club for entertainers in Vegas, and it really didn't get rolling until two or three in the morning.

After a steam and some time in a Jacuzzi, I found out that the ladies too were an optional accessory. You could have it any way you wanted it in Vegas. I might even have gotten around to a lady or two except for the fact that I started to smoke a joint in the hot tub. There was a full-blown panic when the first cloud of smoke went up. The Everly Brothers almost trampled the Righteous Brothers getting out of the place. The hookers were close behind.

There was drug use in Vegas in those days, but nobody flashed it around, and nobody talked about it for one simple reason: It could cost you your job.

Our booking finished after a few weeks with the usual mixture of sadness, premature nostalgia, and relief. When it was over I took my whole crew, including Connie, on a private jet to Oklahoma City for the Stars and Stripes Show, a local extravaganza. I met Tom Stafford, who had played "Up, Up and Away" on his way around the moon in *Apollo 10*. I played "MacArthur Park" with the Oklahoma City Symphony and twenty thousand people cheered their approval. By the time we got back to Los Angeles, Caesars Palace had offered me an eight-week engagement—forty thousand dollars, three times a year. Management wanted me to play an instrumental version of "MacArthur Park" on a white piano once a night "like Liberace." They didn't want any singing; singing would pay less.

I turned the deal down. I wanted to be part of the world that my peers inhabited. The world I'd experienced at the Monterey Pop Festival, playing with Johnny Rivers and the Wrecking Crew. Real rock 'n' roll and higher-consciousness types did not play Vegas in 1969. I faced a significant divergence in life's river.

Past

In Oklahoma before the Second World War, my two sets of grandparents lived on opposite sides of the North Fork of the Cimarron River, a tributary of the sprawling Red River that crosses a third of the United States. In plain language, our part of it was a creek; in the rainy season you could squint your eyes up close and it looked a little bit like a river, even if one of somewhat questionable character. Most months of the year it was merely a musical trickle as it looped in gentle arcs through groves of silver-leafed cottonwoods, its bed paved with a mosaic of round river rocks.

On one side of the river stood the relatively prosperous farm of Joe Killingsworth, who had his own gravity gas pump out by the garage to fill the tank of his Pontiac. On the other side was the Sunshine Ranch where Charlie Webb sharecropped, and where his God-fearing wife, Myrtle, saved copies of the *Sayre Headlight-Journal* and used them to line the unfinished walls of their rough shack, to hold at bay the keening wind of deep winter.

Robert Webb, my dad, was a tall, strapping teen and had a

younger sister, Barbara, who was pretty enough to be a marquee idol. The Webb family contrasted in an austere way to the great clan of the Killingsworths, with their two handsome sons, Joe Verne and Don, and two comely daughters, Ann and Joy, who were long of legs, white of teeth, and rosy of lips and cheeks. Ann, a vivacious brunette; Joy, the younger, an athletic blonde and varsity basketball player.

My grandpa Charlie Webb was an odd duck on any pond. He was a rather short man with red hair and a stout build. His pink face was of the round and cheerful variety that belied a hard-as-nails undercoat. His secret armor seemed to insulate him in a satisfactory way from the inevitable, outrageous slings and arrows of fortune. Behind his back, folks called him "The Dutchman," though privately he claimed—with some pride—an Irish heritage. Down in Southwest Oklahoma "Dutchman" was an acceptable sobriquet for any oddball. For one thing, Grandpa Charlie didn't go to church like the rest. He would calmly sit on his porch at the Sunshine Ranch on a Sunday morning smoking snuff out of a briar pipe—a uniquely vile habit—and waving to each family as they passed, seemingly to bless them in their ignorance. The smoked snuff hung around him like a steel blue curtain, impenetrable and noxious as mustard gas.

Myrtle Webb was of the Nazarene sect, who went in for the occasional ecstatic roll on the floor as part of worship, speaking in tongues. Charlie regarded this practice with some unease. However, on one occasion "The Woman," as he called her, was able to persuade him to leave his pipe on the porch and go down to the First Nazarene. He discovered to his great mortification that the proceedings that day had been laid on specifically for his benefit. Dozens were praying out loud for "poor old Charlie" to come back into the fold. Folks rolled on the floor and recited incantations in indecipherable tongues. Charlie got as red as a Texas tomato and walked out of the Church of the Nazarene vowing never, ever to return.

Joe Killingsworth, who we called Granddaddy to differentiate him from Grandpa Charlie, was another sort of iconoclast. He seemed to embrace the theory that words were a precious and irreplaceable resource that were best conserved, like money or gasoline or cottonseed. He said little to nothing as he worked his six hundred acres and raised his ample family. In summer he would wear a short-sleeved shirt with a clean blue tie and a dress straw hat, which was removed from his head at the doorway of the Sweetwater First Baptist Church every Sunday.

He is still, obscured by all these years, somewhat of a cipher, this tireless farming machine with his code of unremitting dawn-to-dusk labor. His reticence went beyond that of the usual quiet sort of country fellow and crossed over into a philosophy of life, with his conviction, never articulated, that life was filled with way too much talk, and talk was a frivolous and wasteful thing. A Marcus Aurelius of the plains, he was rear guard to his wife, Maggie, or "Grandmother." She was a neurotic and nervous soul who fretted her way through the hardships of life on the prairie, worrying at every turn of fortune, good or bad. Joe followed silent and watchful.

Joe Killingsworth would more than likely have kept to himself if not for certain occasions of dire need or crisis when he found it necessary to call on Charlie Webb. For despite the poverty of the Webbs, Charlie, as many folks in Beckham County knew and discussed in hushed tones, was rumored to be the seventh son of a seventh son and he had *powers*. Some of these claims seemed fanciful but certainly not the ability to douse or as some said, to "witch water."

It is a fact that Joe Killingsworth paid Charlie a visit one drought-plagued summer when my father was a teenager. Proverbial hat in hand, Joe asked Charlie if he would "witch him a well." It must have been a dry spell indeed to send Granddaddy on his errand across the North Fork to the Sunshine Ranch.

My father remembers vividly the early morning that Charlie crossed the creek and walked onto the lower forty of Granddad's farm, pausing to cut a pliant young fork from a cedar tree with his pocketknife and cleaning it as he walked. When he was finished, he held a rough instrument. The two prongs functioned as handles and at the midpoint joined together in a single stick: a wand.

Charlie asked Joe where he wanted the well and Joe pointed out a general area, which Charlie walked across, holding this dowsing rod out in front of his body, casually. About halfway across the space the divining stick plunged as though of its own accord into a dry furrow. Charlie smiled and circled the area a little and then held the humble instrument forth again and walked back across the spot at a forty-five-degree angle. Joe watched with his usual stoicism as the dowser crossed the same spot and the cedar branch plunged anew, as though forced by unseen hands into the parched earth.

My father and young Joe were watching this performance expectantly from the top rail of a corral fence, and at this point Charlie called them over and took two pairs of pliers out of his coat pocket.

"Now this time, boys," he said, "I want you to walk with me. And I want you to clamp down on the handles of this here twig with all your might and if you allow it to bend even a smidge, I'm goin' to thrash yuh." He winked and smiled.

This, the third time, Charlie walked across at a ninety-degree angle with each boy pacing him on a side, gripping the pliers with fierce concentration. As they came to the appointed place, the branches began to twist and bend in the pliers, complaining and weeping. The bending became a tearing and rending as Charlie walked closer to the spot. Then the cedar bent at ninety degrees toward the ground, in spite of any counterforce the two strong young men could exert. Joe Killingsworth stood, doubtless dumbfounded, chewing a stalk of hay. Whatever his true feelings, they would be held in check.

The demonstration presaged good fortune, for Killingsworth dropped a well on that spot within a week and artesian water came bubbling up and flooded the thirsty soil of its own accord. The well itself remains, and I have quenched my thirst there on many a sweaty, humid summer afternoon. So must Robert Webb and Ann Killingsworth have shared the miraculous water. Despite the seeming disparity of fortune and ambition that divided the families as surely as the rambling scar of the North Fork, young love budded under the rustling leaves of the cottonwoods before the war.

1969

I sang in public for the first time on Hugh Hefner's *Playboy After Dark*. My voice was untrained, though it had benefited somewhat from years of hymn singing. I was restless and looking around for some way to take advantage of my notoriety. My closest companions were Fred Tackett and Patricia, my majordomo Jim Beniche, my father, who had come out from Oklahoma to help me with my production and publishing endeavors, and Howard Golden, an ambitious and industry-savvy young attorney. Oh, and there was Satan. Old Scratch. The Devil.

Satan was a semipermanent houseguest, getting a divorce and managing a girlfriend but finding time to lounge by my pool to read *Fear and Loathing in Las Vegas* and works by Carlos Castaneda and Ken Kesey. I had a sauna installed in the old pool house, with a shower and an old gothic church window in the dressing room to the outside. We sat there in the fragrant heat, Satan and I, and had contests to see who could stay inside the longest at the highest possible temperature. It is gratuitous to add that he most often won these contests with ease. We engaged in long meandering conversations, mostly about his philosophy, which was not to have a philosophy. No one, before or since, was funnier or more ready for a bit of rowdy.

He was unimpressed with the new Corvette. He had discovered an advertisement in a local newspaper announcing the sale of a number of cars and other machinery at Carroll Shelby's warehouse. Carroll's years of Class-A sports car racing were winding down and Cobras were for sale. We were among the first on the scene and wandered in well-oiled ecstasy through row after row of race cars, trucks, tools, a Cobra turbojet boat and other pricey knick-knacks, finally coming to a reverent halt in front of a 427 Shelby Cobra, Carroll's personal ride. The Devil flashed his grin.

"Now here's a sled," he murmured reverentially, folding his arms and taking a step back, the better to take it in.

The Cobra crouched in immaculate Shelby racing blue, the embodiment of barely restrained violence. It flat-out scared me. I had seen Cobras from the stands at Laguna Seca. I had seen little red 289s scooting around Hollywood with an impertinent snarl. I had never seen this big block monster 427 up close, especially Carroll's car with its decidedly indecent bulging bonnet and flaring chromed exhaust headers, each one the diameter of a small cannon.

Shelby sauntered over to join us.

"Well, ya want me to wrap it up fer ya?" he drawled, betraying Texas ancestry.

"How much you want for it?" I asked.

"Thirteen thousand." He leaned over the car and looked at his contorted reflection in the curvature.

In today's money that was about $130,000. I looked at the Big D. His grin had stayed in place, so I said to Carroll, "Can you give me 'til tomorrow to think about it?"

He looked me up and down, surely thinking, *No way this kid has thirteen grand.* Then he said, "Okay. Tomorrow."

We walked out of there and crawled into the stifling heat of the Corvette's sumptuous little cockpit. The 'Vette had gotten smaller. It was shrunken and ladylike and didn't sound nearly as gnarly as before. I started her up and looked over into the Devil's cold, gray blue eyes.

"Buy it," he said.

Now known as a Super Snake it was reclassified as a 427 Cobra Semi-Competition. Although many 427 SCs were raced and never saw a public road, they had titles and were legal to drive on the highway. There were only two of these Shelby race-ready cars ever built. One briefly belonged to Bill Cosby, and now one of them was mine.

I had an inspiration to drive that Cobra up to Vegas to see Elvis Presley. Presley was staging a comeback at the International Hotel and the Hollywood cognoscenti were all vying for tickets to witness the second coming of the King of Rock 'n' Roll. Some, it must be admitted, were merely jealous or envious and interested in seeing the King lose his clothes. A casual perusal of rock history will reveal that Presley knew this and was terrified by the prospect of failure. Having missed the Presley phenomenon the first time around, I was mildly skeptical but curious.

As usual, the Devil was amiable to any brand of mischief and readily agreed. It was late afternoon when we got started, wearing leather jackets and carrying a Sucrets box prudently packed with ready rolls to ward off the ennui.

"Well, you must be happy," I said to Satan as the big engine cranked over in a petulant mood, cantankerously launching a couple of blue Roman candles into the air.

"In general, or about something in particular?" he asked without breaking his blinding Southern smile.

"Don't think I've forgotten it was all your idea . . . this Cobra thing."

He beamed brighter and laughed. "I seem to be at my best during moments of indecision, if you haven't noticed."

The car coughed and hacked its impatience all the way down Hayvenhurst to the red light and ramp leading to the Ventura Freeway. We came to a stop, stifling our wild anticipation, and at first did not notice the CHP trooper mounted on a motorcycle as he coasted slowly to a halt beside us. He looked us over with a hard face, the typical Übermensch with his tiny, immaculately groomed red mustache and glossy knee-high leather boots. The afternoon sun was dropping behind the eucalyptus trees that lined the roadway. He looked; we waited.

The Cobra waited as well, but with less patience at the long red light. Behind the wheel I was sweating bullets as the big cam cranked over and each time caused the car to dance its nervous little dance with an ear thumping *whump,* like a grandfather clock with giant stainless steel balls.

I watched the temperature gauge move upward ever so slightly, as the big engine politely coughed and cleared its throat. The electric cooling fans in the intake scoop up front automatically came on and whirred.

"*No!*" I screamed at the car telepathically. "*Don't* . . . not now . . ."

At that second the Cobra launched one glowing, incandescent blue ball of half-burned fuel with a tremendous report like a signaling cannon, and then another: two missiles in quick succession. Both made direct hits on the trooper's polished right boot. He was stomping his boot on the ground trying to get the fire out and almost jumped off the motorcycle but thought better of it. The light turned green. He reached up and keyed his motorcycle off, impassive, and stiffly extended the kickstand and parked the bike upright in the middle of the street. Nobody else moved.

"Turn off the ignition please," he said so softly I could not make it out over the sound of horsepower.

"Excuse me?" I begged politely.

"*I said turn the Goddamn ignition off!*" he barked, suddenly animated enough to place one hand on his gun and the other on my vehicle.

I thought about our Sucrets box full of high-grade weed and looked over at Satan, whose expression was deadpan. His sangfroid was rarely displaced.

"Do you realize, sir, that these baffles are illegal?" He gestured at the side pipes.

"These baffles are factory installed on this vehicle, Officer. Without intentionally contradicting you I think you will find the inspection sticker is in order on this car, sir." When it comes to politeness I am hardly ever upstaged.

He leaned over and stared at the current inspection sticker with jaundiced eye. I had him, I thought.

"License and registration please," he ordered tersely. As I complied he looked at the racer from head to taillight shaking his head in silent anguish.

"All right then, Mr. Webb," he said after inspecting my papers. "I'm going to be writing you a citation this evening."

"For what?" I blurted in an unforgivable loss of cool.

With a self-satisfied smile he handed me the ticket and my license, remounted his iron steed, and rode on to the Ventura Freeway without even a backward glance. I restarted the car and in the dim light of the instruments managed to read his deformed handwriting on the proper line: "For excessive display of speed."

I choked, handing the ticket to Satan, who howled with laughter. We both chortled as I revved the engine and put the hulking Hydromatic trannie in drive. He had written us up for an excessive display of speed while we were stationary and the engine wasn't even running. The Devil and I tooled the Cobra up the Van Nuys on-ramp to the Ventura Freeway and headed southeast toward San Bernardino and Elvis's opening night at the International Hotel.

1941

On a Sunday afternoon, news of the Japanese attack on Pearl Harbor arrived in Western Oklahoma. My dad was visiting in the Killingsworth homestead and by chance, as in hundreds of thousands of American homes, the austere brown radio was on at that exact time. Joe Jr. and my father struggled to find the Navy's huge Pacific base on a map and showed the family where it was.

When things quieted down Joe Jr. and my daddy went outside on the porch. Joe pulled him closer and whispered, "That means us."

Within a couple of months Dad had boarded a Greyhound and taken the ride up Route 66 to Oklahoma City where he presented himself for the draft.

At first the war went so poorly against the superior machines and manpower of Japan that the government misled its own citizens as to the seriousness of their situation and secretly prepared for a physical invasion of the westernmost states. Down amid the whispering cottonwoods Robert and Ann spoke often of impending catastrophe; Robert would be taken soon and sent into the maelstrom of total war. They had no illusions as to the outcome.

At some pivotal moment they decided they would marry before it was too late, even though Ann was only a sixteen-year-old junior at Sweetwater High School. At seventeen, my father's dates with Ann to this point had been carefully monitored. The only way Dad could date my mother was with her brother Joe Jr. and his girlfriend Jean along, including the caveat that all traveling must be done in my granddad's '42 Pontiac.

A conspiracy was hatched. My dad went to his uncle Ernest, a persistent black sheep, even on the Webb side where it might be said that standards did not run quite so high as they did across the creek. Ernest had a beat-up old Ford that he loaned to my dad for an afternoon drive to the high school. In an amazing display of testosterone-charged hubris, Dad picked Ann up at school and took her up the road twelve miles to Erick, the scene of a hastily convened wedding party at Uncle Virgil's place. The group made a short trip to the Methodist minister's home and there the two kids were married, my mother in her school clothes and my father wearing a pair of blue jeans and brown shoes, tall and lithe and good-looking but now on the wrong side of the law.

With thirty-five dollars between them they headed for Lubbock, Texas, cuddled in the backseat of a Greyhound bus. But when the cooing newlyweds arrived in Lubbock, the terminal was crawling with cops. Dad was promptly clapped in irons and charged with kidnapping.

The next morning Ann was driven home by her indignant parents, her dreams betrayed by a girlfriend in whom she had foolishly confided details of the plot. For my father, alone and behind bars for the first time, life had taken a sudden depressing turn.

Voices were raised on the Killingsworth estate. Ann was in a high temper over my father's predicament in the Lubbock jail and for once laid down her own version of the law to her normally unassailable father and his equally phlegmatic counterpart. If they didn't get Robert out of jail immediately, she said, they would have to watch her every second for the rest of her life; otherwise, at the first opportunity she would run.

She meant it and they knew she meant it. Dad was released from jail and drove the old Ford back to the Sunshine Ranch, still smarting from his first encounter with the law.

He went to work as a hired hand up on the highlands east of the creek, and he and Ann lived together in a one-room shack with an outdoor lavatory. To hear him tell it they were happy, even though their time together was of the borrowed variety, and too soon the day came for him to pack a single suitcase full of essentials and make the trip to the train depot in Sayre.

The morning was pleasant and cool, and both families, after all that acrimony, turned out to say good-bye. They were all dressed in their Sunday best except Charlie, who for reasons of his own, was elsewhere. There were tears, kisses, and hugs, and then the big Santa Fe locomotive took Robert away.

He finished basic training two months later. He had excelled, particularly with a rifle, earning a marksmanship badge. Ann settled herself with relatives near Camp Matthews on the outskirts of San Diego. They were able to see each other in almost painful intervals of intimacy knowing Dad was destined for the South Pacific. Perhaps there was no other way, but high in the government, great men were impatient to have the war over and done with, and the most expeditious, not the most humane, tactics were employed.

Such were the anxieties and fears that filled the waking and sleeping hours of the young lovers until the night my father was ordered overseas. The soldiers received no warning. They were told to pack and pray and present themselves at the trucks that would take them down to the great harbor and the ships of war. As the trucks trundled along the highway that by chance ran just past where Ann lived, Dad agonized over not being able to leave a note or even place a phone call. He eased his KA-BAR out of his duffel and carefully cut a small peephole in the canvas that covered the back of the truck. Through the tiny hole he saw Ann's little house come into view and as quickly disappear. It was the last he would see of her for thirty-seven months.

1969

The Cobra went up to one hundred miles an hour as easy as cream goes into coffee, still grumbling and launching fireballs from time to time, betraying an insatiable appetite to be in her comfort zone, which was another fifty miles an hour faster. Real race car driving was trickier than it looked on television. It took all my focus to keep it straight and between the white lines as we penetrated out into the Inland Empire on Highway 10, past Ontario and its gigantic speedway, eventually toward Colton, home of my alma mater, and birthplace of my muse, the lovely Susan Horton.

Night fell. Now we were cruising. Past San Bernardino on Highway 15, then onto the wide, buff-colored Mojave Desert. The evening chill and increasing altitude seeped into our clothes as the engine bit into the colder air. We homed through the desert on a mostly empty road. No gas stations, no houses, no roadside phones or rest stops, just the cacti, mesquite, and tumbleweeds of the high desert.

There, the Cobra powered down and slowed to a crawl in a slight depression, and then stopped. Even the Devil looked stunned.

We waited, the only two figures in an otherwise lifeless tableau. Hours crawled by and no assistance came. The questionable novelty of our situation quickly turned into fathomless boredom and irritation, punctuated by fits of temper directed at the Cobra ("fucking piece of shit") and the desert ("my left ball just froze off"). Finally the Devil got so cold he stood in a tumbleweed and ignited it with a cigarette lighter. There he stood, his feet and legs swathed in boiling flames, smiling his enigmatic smile.

"Does that work?" I asked.

"Not really. I'm signaling."

Eventually a kindly driver chanced upon the pathetic scene and agreed to take us, shivering and babbling our gratitude, into the nearest town, humble Barstow. We checked into Leon's Lucky Deuce Motel, a dung heap, and fell asleep. I dreamed that I was in Las Vegas and meeting Elvis.

The next morning the Evil One and I staggered to Leon's Lucky Deuce Garage. Leon was hunched over the engine compartment, undoubtedly challenged by the Gordian knot in the guts of the Cobra. "It'll be ready when it's ready," he grunted. We headed to Leon's Lucky Deuce Grill and Grocery for breakfast.

"Places like this will be history soon," said the Devil. "Soak it up while you can. In ten years that garage will be a parking lot and this joint will be a strip mall." The Devil was always throwing that kind of shit in my breakfast.

We went back to the garage and noticed with satisfaction that the bonnet was closed on the Cobra. Leon charged a thousand dollars for his work. I grudgingly handed it over, anxious for the bellow of unfettered power moving ahead. Moving ahead was all.

By the time we got into Vegas, we were beaten down. Ears ringing, hair greasy, a slight film of oil covering our faces, not looking or feeling our best. I drove to Caesars Palace, where I was a regular, and the parking guys gawked at the Cobra and parked it out front where everybody could see it. They asked us if we wanted broads and we stared dumbly into each other's glazed eyes and shook our heads in negative unison. We went up to a big suite that was furnished like the best little whorehouse in Herculaneum, and we crashed.

When the shadows grew long and the towering hotel blotted out the descent of the merciless sun through the unadorned sky, we donned expensive Italian suits with silk shirts and Gucci loafers for the Elvis Presley show. Our hair was shoulder length, however, and we got looks from some of the casino bosses as we exited the elevator and walked through the lobby. Hippies were objects of suspicion at the big hotels back when "The Family" was running things.

Out front under the huge arching canopy, under a thousand glistening spotlights and exuding a silent belligerence, sat the Cobra. Without discussing it, we opted for a cab. It was a short hop from our hotel to the International, barely time to smoke a ready roll and split a couple of caps of mescaline.

Reality was already morphing when we exited the cab into a mass of celebrity and journalistic chaos. Outside and inside the huge lobby of the International were sensational billboards announcing the "Elvis Presley Summer Festival" to an elbow-knocking crowd of DJs, high-rollers, hookers, greats, near-greats, not-even-greats, ingrates, would-bes, hustlers, hucksters, hoodlums, honchos, and some fans. In the faces of the middle-aged women who had worshipped Elvis in their teens, there was a holy light. Not on any other evening of their lives, be it unbearably long or tragically short, would they experience the transcendent ecstasy that was visible all around their persons. No mean thought marred their beauty in this hour, however sordid or plain their lives may have been, as they moved in a hushed mass toward their Source, their Fountain and High Priest of Youth.

I was carried along with the current of unmitigated enthusiasm, into a showroom that glowed like the interior of some impossibly vast spaceship, emblazoned high up on the walls with idols: unforgettable, gigantic golden angels. Why angels? I did not know, nor did I know for a certainty they were really there. And then I had it. It was Elvis! Elvis was the angel. And around me the world swirled in joyous pilgrimage to see a real angel.

Security persons blocked the way but the Devil whispered in their ears, money changed hands, and ropes and barriers parted magically as the elite were filtered onward, down the seemingly endless platforms of the indoor amphitheater, past the leather upholstered divans and booths, all the way down, until I thought there must be some mistake. Down to the linen-covered long tables situated in parallel rows right in front of the stage and then, unbelievably, further still, to the first seats at the very front of the crowd, the stage looming a couple of feet above our heads.

I stared across the table right into the face of All-Pro fullback Jim Brown.

"Howdy," I said.

He acknowledged me with a curt nod. Still, I was impressed. Even a cursory glance around us revealed an essentially all-celebrity crowd. Hollywood had come to Las Vegas.

Softly at first, but with increasing urgency, the *Thus Spake Zarathustra* theme of Richard Strauss began to play on huge speakers overhead as the lights dimmed. The throbbing engine of the rhythm section was engaged and the metaphor of space travel was evoked again as the floor trembled under the influence of some vast psychic motor. Then, to put it simply—though it was not a simple thing—Elvis Aaron Presley walked onto the stage.

Putting all criteria regarding tessitura, style, presentation, and all the other boxes on the scoring checklist of the professional reviewer aside for the moment, Elvis had a superhuman, metaphysical presence on stage that bowled me over completely. I felt as though he knew I was there and was singing to me, talking to me.

I looked around me and could see that everyone else felt exactly the same way. He was wearing a black, close-fitting costume with a long piratical red sash around his midsection. His hair was loose and styled much like a Beatles cut, not sprayed into a pompadour as I had expected. His physical condition was superb as he gyrated through "Train" and "All Shook Up," stopping to indulge in some questionable comedy, such as bending over too far and allowing his guitar neck to get "stuck" on the toe of his boot. He goofed around with a little foot-long Fender guitar: "When I was a baby I played this little bitty guitar!" Dumb joke. But nobody cared. I felt the electricity lancing through the room in great jolting bolts. It wasn't a performance as much as a special effect or an induced epiphany. He possessed the audience and made it his.

He looked up at the gigantic figures on the walls and stared thoughtfully before saying: "Boy, those are some pretty funky-looking angels up there!"

Everybody laughed hysterically. It became obvious to me, somehow I knew in the way trippers always know, that he was high as a kite on something.

Looking back into the room I could see the beginnings of mayhem. Hundreds of women were leaving their seats and migrating toward the front as the show progressed. Quickly they penetrated the A-list conclave and were all around us, tears streaming down their cheeks, faces filled with a ghostly light and tranquil reverence as though they were witnessing a miracle: a perfect outline of Christ appearing on the wall of a grain silo.

"Wise men say, only fools rush in . . ."

Like the invitational at the end of a revival service, the hymn-like tune of "Can't Help Falling in Love" (w. Peretti, Creatore, and Weiss) caused many to cry openly.

Elvis was now working his way from stage right to stage left along the footlights, fifteen or twenty silk scarves draped around his neck. He was stopping to kiss the girls and drape a souvenir scarf around them. He took his time and the kisses were real. A beautiful supplicant near me sighed and dropped like a stone, while others tried to support and comfort her.

Eventually I looked up and saw he was standing over me look-ing down. If he had wanted to kiss me and give me a scarf it would have been okay. Instead he reached out with a little scrap of paper torn from an envelope and dropped it on my table. I was looking straight in his eyes and they smiled as he moved on. There was much more kissing and scarfing to be done!

I squinted at the little torn out square of paper and saw scrawled there in a rough hand: "Dear Jimmy, come backstage."

Suddenly the house lights were up. The show was over. The au-dience stood applauding, all of them, waiting for an encore that would never come.

The famous epithet "Elvis has left the building, ladies and gen-tlemen. Elvis has left the building!" sounded through the P.A. in an attempt to dissipate the crowd, which was stubbornly holding its ground, reluctant to consign such a moment to history.

Two burly security guards appeared out of nowhere and I had a momentary notion that they were there to throw us out of the place.

Instead one of them growled, "Are you Webb?"

I nodded.

"Let's go!" they both said, and bracing us on either side as we penetrated that mass of humanity, stubborn as a hedgerow, they half escorted, half dragged us to the side of the stage and through a double door that led into the labyrinth of hidden passages that honeycombed the inside of the hotel.

Eventually we came to an unprepossessing doorway that led into a smallish dressing room full of Elvis costumes on racks, glittering suits with big collars. Then the guards stopped at another door and beckoned us inside. A short, fat man chewing on a cigar was glad-handing us from the moment we stepped inside.

"I'm Tom Parker," he chewed in a Southern accent. "I s'pose y'all here to meet Elvis."

We nodded dumbly, the mescaline wearing off now, the neon lighting harsh as we went through yet another door, and suddenly there he stood. It was Elvis, already changed into tight faded jeans and a loose coat of many colors. The customary sunglasses were forgone. Surrounding him, in a flying wedge, as though they possessed him in some way, was the Memphis Mafia: Red, Charlie, a half-dozen of 'em. The tableau had a psychological effect. We shrunk; he expanded.

I approached and shook his hand, the Devil and I mumbling words that I don't recall except I do recall Beelzebub saying "Howdy, El!" which seemed a little familiar, but the Devil had a pair and he wasn't going to kowtow to nobody. In close proximity to Elvis his animus, his mana, became almost suffocating. I forgot what I had planned to say. It didn't seem to matter. Only he mattered. He was saying something about Glen Campbell, and they were saying he had to pick out another outfit for his next show, and we stood there in La-La Land just staring like tourists from another planet. Elvis must have endured millions of such stares.

Phone numbers were exchanged through intermediaries as though he was going to be calling me or vice versa. What a laugh. The last thing I remember before I left, hustled out by the officious and ever congenial Tom Parker, was gazing in awe at the diamond-studded belt that marked Elvis's physical and spiritual center. It lanced, glittered, and sparkled with the only word that needed to be said: ELVIS.

1945

After thirty-seven months in the combat zone my father de-shipped in Long Beach from the USS *Maryland* and walked down the long gangway with his duffel bag over his brawny shoulders into a milling crowd of brother Marines and sailors, and civilians—mostly women—intent on finding that one special person, to re-make a pairing in a ritual as old as warfare and waiting. The crowd was thinning before they found each other, it having taken them a long time to recognize each other after all the years and the physical changes on both sides. He was twenty pounds of hard muscle heavier and two inches taller. She had always been a pretty girl but had flowered into a curvaceous pinup in his absence, a fact she had not been shy to advertise in an occasional black-and-white photo posed demurely in a one-piece bathing suit and sent like a promise into the maelstrom of war. Finally, they came hesitantly face-to-face.

"Bob?" she asked uncertainly, looking up into his hard, browned features.

"Ann?" he replied unsteadily as he dropped the duffel bag and swept her up into his mighty arms.

My father, a man of considerable wit, says I was born "nine months and forty-five minutes later."

1969

I soon returned to Las Vegas. It was the end of August and the Presley show was closing for the year. I couldn't miss that. I was alone, the Prince of Darkness having gone off on some nefarious mission.

I was in the lobby of the International Hotel, which had been closed for a huge private party. A corridor had been roped off through which the regular guests could travel from the front door to the registration desk and then to the massive elevator banks. The rest of the stadium-sized lobby was reserved for Miss Nancy Sinatra's opening night party, commingled with Elvis's closing night party. Elvis and Nancy had just appeared in 1968's *Speedway* together. Mr. Sinatra was hosting for his suddenly famous daughter, riding high with Lee Hazlewood's production of her hit "These Boots Are Made for Walking." In attendance was every singer on the Strip who wasn't working, the celeb contingent up from Hollywoodland, hundreds of record company brass and high rollers, and cadres of undercover security guys packing iron, which made them so conspicuous it was laughable.

There was so much glad-handing, bullshitting, ass-kissing, ego-schmoozing, and showbiz circle-jerking going on that you could have easily mistaken it for a political fund-raiser, but it was just the usual Vegas Vamp. I had neither the will nor the skill to play this kind of chess. I was only learning insincerity, slowly but surely.

I drifted from the center of the room, where I greeted Nancy

Sinatra, a sweet, straightforward kid my age, and her father, who wasn't really known for long frivolous conversations. Nobody knew who the hell I was unless they were telepathic, which made it easier to slide through the seekers and sounders and find a friendly barstool in the corner. I ordered a beer and swiveled to face the crowd, which had reached maximum spatial saturation, a point at which literally no person in the room can move in any direction for any distance. Networking shuts down. Now people just want to get out alive.

I laughed and wheeled around to devote my attention to the gold veins in the black mirror behind the bar. "These Boots Are Made for Walking" was just short of deafening on the sound system as I felt rather than sensed, a person immediately to my right.

A familiar baritone bourbon voice reverberated in my ear: "Jimma!"

The guy had bent over and put his elbow right down on the bar to talk to me. I eased my head around cautiously, not sure who had managed to move in so close.

"Jimma!" he said again, and I found myself nose-to-nose and eyebrow-to-eyebrow with Elvis Presley.

"Hey!" I shouted involuntarily, as all my ass-kissing solenoids kicked in at the same time. I skewed the barstool around to face him. He was wearing dark glasses, a white shirt open at the throat, jeans, and a black velvet jacket.

"Don' geddup, Jimma," Elvis said. "I jus wonna talk to ya fo a minute."

I mumbled something about that being an honor and asked him if he wanted a beer.

"Nah, I don' drink." He laughed and I laughed, too, as if I knew the joke but I fuckin' didn't.

"Jimma, I jus wanna ask you how many French horns you use in your orchester." I didn't think of myself as someone who "had an orchestra" like Harry James or Nelson Riddle, but so earnest was his expression and tone of voice that I let that slide.

"Well, I tell you, Elvis," I said, "when I first started out I used three because there's basically three notes in a chord."

He snorted. "Yeh, I know that!" His lip really did curve up on one side, like a friendly snarl.

"Well," I continued, "when I started writing more complicated chords I found out three French horns just didn't always get a full, rich sound."

Now, I was talking to the guy about something I cared about. He thought about it as I studied his reflection in the bar mirror.

"Okay, Jimma, that seems about right to me, too."

So the Big E lies in his giant white bed and thinks about orchestration? Mind-blowing.

"You know," I added, as I nodded toward Mr. Sinatra across the room, "Nelson Riddle uses four French horns."

Elvis slipped off the black glasses and reached over to shake my hand.

"Hey, Jimma, thank ya vermuch. Just wait'll yuh hear ma new orchester."

He smiled and I said, "Hey, anytime!"

And then like a wraith he was gone. I mean gone. I did a 360-degree scan of the gigantic lobby and there was no sign of him. All my life I've felt a moment passed, a chance to say: "I mean anytime, or anything! Any of those monsters you're wrestling with, 'cause I have monsters in my closet, too! I like you. I would like to tell you every goddamn thing I know about music! I think I could turn you on to stuff. . . ." But he was gone, and like Melville's Moby-Dick I would only see him again once more.

Jimmy Webb with Robert and Ann Webb, 1946. *(Courtesy of Janice Linnens)*

CHAPTER TWO

There's something happening here
What it is ain't exactly clear . . .
—Stephen Stills, "For What It's Worth," 1966

1969

I was one of a rarified few who had offices in one of the old-fashioned star system–era bungalows clustered in a grove of palm trees on the Universal Film Studios lot in Universal City. Only well-known production companies had them, or high-budget pictures in progress for the duration of their stay, or individuals bound directly to the studio by exclusive contracts. I was one of these.

My attorneys, among them some fine men like Howard Golden, had labored long and hard to negotiate a filmed musical project and a television special among other things, including the private bungalow, a substantial sum of money up front, and at the last minute, well, Beelzebub insisted on everyone getting a Cadillac. A brand-new

El Dorado for me, one for the Prince of Evil, one for my father, and one for Howard. This was one of those asinine last-minute conceits almost guaranteed to spoil a deal, and Howard turned white when Patch and I told him about the Caddies.

"You're fucked" were his exact words.

All in, I guess it was $150,000 or so worth of Cadillacs, but in Hollywood when you're hot, you're hot, and like the Leigh Harline and Ned Washington song says, "No request is too extreme." Everybody got a Cadillac. We could have said, "*And* an airplane!"

Civilized restraint prevailed and we settled for our own personal secretary, new rugs, and a custom letterhead. Oh yes, and a fresh paint job for our bungalow, handily located right next door to the Universal recording facility. I could look out the window at my Cobra parked in my private parking space with a neat black-on-white lettered sign that said WEBB. Parking space on the Universal lot was not so much a place to put your car as it was a symbol of exalted social status, a subtle badge trumping the mojo of the hoi polloi of producers and mere stars who crowded the cafeteria and shooting stages and walked out to the parking lots to get their cars. Revered film director Abraham Polonsky didn't have a parking place, but I had three.

It was the first week of August and I was just settling in. I was working in the back room of the ranchette, which was my territory, replete with a big desk, a couch, and a skinny spinet of an upright piano that sounded like a Tin Pan Alley reject. I had a plum of a project. Universal had asked me to write the score for a new Herb Ross–directed musical based on James Barrie's *Peter Pan* and starring Mia Farrow. Mel Ferrer, an affable B-list actor from the 1950s with a tall and dignified mien, would take the helm as producer. Mia and I exchanged phone calls frequently about *Pan* and the underlying philosophy and deeper meanings of James Barrie's warhorse. I was in there chopping away constantly on pirates and crocodiles and flying pixies. Truly, I was having at it and writing a goddamn fine score, enquiries welcomed.

Simultaneously, I was visited occasionally by a young director named Philip Kaufman, a soft-spoken gentleman about my age who had been chosen to create the shooting script for a new television special starring me and just about everybody I was recording with at the time. He had some fine ideas about suspending a magical pipe organ from a giant balloon and flying all over a psychedelic landscape populated by various recording artists who would sing my songs while I played along. In the props department at Universal, special effects craftsmen were already constructing sets and special equipment. This included a balloon more than four stories high in consultation with balloonist Don Piccard for the "Up, Up and Away" flying sequence. It was, at the time, the largest hot air balloon ever constructed.

Rarely did anything intrude on my dreamlike reveries of Peter Pan's hijinks or my giant hot air balloon. Ergo, I paid little or no attention to business matters or practicalities or even the news. The world outside my citadel in Encino or my bungalow at Universal began to shrink. My largest worry at the time was whether or not I could persuade Mr. Frank Sinatra or Aretha Franklin to appear on the proposed TV special, because that's what the ties in the tower wanted.

Phil Kaufman and I were lounging on couches at Campo de Encino, talking about the incongruity of me dangling underneath a huge balloon playing upon my magical organ when in fact the instrument I performed upon was a piano. But he had a good argument with the elaborate organ because it could do phantasmagorical things such as whisking the balloon to far-off distant lands or other dimensions. I was smiling at bearded, brilliant Phil as my stepbrother Garth walked in through the kitchen entrance with a grim face, teeth tightly clenched.

"Turn on the TV," Garth barked as the birds sang sweetly, flitting from windowsill to branch around the sunny old house.

I walked past my rock 'n' roll heaven stained glass windows over to the entertainment center. I flipped on a screen that came alive with a shot of Cielo Drive in Beverly Hills and an announcer speaking in low, shocked tones about the murder of Jay Sebring, Sharon Tate and her unborn child, as well as Abigail Folger, Steve Parent, and Wojciech Frykowski.

Phil and I looked at each other aghast, all thoughts of transcendental journeys to fairy-tale kingdoms blotted out in a split second. Sad-eyed and tongue-tied journalists managed to blurt out that all those at the horror house had been stabbed and mutilated before death. An image of Sharon flashed in front of my eyes as we trained at the Beverly Hills Fencing Academy, her forehead wrinkled with concentration as she thrust and parried, deftly manipulating her foil and oblivious to my admiring gaze. Then another vision of her dancing with Roman Polanski at a party at Victor Lownes's in London; happy and at ease, clowning around with Bill Cosby, who had been wearing only a towel.

I remembered Jay Sebring with his screen-star handsome face, hands quick and expert as he sculpted my hair, simultaneously offering shrewd and compact advice about making a smooth passage through the wilds of Hollywood. I thought of the night I blew up his 427 Cobra and smiled in spite of myself, remembering his aplomb as he inspected the smoking collection of charred parts in his engine compartment. He had never raised his voice or displayed the slightest annoyance or anger that night. In fact, he and Sharon were seemingly two of the gentlest souls.

The Flower Children died that day, irrevocably and forever. The stereotypical long-haired hippie in tattered jeans and tie-dyed T-shirt, thumbing a ride on the freeway with a guitar case over his shoulder, became suddenly an object of suspicion and dread.

The primary subject of most conjecture was: Why? Why these celebrities? Later it would become apparent that Charles Manson's objective went far beyond such a limited agenda as celebrity. Yet it remains ironic that such a horror had at its ground zero issues as prosaic as the frustrated dreams of an inept and ignored songwriter.

In the aftermath, flying keyboards and magical mystery tours seemed strange fare for adult conversation. All of Hollywood, especially the celebrated and famous sector, seemed to be shifting into a new gear as panicked phone calls were made in shocked tones, meetings canceled, children rushed home from expensive schools, and business in the bodyguard ranks and gun stores skyrocketed.

An early version of a black-and-white security camera was installed at my gate in order to see callers before they were admitted. In our neighborhood lived Sergio Mendes, David Cassidy, Billy and Marilyn Davis, Aretha Franklin (who would soon sell her house to Michael Jackson), and many other persons who thought they had cause to worry. The Spahn Ranch, Den of Assassins, lay only a twenty-minute drive west of Campo de Encino.

Years later I would be sitting in a quiet London bar with Cass Elliot, a cherished friend who was always seeking a special song I seemed unable to write. She confessed, in a whisper, that unknown to Vincent Bugliosi and the judicial world at large, or for that matter anyone else except her sister and the two of us, she had been the first witness to arrive on that bloody one-sided battlefield in the early hours of Sunday morning, a party in the offing and looking forward to seeing her friends Sharon and Jay. She had walked like an automaton past the slain pizza boy in his car, up to the desecrated body of Abigail Folger and stopped, knowing she did not want to see what lay in the house beyond. Suffering from paroxysm and shock, she had retreated home to her bedroom and stayed there for days.

She had told me, as we both smoked and consumed shots of tequila, that she felt to have told the story would only have further validated its bizarre reality, making it more indelible. She was still, five years later, crazy from it and having recurring nightmares. It had become to her a vivid, yet unreal, silent vignette; a scene clipped from a horror movie and left by the cleaner, curled on the cutting room floor.

1949

Robert Webb brooded and worked as a farm laborer, disappointed with the economic opportunities afforded returned heroes.

One day, while driving a tractor out on the north forty of the Killingsworth farm, God paid him a visit. According to my father's testimony, God appeared in front of his tractor and said, "Robert! Get down off that tractor!" My father complied and fell to his knees in the furrow. "Robert, I want you to be my preacher!" God said. "Get yourself out of this place and into a place of learning. You will not be a farmer!" There was a bright light and a crash of thunder. Dad had been called. This was classic New Testament stuff.

Dad packed up his little family, grown to four with the arrival of baby Janice, and moved to Wichita Falls, Texas, where he enrolled in J. Frank Norris's Bible Baptist Seminary. Eschewing the rigorous discipline of Grandma Myrtle's Nazarene sect, which tolerated no movies, dancing, makeup, or hair cutting, he opted for the promising field of evangelical oratory. J. Frank Norris was one of the country's first radio preachers and a role model for my dad. He broadcast nightly from Dallas, Texas, shivering the rafters in a hundred thousand houses with reverberant promises of death and destruction in an eternal burning lake of fire for the ungodly. These threats paid well. Norris lived the high life in a mansion as president of the seminary and all-around religious big wheel. We lived in a trailer the size of a rowboat, situated at the end of the runway at Sheppard Air Force Base. When the B-36 Peacemakers would rotate and climb reluctantly skyward with all six pusher props and four jets screaming, the noise would rearrange the knives and forks in the flatware drawer. I remember the plane's primeval throb somewhere deep in my chest even though I was only four years old.

Mother must have sweated out the hot, humid nights trapped in that sausage can of a trailer with two growing, demanding kids, wondering where were we going, what were we doing. But Dad's answer was that God always knew where we were going even if we didn't, and she was enough in love with him to go along.

While researching a paper, my father discovered a yellowing news item from the *Fort Worth Star-Telegram*, dated July 17, 1926. It seems J. Frank Norris had put three .38 caliber kill shots right through parishioner D. E. Chipps's chest. The result was a trial in Austin, Texas, on a scale with the O. J. Simpson circus. He was found not guilty. I think my father felt like an idiot in his ignorance of this gargantuan scandal even though it had happened about the same time he was born.

When the sun came up the next morning my father was on the road north towing his tiny trailer and busted dream back to Red Man's Land. My father's vision of being a preacher was momentarily shattered. But not his will to make himself one. That trait I inherited from him. He would figure it out. He would ordain himself.

1969

In September a peaceful missile from abroad descended on Campo de Encino with an airburst of possibility and excitement in the form of a letter from the Festival Internacional da Canção Popular in Brazil. Though not well known in the hippie culture, this was a popular and globally televised songwriting and performing competition.

Songwriting was something I had most often done for no audience in a barren practice room or garage. But I was cocky about my abilities and appreciative of a solid excuse to get out of Los Angeles and the onslaught of the Tate murders news coverage.

As I dallied over the idea, the committee from down south became more insistent on an answer. Who would go? The event called for a composer as well as a starring performer, and I couldn't think of a suitable choice immediately. I would take my guitarist Freddy Tackett; that was a given. So that meant his flower-child bride, Patricia, and their brand-new son, Miles, would need passage. When I decided to go, my father and Howard Golden volunteered to go as well. And, oh yes, His Dark Eminence would want to go, too. I was informed that I would be officially representing the United States. My father was duly impressed with the gravitas of my having a chance to represent my country.

The real problem was I needed a song. It was not permitted to go down to Brazil with a warhorse or used hit. "The Girl from Ipanema" was one of the most-played records of the decade in the United States and had been a hit twice, once as an instrumental with saxophonist Stan Getz. American interest waxed in all things Brazilian. I didn't have the salt to take a bossa nova to Brazil, but I knew it must be something new, chord intensive, and melodic, possibly even sad. Enter "Evie."

It was a two-verse form, too brief in hindsight, and abysmally morose. No sing-along here, but the real problem would prove to be the subject matter. I had written the song during my entanglement with Evie Bricusse, wife of Leslie, a lyricist well known in Hollywood. A slight hint of judgment or good taste would have told me to leave it in the locker, but who had any?

I decided I would debut "Evie" at the Canção Popular with Righteous Brothers superstar Bill Medley. I had auditioned many a song for Bill and had followed his career with Bobby Hatfield in a jealous fervor through a series of the greatest hits the country had ever seen. They had recorded possibly the greatest rock 'n' roll milestone of all time, "You've Lost That Lovin' Feeling," produced by Phil Spector (w. Barry Mann, Cynthia Weil, and Spector). Nothing like "Evie," but never mind. Bill's voice was a smoldering baritone and unforgettable on record. He was unflappable, rail thin, and movie-star handsome. He signed on.

Meanwhile, unknown to me, sprawling, continent-sized Brazil, awaiting titans of music and bevies of movie stars, sweltered in the iron grip of a despotic military triumvirate. For five years its population had struggled and writhed under a constitution that could have been written by an ex-Nazi. The fascist regime tortured, imprisoned, and jackbooted their way toward "economic opportunity," crushing journalistic freedom by deporting anyone who dared to dissent. The populace grumbled darkly about the United States and its laissez-faire stance, if not outright support, of anticommunist thugs, while soldiers stood on every public street corner brandishing machine guns. In response, the death squads kicked in favela doors at midnight to take potential mutineers up the road of no return. As a typical American with "International Attention Deficit Disorder," this sordid state of affairs had missed my review. Our audience was waiting for us.

1952

I was six years old and standing in front of our house in Lutie, Texas, which was little more than a four-way stop with a blacksmith shop on one corner and a Baptist church directly across. The church was a double shotgun shack that had once been a derelict supported only by rotting two-by-fours. My father climbed up on it wearing a leather nail belt, wielding a hammer, and put it back together. Some of his parishioners came by and helped him roof it with tar paper and cheap green asphalt tiles.

It was his first pastorate and he was making a hundred dollars a week. Little brother Tommy had arrived somewhere along the way, a charming tyke with ears like car doors. That salary was now split between Mother and Daddy, little Tommy, Janice, and me. Mother managed to put aside a couple of dollars a month for piano lessons. Out in the middle of the parched prairie, surrounded by rattle-snakes, tarantulas, and jackrabbits, somehow she had a thought for my future.

In spite of a paucity of income, the family was growing and try-ing to better itself. Daily I stood waiting for the school bus on the road and must have presented an absolutely forlorn object to my mother, who watched from the windows of the little parsonage. The West Texas wind continually blew across the sandy, featureless landscape and carried dust under the door and into every crack and crevice of that long-neglected one-room house.

I would remember our teacher all my life. She was a sadist named Mrs. Sakker. On the first day she called me to the blackboard two times and twice she got a refusal. The first time I demurred, she grabbed my elbow, twisted it behind my back, and turkey-walked me to the front. The second time I declined to recite, she grabbed me by the lobe of the ear and dragged me the length of the class-room. Next she called on a sweet little girl I had looked at admir-ingly more than once. The girl stood up but couldn't manage a response, merely chewing on her thumb as she stared at her feet. Mrs. Sakker doubled up her fat fist and punched the girl square in the stomach. The first-grader sat down on the floor, white and lean-ing against her desk. I arrived home in a near catatonic state and haltingly described what I'd been through to my folks. Nothing hap-pened.

In a couple years, Dad moved us down the road thirty miles to

Wellington, a proper little town. He was coming up in the world. Wellington had a cinder block church house, though for the life of me I can't remember the inside of that building or anything about it. I remember the piano lessons, a different teacher, and a new upright piano that was bought and moved into the house. Other than that, not a song, not a picture, nor even a conversation. I was eight years old.

1969

When we landed in Rio, we were met by representatives of the Canção Popular, U.S. Consulate officials, police, reporters, photographers, and our handlers, who were exceptionally pretty young girls in red uniforms and berets, who would be interpreting and helping us enjoy our stay in Brazil.

"My name is Monica!" our girl said with a good deal of pride in her excellent English. She went into the limousine with us. It was an old, scratched, black bastard with flags flying from the fenders, preceded by a noisy escort of carelessly groomed cops on Harley-Davidson shovelheads.

We rode the modern-looking highway into the Ipanema district of Rio, where a series of *grande siècle* hotels fronted the famous beach, glistening in the moonlight and rising like elaborately carved monuments by the ocean. Jeeps with fat radios, whip antennas, and .30 caliber machine-gun mounts were stationed on street corners. Wary guards stood in nearly every public square with Uzis on shoulder straps.

"Uh, did we forget to bring our guns?" Fred drily inquired in his Arkansas patois.

As we pulled up in front of the magnificent Hotel Glória Praia do Flamengo, we saw candles and bits of food laid out on huge green palmetto leaves that illuminated the center divider of the boulevard for the length of the street.

"Oh, look," said Patricia. "They are welcoming us!"

"That's Macumba," said Satan at my shoulder. "Voodoo. They've put a curse on us. These people don't like the U.S., get it?"

Our keeper was suddenly overly attentive and busy opening doors, hailing porters, and hustling us out of the limo and into a "Photo Phrenzy" of paparazzi shouting in Portuguese.

Upstairs, after a chaotic check-in, the Walkin' Dude and I sat in our grand apartments and for once did not smoke a joint. We had not dared to bring marijuana through.

The next morning our contingent gathered in the lobby at eleven sharp, as ordered.

"Good morning!" Monica bubbled to the group. "We will now go to the Tour Internacional for our famous welcome luncheon with . . ." She reeled off a slew of foreign names I did not recognize, including some English guy named Malcolm Somebody, who I knew was representing Great Britain, but I wasn't listening. I yawned. I looked around at my crew. Patricia was beaming and pretty, in her element, on the edge of a great discovery. She held baby Miles, who was toddling and had a pacifier for the duration. Fred stood beside her, his hair profuse and his beard sprouting like a giant garden plant out and down and past his sternum. He was a sensation with the paparazzi. They had themselves a hippie.

Bill Medley stood there in a dark blue suit looking for all the world like a Baptist preacher in his white shirt and black boots. He was a devout Christian and a teetotaler, his hair dressed back in the manner of a young Billy Graham. My dad was there, putting on a little weight, wearing a diamond ring the size of a carbuncle and not looking much like a Baptist preacher anymore. The Devil stood in our circle. He was carefully tailored, in his usual gear: sparkling brown, stitched cowboy boots, light-colored scalloped cowboy shirt with pearl buttons tucked into a pair of crotch-tight, faded Levi's cinched up with a silver rodeo belt buckle. I looked at them wondering how big of a mess we were in.

The convoy set off, a series of black limos a quarter of a mile long headed, flanked, and shadowed by rakish cops in cartoon blue on their old Harleys. They were everywhere and all over the road.

No decorum wasted here. They rode with flagrant disregard into the crowds that lined the route, screaming and shaking their fists and coming to a full stop occasionally to shove someone out of the way. They would pull up close beside the limousines and stare insolently through their mirrored aviator specs into the car hoping to see what? A star? Some titty? They were half-shaved, disreputable-looking characters, reveling in the power and authority of their big motorcycles with their sirens and flashing lights.

To their credit, we went at a good speed through the streets unimpeded, until we could see an incongruity becoming larger and stranger as we closed the distance. It was a modern skyscraper, grown up out of the garish hillsides of impoverished housing like a silver rocket ship standing on a tatty moonscape. With lots of sirens, Portuguese cursing, and clearing of riffraff, we penetrated underground into the garages of the colossus to be herded by Monica and her sisters into elevators with brushed chrome doors.

A James Bond villain's hideaway revealed itself as we exited on the roof into a scene busy with songwriters, singers, actresses, and paparazzi, with hooch dispensed from multiple bars. A great foo-foo-rah and hubbub was in progress over a sex queen who poured bottles of cold Champagne over her bare body, arousing her nipples as she stood half revealed in the shallows of the pool, the focus of a thousand lenses. We were jostled by the crowd as a dozen more half-naked felines appeared, pouring magnums of Champagne carelessly into the pool, uttering sexy *oohs* and *ahs*. Devilman grinned in unconcealed delight.

I pulled away from the center of the Nijinskyesque revel, taken aback, and found a perch from which I could look over the edge of the building.

The favelas hit me in the face like a physical blow. Corrugated tin sheds, cardboard boxes, sewage pipes, and shipping boxes—any detritus that could be fashioned into some semblance of shelter—spread out below our Shangri-La.

Surprised, my eyes encompassed the brown ragged multitudes staring up at the top of the wondrous silver skyscraper, no doubt in earshot of the music and the laughter, if not of the popping of champagne corks. Open latrine ditches veined the hillsides, the smell of effluvia and rotting garbage borne aloft, high enough to reach the nostrils of the rich and powerful. Satan was there. I could feel him at my side. I tried to grasp the concept of an ancestral and eternal poverty.

There was a friendly Brit hanging about, a blondish reporter toting a camera. He came over to us and asked if he could shoot some pictures, and I told him to go ahead. He said his name was Ritchie, and he was a freelancer who picked up local entertainment and human-interest photos for the papers back in England. He said the Brazilian people were good-hearted if you could get out of the artificial dome of military control and into the favelas. The famous Brazilian Samba School was there, and he didn't know if we were interested, but there might even be a smoke. Freddy was all over it. Get out there with the common man and find out the haps? Local musicians? Some potent herb? Patricia's liberal heart leaped at the opportunity to interact with an alien culture. I told the young journalist to come by the hotel and have a drink.

That is how Ritchie became our mascot without portfolio in Rio. He took a picture that was to be a minor sensation in the Brazilian papers: a front-page shot of baby Miles Tackett standing inside his father's open guitar case, with a big smile for the public. I was trying to decipher the caption as I waited for my elevator, which opened on a covey of American ladies from the floor above. They saw me and suddenly clammed up good with reddening faces. I nodded politely as we rode together. I could hear them breathing and smell their high-end perfume.

This conversation would no doubt have been about Evie, who I had called the night before in order to greet her from such an exotic and novel place. I said I was proud of the song but it didn't seem to be coming off too well. She told me, "Don't worry, darling. It won't win anyway. It's too sad!"

Patricia had asked the Red Berets if we could go out into the country and "see the real people and visit with them." We had to wait for an answer.

Meanwhile, the Canção Popular got ready for the first round

that would decide the final ten winners. Only the first three places received the diamond- and ruby-encrusted golden rooster that we irreverently called the Chicken.

Ritchie laughed when we asked him about our chances. "Well, this is Brazil. And Brazil always wins!"

Freddy and I sounded Ritchie out about the possibility of some Mary Jane. He answered that it would be dangerous as all hell but that he would sniff around and see if some of the musicians would take a chance on getting busted and going to a fascist prison for the rest of their natural days, or worse. As that did not sound too promising, I hit on the idea of sending back to the United States for a packet of cassettes, lead sheets, and bullshit music gear under the pretense that these were needed for the performance, only these cassettes would be disassembled, carefully packed with high-grade seedless colas wrapped in tinfoil, and put back together with forensic precision.

I did not concoct this harebrained scheme alone. The Devil collaborated. Fred looked dubious. "These are not the kind of people you want to screw around with," he said.

We did it anyway. Keeping the plan secret, we informed the Red Berets that a package would be arriving from the States with essential musical materials we had left behind. Then we called Garth at Campo de Encino and described the exact procedure for concealing the drugs in audiocassettes. It never occurred to me that there was a possibility the military had a tap on us.

That night we traveled to the first performance of the Canção Popular in our government limo. As we approached the Maracanãzinho, we began to receive our education in the real internal politics of Brazil. We were hemmed in by large, almost impenetrable crowds of demonstrators. They were chanting something rhythmic, loud, and fast in Portuguese.

"What are they saying?" I asked Monica.

She blushed. "Oh, well, that is nothing!" She smiled brightly. I caught a glimpse of placards waving in the mob: "America Out of Indochina!" "No More War!" and such. A shower of stones splattered over the top of the bodywork, which elicited cries of alarm and surprise from our crew. Faces plastered against the outside glass distorted into grotesque masques: "Nixon is shit! Nixon is shit!"

"Right on!" I wanted to shout out to them.

We walked into the backstage area of the arena and out in front of 15,000 people, some of them actually music fans already rabid to get to the action. Through the tornadic roar of the crowd, one could see the flags of Brazil waving and hear the songs and chants of Brazilian football.

Approximately twenty-two countries vied for the first ten places at the festival. Benny Borg was there with "A Wind Sang in the Trees" from Sweden. A young Phil Coulter with partner Bill Martin had brought "Poundstone River" from Ireland. America's "Evie" wasn't the only lady represented; there was Brazil's "Luciana" (Tapajos/ Sauto) and "Penelope" (Alguero/Senat), a lady of Spain. Well-known folkie Roger Whittaker was there for Kenya with a song of hope, "New World in the Morning." Most are forgotten now, but the night we walked into the dome all these anthems were ringing from the walls.

Bill and I sat in folding chairs backstage, watching the monitors through a couple of unremarkable entries that the Brazilian fans greeted with a fine display of diplomatic politeness. But then Britain's Malcolm Roberts took the stage in a white sport coat and black bow tie, a blond god of a man. From the first notes of "Love Is All" (*w.* Les Reed and Barry Mason), a crafty Humperdinck-like sing-along with dramatic roller-coaster high notes, the crowd was in a frenzy. They stomped and clapped. They spontaneously erupted in tsunamis of hurrahs as Malcolm crested each high note building toward the climax. At the moment of truth he opened his arms and belted an A above A above middle C that precluded forever any of *American Idol*'s supposed vocal triumphs.

"We have to follow that?" I said to Bill, who smiled his gunfighter smile even as the uproar crescendoed outside, but no, Malcolm wasn't finished. He went back into the last chorus, picked up the now familiar melody, and did it again. The Brazilians went berserk.

They sang with him, they wept, they passed out. Huge hand-lettered white banners were waved by fanatics on the little monitors: "Angle-terre," "Malcolm," "America Out of Indochina!"

When our turn came, Bill fastened his clear blue eyes on me and said, "Don't worry. We'll get ours."

Backstage the managers yelled: "Go! Go! Go!" We scattered to our respective positions, dozens of feet from one another on the sprawling stage, as every eye in the arena fastened on Bill Medley. There was a hush. From the crowd there was a small chorus of boos and a curse or two. I heard *"Bisha! Bisha!"* and wondered what that could be. The orchestra started up and I concentrated on the music in front of me. Bill's voice, that haunting, spectral baritone from the opening verse of "You've Lost That Lovin' Feeling" that had in-toned "You never close your eyes anymore . . ." That unmistakable sound was superimposed over the first lyric of "Evie":

"There ain't no future in it, Evie
We never should begin it . . ."

A shout of recognition and approval rang through the crowd. The women swooned and shouted. Bill flexed his tall, thin frame and smiled his thanks to the crowd, who came to renewed life at this dose of genuine Americana. My little two-verse song had a good emotional line. The chords would have been somehow familiar to the crowd as I was mimicking some of their greatest composers. It was composed of two almost identical verses except that the sec-ond verse had a second ending similar to the structure of "I Left My Heart in San Francisco."

"Something in me can't stop trying, Evie, it's up to you."

As Bill nailed the high note, pandemonium arose from the aisles to the rafters of the arena. Perhaps not the hysterical reaction that Malcolm had provoked, but plenty boisterous and loud just the same. All the players met backstage beaming as the bedlam rose to a peak out front. There were some boos, and some shouts of *"Bi-sha! Bisha!"* but these were drowned out by a great rush of excitement at the rising tide of extended applause, convincing us that there really was going to be a contest.

Upon returning to our rooms we were informed by Monica that our request to go into the country and see the people was not accepted, due to security concerns. It was clear we were only allowed to see exactly what they wanted us to see. We resolved to take Ritchie up on an adventurous proposal. He had promised he could get us away from our handlers, out of the hotel unnoticed, and into the favelas.

Early the next morning we made a run for it. Our cadre rolled out of bed, giggling and shushing one another like a bunch of college kids preparing to occupy the administration building. Miles let out a yelp and there was a moment of panic as Patricia stuck a pacifier in his mouth. There was a soft knock at the door and Ritchie slipped inside.

"Okay, cats and kittens," he said under his breath in his musical London accent. "We're going to the freight elevator, not in use right now. Watch out for staff, everybody's a spy. If they see us pretend to be hopelessly lost."

He stuck his head out the door for a quick peek and beckoned us out. We rode down the freight elevator, our mood subdued by the magnitude of our crime. As we cleared out we saw a nondescript red van with its sliding door open wide in the alley. Within seconds we were inside, giggling again.

"This is not a game, my American cousins. Put your heads down and try to behave," Ritchie scolded good-naturedly, but there was tension in his voice and we pulled ourselves together.

Traffic in Rio was tangled and slow, but we eventually made our way into the favelas and the poverty was laid out close-up. I suppose the most amazing thing about it was that the residents seemed to take no notice of any special circumstances. They were smiling. Feeding their kids, and laughing, one wary eye on the bandoliered, machine gun–toting guards that stood on every pedestrian island. Involuntarily, we crouched down when we passed that lot, but they took no notice of us. We were no longer celebrities or anything special except a van full of hippies.

We were out all day. We ate Brazilian street food and clowned on the beach at Ipanema and took pictures when we could. The Devil and I rode the suspended cable cars to the top of Sugarloaf and looked down on the whole city. Up on a higher peak and inland was the famous megalithic statue of Christ of Corcovado with arms spread wide, 250 feet tall. The Devil promptly dubbed him "Corky" and called him that for the duration, which bothered me more than a little.

After a dozen false starts, we finally got into a little alleyway that led to The Man. Ritchie got some currency from us and said, "Okay, sit here for a wink and I'll go up and get some ganja. Try not to get arrested in the meantime. You know, fit in!" He smiled and went up a garbage-festooned path that climbed the side of a hill.

It was lonely for a while. There was something very nearly like a crowd forming around the rusty Volkswagen and I wondered how far and quickly word had spread through the long afternoon that there were foreigners, strangers with money and cameras, in the favelas asking questions.

The police would know by now, I decided. They could be here watching us. Then Ritchie came up with a big English smile on his face and a little packet and we drove off happily, worries banished for the moment. Ritchie said, "The best thing to do is to go through the lobby and upstairs as though you've been to the chemist's. Nothing to hide! Concert's tomorrow, remember. They won't let anything interfere with that." And sure enough, no one said anything as we navigated the lobby and went back upstairs. There were sharp looks from some guys we already had pinned for cops, but what were they going to do?

That night we had a pot party in my sitting room. I don't know what the penalty was for smoking dope in Brazil under that regime. I just know it scared the shit out of everybody, and it was pretty much just me and Fred, His Dark Eminence, and Patricia around the piano. I played "Muskrat Ramble" loud and raucous. Ritchie stopped by but quickly left when the joints came out. Bill stuck his head through the door and wrinkled up his nose. "No thanks." It was pretty rough street-grade weed, but since none of us had had a toke since the L.A. airport, we scarfed huge caustic lungsful and congratulated ourselves on getting into the finals of the competition. The top three were tied: England, United States, and Brazil.

1956

Dad moved us north and west into the badlands of the Texas Panhandle. My siblings reacted to the announcement of every new exodus with a chorus of tears. We moved like gypsies every two years, whether we needed to or not.

We arrived in Pampa, a smaller, cheaper version of sprawling Amarillo, and into our first tract home, which was to our eyes a mansion. It had an attached double garage, a porch, a kitchen with built-ins, and a fenced backyard. In that plaster-on-chicken-wire off-yellow-colored tract house we finally became real Americans. This was commemorated when Dad brought home a television set. Janice, Tommy, and I thought we had discovered alien technology from another planet, even though the picture was grainy and snowy and some days would disappear altogether. We would stare at it even if it wasn't on.

When it came to television, my parents frowned on gunplay, smooching, and people having a good time. At one point my father, disgusted with the ungodliness he had brought into our home, took the precious television away. The grieving was horrendous, even for him to behold. He brought it back.

Pampa was another faceless church house on a featureless landscape with no interior detail, like a movie set with a false front. The desert missions, half concealed by ribbons of blowing sand and possessing no architectural identity, no steeple, no stone, no stained glass except the plain yellow variety, no landscaping, no music of any quality (certainly no organ or decent piano), all of these had blended in my nine-year-old consciousness into a prototypical one-horse Baptist church. In my private sanctuary, the inner room hidden behind a thousand doors, I supposed life, if it continued, would be an endless series of ghostly tabernacles, rising like abandoned dreams from the white chalk of the West Texas back roads.

On our next migration, to Eldorado, Dad's luck changed. Eldorado was no fabled city of gold but it was back in Oklahoma, my home state, at least. Nice homes, some of them even large, surrounded a one-street business district with a proper traffic signal working at the main intersection. There was a movie theater with a neon-lighted marquee advertising first-run films and a factory that hand-manufactured polished wooden ski boats under the brand name Indian.

The church, in my starved imagination, was a cathedral: a redbrick edifice with a flight of graceful, wide stairs climbing to the front door. A steeple, an organ, and plush carpet on the dais. I have a picture of Mother and Dad standing on those steps, her in a fittingly formal black dress and wearing heels with her faux pearls, Dad in dark suit and tie. They are in their late twenties and the look is successful. We lived in a dignified redbrick parsonage, hemmed in by a couple of maples and an elm tree that cooled the front porch in the summer. I was now reading hymns easily from the Baptist Hymnal and playing simple classical pieces, like Beethoven's "Moonlight Sonata," if with a decided indifference. Though my mother spoke with great confidence about my future on the piano bench at the First Baptist Church, I suffered through practice; it seemed such an unmanly thing. But she would put the kitchen egg timer on the upright in the living room, a cheeky little chicken, and until it clucked at the end of thirty minutes God help me if I was to quit.

I was in fourth grade and from our front porch I could see across the street to a wide, grassy athletic field and the schoolhouse, an ugly multistoried affair. Schools had not been kind to me. But in a hopeful augury my fourth-grade teacher was named Mrs. Wise. She was in fact wise and kind; the first teacher I ever had who seemed to care for the children she tended. She played records in class. Records? In class? She played Rodgers and Hammerstein's *Oklahoma!* and all the kids sang "Where the wind comes sweepin' down the plain!" Well, most of them. There was a gang of toughs in the back of the room who just smirked, not seeming to relate to the music at all, launching heavy paper wads from rubber bands that would bang into the back of my head hard and wet. But the music was insinuating itself into me, making me want to cry sometimes because it was so beautiful. I would look into Mrs. Wise's spectacled round face beaming with a smile, her silvery head nodding in time to the music, and think, *She feels it, too! She's not even in this classroom just now.* Mrs. Wise was teaching music appreciation, and very well, too.

One spring morning I ate my breakfast quickly, not forgetting to scrape the plate and drop it into the sink, grabbed my books, and jumped off the porch from the top step, landing in one great bound singing: "Oh, what a beautiful morning," and it was! Oh, it was so fresh and clean! "Oh, what a beautiful day!" I sang as I ran across the grass toward the school playground. "I've got a beautiful feeling . . ."

They jumped me from behind a utility shed. Four or five of them. They beat on me yelling, "Damn preacher's kid! Go to Hell, preacher's kid!" They shoved me facedown into the asphalt, grinding the gravel deep into my face and left me there, books spread to the four winds, my lip busted.

1969

The next day a couple of plainclothes cops came up to our suite with a cardboard box full of cassettes, lead sheets, and other crap, and put them down on the coffee table in front of the couch.

"These are the materials the maestro requested through the air mail," one of them said, and smiled as wide and avaricious as a jailhouse door.

"Let us know if we can be of any further assistance to the maestro," the other one said in a dead tone, eyes as cold and hard as a mass grave.

They had broken into the package and the bogus audiocassettes had been dismantled. All the pieces were left in disarray and handfuls of curly recording tape decorated the warning.

They had been gone for all of five minutes when Fred and Patricia came through the door looking for Ritchie. He had disappeared. "I think something's wrong, man," Freddy said. "I think something's happened to Ritchie. He hasn't answered his phone since last night."

Big D put his finger to pursed lips, went over to the window, and lifted the heavy sash. We both knelt and put our heads outside in the roar of afternoon traffic punctuated by two-cycle engines and snorting diesel buses.

"That's better," the Devil said. He looked at me with bland simile. "We're made," he said. "They've got our dope. They could nail us right now. The way I see it the only thing between us and the Brazilian big house is 'Evie.'"

My stomach turned wrong side out. "What about Ritchie?" I asked.

"He's either in jail or maybe trying to get over the border somewhere. Of course there is the unspeakable third possibility."

We strained to close the ancient stiff sash and pulled our heads in, giving Fred and Patricia the "no talking" sign and tried to play it casual.

That night was the final round of the Canção Popular. Ritchie was still missing. We lived all day with the tension and worry of it. No polite attempt to locate him through channels elicited any response. He seemed to have passed through a doorway into the land of the "the missing ones," as they called them down there.

The contest teetered toward its climax. But for some of us there was a burgeoning dread of what would happen at its conclusion. Were they just going to let us go home without repercussions? We prepared for the concert in a somber mood. All the giddiness that comes with flaunting authority was gone and forgotten, replaced by a sickness in the gut. The novelty of being stoned and yelled at, like the "capitalist pigs" we supposedly represented, had fled. We rode down to the arena in silence, the close escort of a dozen police taking on a more sinister aspect.

In the arena that night there were some preliminaries. Then our nemesis Malcolm Roberts hit the boards and the crowd shook the house, clapping in time, singing the whole song with him, flinging bravura cheers to the heights of the dome and generally behaving as though Corky himself had come down in a white sport coat and a pink carnation. He did the fake ending. They bought in. They pretty much crowned him right there.

After what seemed like a long period of agitation and excitement, the crowd had quieted enough for our lot to be introduced. I went straight to the piano and sat down. Freddy smiled tightly at me from behind his big acoustic guitar. I smiled back; what the hell! Just one more time. *"Bisha! Bisha! Bisha!"* echoed as always, still a mystery. Bill's female adherents shrieked as usual. We had that going for us. Bill bent slightly as he took the weight of the song:

> *"There ain't no future in it, Evie*
> *We never should begin it, Evie."*

There was tumultuous racket going on from the very first note. It was not the sound of singing or clapping but a grousing rumble of ill will that seemed to gain momentum as Bill moved through the second verse:

> *"If time was half a nice guy, Evie*
> *We might have had a nice try, Evie, oh, Evie . . ."*

Bill was giving his best performance ever, but even as he stood tall and began the ending couplet, the most bittersweet of all the lyrics, there was a roar of real anger from the crowd. The ending of the song could not be heard over the screams of thousands of people bent on ending the performance early. Bill tried to finish and never stopped singing. They were screaming, weeping, stamping in one prolonged howl of outrage and Bill Medley stood there completely disarmed. What had he done to provoke this?

Suddenly, out of nowhere, came white-coated Malcolm Roberts dragging a Union Jack as big as an outdoor billboard onto the stage.

Broad-shouldered Malcolm manhandled the great hulking mass of red, white, and blue stripes out into the middle of the stage. Gamely, we ventured the closing lines:

"Though it's doomed and damned and dying
Something in me won't stop trying . . ."

Malcolm chose this moment to throw the giant British flag over Bill's shoulder in a protective gesture, a move that almost brought the tall, thin Californian to his knees. The flag's weight was immense. Bill shifted his center of gravity underneath the great awkward bundle to hold it up. For one nightmarish second I thought Bill was going to shrug the Union Jack off and drop it onto the stage. I said, "No!" He never heard or saw me.

"Evie . . ."

It's a long note and Medley used it to hitch up the burden of the flag.

"It's up to you . . ."

He finished like a gentleman, standing straight and tall under the flag of our mother country. If a bomb had hit the place it couldn't have caused more furor, uproar, or consternation than Malcolm's split-second decision to save the American. We came backstage, exhausted from the withering reception. Not anxious to hear "Lucinda" again, as only Brazil remained to perform, we retreated to the hotel.

The next day we got the results, and just as the punters told us from day one, Brazil won first prize. Unbelievably the United States was second. Malcolm Roberts, selfless gesture and all, had come third for the U.K. Any analysis of this baffling outcome is unsatisfactory.

The ride to the airport took a thousand years. There was nothing encouraging about the military Jeeps in front and behind our single car. The motorcycle cops no longer showed interest in try-ing to view us through the tinted windows; their formality was unnerving.

We were met at the airport by police and customs officials who took hours to go through our luggage, searching every shaving kit and medicine bottle. Our passports, our declarations, the minutiae of bureaucracy, took hours. At intervals, there were unexplained delays that kept us waiting alone or in small groups. They were sweating us.

When we were finally on the aircraft I looked out the small win-dow to see military Jeeps and police cars in a cordon around the plane, blue lights flashing. Officials glared at us from behind avia-tor shades with no attempt to disguise their deep unhappiness at our departure.

As we taxied down the strip, every moment a small eternity, ve-hicles followed on both wingtips as though hoping for one last slipup, anything that would put us back in their hands. I breathed a silent prayer to the God of Engines and looked over at Mr. Satan. He smiled benignly.

"They could still arrest us anytime, you know!" he assured me.

"Thanks, pal."

"Also, I have to tell you, buddy," he added with a grin, " 'bisha' means 'homo'!"

I looked across the cabin at Fred and Patricia. They were lean-ing back against the headrests with their eyes closed. Miles was sleeping peacefully on Patricia's lap. I figured they were praying like me.

Outside, the waiting police, the suffering city in the distance, and a memory of a guy named Ritchie were still in frame. The throttles opened, the bird rolled, and just like that we were out of it. In the first-class cabin there was a massive synchronized exhale from everyone, including the innocent, and then an involuntary laugh and a guilty round of applause. A relief washed over me that tasted like all the rest of life, tempered by regret as to what could have become of our good friend and guide Ritchie. To date there has been no contact.

1956

Dad raised chickens out in the back of the parsonage. It was fun at first, lots of tiny balls of peeping yellow fuzz running around in cardboard boxes warmed by sixty-watt lightbulbs like wonderful Easter presents. When they got older, gawky and teenage looking, he went out back wearing old jeans, shirtsleeves rolled up, and wrung their necks in a bloody massacre, while we watched in stunned disbelief. They flapped and convulsed around the yard in a macabre corps de ballet of death. Then, gathered around an oil drum full of boiling water, my brother, sister, and I were forced to dip and soak the decapitated bodies until they were waterlogged, at which time we pulled the sodden feathers from their bodies, every single quill, until they were naked and still. Feet were lopped off. The rest of the carnage was rough surgery. By any measure it was a bloodbath and even the memory of the smell was nauseating.

There was an old man in Eldorado, who lived across the alley from us. His grandchildren visited from time to time. I thought nothing of it that my little brother and sister played with them along the alley between the houses, hiding in abandoned henhouses and acting out Cowboys and Indians. One day the eccentric neighbor came across the alley yelling at the kids and told my dad that Tommy and Janice were trying to "play doctor" with his grandkids. This was an unlikely allegation.

Without asking my siblings for an explanation, Dad marched them into the front bedroom downstairs. Pressing them facedown on the bed he took his belt to them. Seeing my sister Janice flogged within an inch when I knew she was perfectly innocent knocked the breath out of me. I figured a guy like me just had to take his chances with my dad, but a little girl? I felt in that moment that I hated and feared him, I just didn't know in what order.

Jimmy Webb in London. *(Courtesy of* Penthouse)

CHAPTER THREE

The theme song will not be written by Jim Webb,
Francis Scott Key nor sung by Glen Campbell,
Tom Jones, Johnny Cash, Engelbert
Humperdinck or the Rare Earth.
The revolution will not be televised.
—Gil Scott-Heron,
"The Revolution Will Not Be Televised," 1970

I never got Jimmy Webb. —Gene Pitney

1969

For all practical purposes I had been commuting to London since
1967. There had been trips for various projects and vacations, but
for the most part I went there to see Richard Harris and to work

on our albums. The 1968 follow-up to *Tramp Shining* and the stunning performance of "MacArthur Park" had been an album called *The Yard Went On Forever,* a critic's darling that did not produce a single.

There were other overtones of dissonance between the physically imposing and irrepressible Harris and myself. I needed to know if he had any problems with his share of the proceeds from our records, even though I would rather have put both hands in a sausage grinder than take a wayward penny. There were rumors, however, that he thought I was giving him the short end of the stick. It was painful. Still, I sincerely wanted to do a third album with him.

We feuded in a polite sort of way over a promise he made me during the creation of *Tramp Shining,* his debut solo album—containing my songs and arrangements—after his singing movie role in Lerner and Loewe's *Camelot.* In the backseat of his Phantom V, a car I understood to have been purchased from the Royal Household, in a fever of excitement and after a pitcher of Pimm's, he had clasped me around the shoulders and said, "Ah, Jimmywebb! This album's goin' to be a huge hit! We're going to fool 'em all, Jimmywebb! And when this fucking album is a hit . . . ." He paused dramatically in his Shakespearean-flavored Irish brogue. "*I'm going to give you this Phantom V!*"

I demurred and told him I was sure he didn't really mean that. He continued to insist in the strongest possible invective that he fucking well did mean it and I should clear a space in the driveway. We had been so close in those days. He was a tough guy, a human monument and someone I openly revered. Richard had a strong temper and after a couple of Black Velvets it was better to avoid talking about religion or politics or even his beloved Ireland, except perhaps to say that the bloody British should get out. "Up the Rebels!" he would shout, and smash an empty glass into the wall.

So this was the loving, mercurial, adopted older brother I was flying over to visit with some trepidation. He would no doubt have a half-dozen photographs of Rolls-Royce limousines to show me, some of them quite impressive. I would politely decline and look at him, shaking my head and saying, "I don't believe that's the car I ordered." I was devastated that he didn't want to give me his Phantom V. I didn't need anyone to give me a car. I had cars. Nor did I want just any old Phantom V. More than anything in the world I wanted *Richard's* Phantom V. And, though this may have been too much to ask: I wanted him to give it to me with joy in his heart.

There was something uneasy in the wind. The Irish can silently bury a grudge deeper and hold it longer than any other creatures under Heaven. I was sure there was something festering deep and agitating Richard that he had not told me about.

1958

Not to be tethered in one place—even a nice one—too long, it was hey up and throw me over yet again, when my father moved us out of the agrarian prosperity of Eldorado and into an urban and almost alien landscape, the Boom Town, the Oil Town, the Cattle Town, the Capital, and the storied center of the state: Oklahoma City. We settled in a dilapidated suburb on the four-lane Grand Boulevard. Dad pastored a cinder block Baptist church called Rockwood, right next to Rockwood Elementary School, a small urban prison for kids. Backhoes were digging huge openings in Grand Boulevard, probably in the faint hope of making it grander, and large piles of red clay clods were piled willy-nilly, marking our route to school.

The bullies would materialize from behind these tall mounds, flinging clods at my little brother Tommy and me. They would pepper us with a stinging barrage and then move in for a kidney punch or a slap to the forehead. "He yah, Four Eyes!" "It's Preach! C'mon, Preach, eat this clod. Eat it or I'll kill you, you little son of a bitch!" I peered back through my thick eyeglasses, congenitally myopic. They were bigger, older, and mad-dog-mean oil field trash. The biggest one of those bastards I really wanted to hurt. I patiently explained military strategy to my little brother: I would open with a machine-gun burst to the face, and at this point I would "hit him high" and Tommy would "hit him low." Tommy, a brave little soul, nodded in sage comprehension. "Then," I said, "when we've got him down, we'll pound him in the face and balls with our fists." He nodded. We rehearsed the tactics a few times and prepared for our attack the next morning.

The rangy redneck came over the top of one of the dirt piles in a surprise frontal assault, almost as though he was privy to our plans. I emptied two handfuls of small rocks at his head and jumped off my feet to meet him head and shoulders. I started swinging. Tommy stood and watched the bully pin me to the ground and tenderize me from stomach to forehead with impunity. When he got tired of jackhammering me he stuck a handful of red dirt in my mouth and went on his way. I picked up my soiled and torn schoolbooks, found my glasses, spit, cast one reproachful glance at my kid brother, and we walked silently on to school.

In fairness to the bullies and baboons, I was a fairly odd kid. I had one friend, a grown-up named Bob, who had no proper job but hours to burn building and crashing engine-powered model airplanes. He was a nerd before they invented the word, always covered in glue, oil, and glow fuel. But he had a cheerful, feckless soul, as well as my admiration, though I was witness to many a shouting match between him and his young wife, who supported his plane habit and a couple of diaper-clad babies.

Bob especially loved Sterling Ringmasters, a stunt plane of the day with a forty-inch wingspan. He'd crank the plane's .35 engine with a wooden prop until its tremulous wail echoed around the neighborhood. The whining bird would leap up and into an endless circle, Bob whirling in the middle like a dervish.

Dad referred to Bob as "The Model Bum," and whether he realized it or not, he began to feel a little jealous of all the time I spent with my new friend.

With a handsome, fiery young minister in the pulpit, Rockwood Baptist flourished. I tended the piano bench. As the only musician at the new church, I felt pressure to provide as massive an accompaniment as possible for the choir and congregation. I started seeing a new piano teacher, Susan Goddard, who was unique in my experience, as she specialized in improvisation, the catalyst for a logarithmic leap in my musical comprehension. This training consisted of exercises with the Baptist Hymnal; arranging and harmonizing familiar tunes by using what Leonard Bernstein would later call "transformational elements." She taught me to play in octaves and "fill in" the third and fifth tones in order to make a more massive chord. She taught me chord "substitution," which is the alchemy of substituting exotic and unfamiliar chords for more prosaic ones. Arpeggiation, dissonance, alternate basses—all of these techniques enriched my playing in a way that helped me create richer, more classically textured arrangements.

Occasionally I pushed it over the line. A current box office smash *Ben-Hur* featured an Oscar-winning score by Miklós Rózsa. It was a tour de force of Roman military marches and transfiguration themes representing a Christ who was never actually seen. It also had a dynamite love theme. One Sunday morning I coolly slipped the Love Theme from *Ben-Hur* into my offertory. The blue-haired music committee marched into my father's study immediately after service. Dad later informed me I was clinging to the organ bench "only by your fingernails."

I began my first year in junior high at Stonewall Jackson Jr., only a few blocks' walk from home. I also began to write my first pop songs, a practice that irritated my father within a micrometer of his self-control. The radio I listened to at night covertly, under the covers of my bed, was rich with Sam Cooke's "You Send Me" (*w.* Sam Cooke), Pat Boone's "Love Letters in the Sand" (*w.* Nick Kenny and Charles Kenny), and a peppery mix of other music. Elvis dominated with "All Shook Up" (*w.* Otis Blackwell), "(Let Me Be Your) Teddy Bear" (*w.* Kal Mann and Bernie Lowe), and "Jailhouse Rock" (*w.* Jerry Leiber and Mike Stoller). There were unlikely records such as Belafonte's "Banana Boat" (*w.* Unknown), and Perry Como's "Round and Round" (*w.* Joe Shapiro and Lou Stallman). There were songs that defined the era such as Marty Robbins's "A White Sport Coat" (*w.* Marty Robbins), and Debbie Reynolds's "Tammy" (*w.* Jay Livingstone and Ray Evans). I pecked a song out on the family's old upright that I thought would be good for the Everlys. It was called "Someone Else" and I was twelve years old. Years later Art Garfunkel would record this song.

> It's someone else
> I saw you out last night
> Holding him so tight
> And it's someone else

It drove Dad crazy. He had developed a notion that all kids' music, especially rock 'n' roll, was about sex. What a concept. Dad was not, however, universally opposed to the idea of sex. Two little girls, Little Susan and Baby Sylvia, joined our family in rapid succession.

1969

I planned to meet Evie in Venice and then return to London to spend time with Richard Harris. Evie proposed a meeting on the Grand Canal at the Hotel Metropole, rightly calculating that it was probably the single most romantic place in the civilized world. I was only a little surprised to learn she had also invited Ron Kass and Joan Collins. Ironically, Joan's second husband, Tony Newley, was the songwriting partner of Leslie Bricusse, Evie's husband. It all seemed not a little bit incestuous to me but Evie said, "Darling, everybody in London is having an affair! No one makes a fuss!" I had been hurt by that. When we had met the previous year, she was quite fussy about it because, she told me, Leslie was rumored to be having an affair with Lana Wood, Natalie's stunning sister.

At dawn I arrived on the dock right in front of the Hotel Metropole. I stood unsteadily a few paces from the Piazza San Marco and the winged lion high atop his pedestal. Evie was standing there. She smiled and tossed her long black hair and fussed over me on the short walk to the hotel. I breathed her in, the exquisite olive skin and deep brown eyes of this exotic being from Malta. In the early dawn the gondola lamps still burned outside the millionaires' row of exorbitantly expensive hotels that fronted the Bacino di San Marco.

We sat on the balcony of our suite and sipped bloodred Mediterranean orange juice. We watched the sun rising up on the rhythms of the water traffic. We walked to a small espresso shop, one of many on the sprawling piazza, and sipped the hairy-chested coffee, watching the Venetians stop in on their way to work. And then we slept.

Reluctantly, we dragged ourselves out of the deep downy mattress around nightfall. The four of us met for the first time at a restaurant that night. Joan was strikingly beautiful, and her fianceé, Ron Kass, who became her third husband, was a virile-looking specimen, what women like to call a "hunk." Physically imposing, open-faced, and quick to smile in a shy sort of way, Ron was CEO at Apple Corps and manager of The Beatles. I didn't know much about him except the London papers had been hinting at trouble within The Beatles' famous company for weeks.

It was odd, even in the swinging '60s, to be sitting there openly in view of the international jet set, a foursome with so many complicated and intertwining connections. The four of us looked at one another in quite a sober fashion for a minute or so, and then we all laughed helplessly and proceeded to get rip-roaring smashed on Dom Pérignon. Joan turned out to be a hoot, like most British theater folk, and one got the feeling that for both women the immediate past had been sad and stuffy enough. It was time for a little fun.

Theretofore, Ron had enjoyed near superstar status. He was thirty-four years old and a corporate success symbol even though Apple had been hemorrhaging money for months on schemes that at times bordered on the absurd. It was a rough spot to be in. Apple had been founded by The Beatles as "a new kind of corporation," one that would provide funds to impoverished artists who had the will but not the way. The Beatles were a moneymaking machine whose public stance was antiestablishment and whose private machinations were a dicey mix of group politics (Paul and John were senior partners; the other two had to scuffle) and virtually unfettered personal spending on a scale with any newly minted capitalist. John and Paul fought an ongoing private war over group supremacy and conflicting girlfriends and such, each reserving the right to okay expensive and risky ventures outside the control of Ron Kass or anybody like him. Enter Allen Klein. Klein was a New Jersey–born hustler who had managed the Rolling Stones in the early '60s and ended up owning their publishing company (all songs before 1971) thank you very much. Klein had contacted John Lennon after Lennon had complained in the London papers that the band was "going broke." By early 1969, John had convinced Ringo and George that Klein was their man. Paul refused to warm up to Klein and never signed the contract. This bone of contention continued as a significant factor in the band's slow-motion dissolution.

On this night, while dining with us in Venice, Ron received a call informing him that Klein was charging him with "financial impropriety." I remember Ron's and Joan's faces went pale, and he charged out of there with barely a wave. He was going to try to fight Klein off. Ron canceled his lavish room at the Metropole and flew straight to London. Joan decided to stay over with Evie and me so as to try to make the best of it. It was a chaotic moment and suddenly Joan was moving in with her cases and wardrobe. The bed was roughly queen-sized, so I offered immediately to take the couch. The ladies would have none of it. I suppose I could have entertained a couple of James Bond–like fantasies about sharing a bed with not one but two of the hottest chicks in London. But no. I loved Evie, to distraction.

As we prepared for bed, any exotic thoughts I may have retained became ludicrous. Off came the false eyelashes and makeup. Out came the rollers and the bobby pins, green masques, serums, and Mother Hubbards. I tried very hard to maintain a contact-free zone in the middle of the bed; but as the night progressed, arms and legs were thrown about and it became a kind of wrestling match. It was not very unlike being in bed with my brother Tommy and sister Janice. So much for the romantic weekend in Venice.

The three of us flew back to London the next day. There was much upset as Ron was unhorsed at Apple. Klein was ousted scarcely two years later when Paul McCartney sued the other Beatles, and Apple went into receivership. Klein subsequently went to jail for defrauding the Bangladesh concert and UNICEF. On top of it all, the bastard ruined our weekend in Venice.

I had learned in Venice via telegraph, somewhere in the confusion and departure of Ron Kass, that I had won a Best Orchestration Grammy for Richard Harris's recording of "MacArthur Park." My father had accepted for me. I'd gone the previous year and won for "Up, Up and Away" but still somehow couldn't get myself into that self-aggrandizing room again. The lens of hindsight clearly focuses my priorities at that time of my life. At any rate, had I been there, I still would have been disappointed. *A Tramp Shining* wasn't Record of the Year? "MacArthur Park" wasn't Best Single? When had there ever been anything as remotely ambitious and well recorded? Looking ahead to our meeting, I realized Richard had probably been disappointed that only the orchestration had been deemed good enough for a Grammy. He had poured his heart into his vocal performance but lost Best Pop Male Vocalist to José Feliciano, for his cover of the Doors' "Light My Fire."

After the unavoidable slog through immigration and customs at Heathrow, I parted ways with Evie and Joan and waited for the arrival of my favored driver, Terry Naylor, who appeared smiling to beat the band and displaying some very dodgy dental work. He helped me with my large case, which had already been to Brazil and back, out to a chilly world of visible exhalations and into the backseat of a Phantom V idling at the curb.

Richard and I had agreed to meet at a country house he was renting in Sussex. Totally unlike Richard was this change to a bucolic environment, but it sounded as though it might be the very place to get a few things straightened out.

Hours passed and we were on a farm road with fences close aboard and hummocks of tall grasses frosted with white. We slowed to make a turn into a long driveway and I just caught a glimpse of a weathered sign tacked to a fence post: COTCHFORD FARM.

1958

There was a talent show at Stonewall Jackson High. It happened once a year, qualified competitors or not. I was mature enough to go out on the evangelical circuit with my father. What was the difference in performing in church and performing on stage? Same adrenaline, same nerves, and for most people, a healthy dose of fear combined with a tremendous impetus to hit the notes and hit them right. I auditioned my jazz piece one day in the school auditorium. To the school's credit they had a proper proscenium arch and as my hands moved over the real ivory keys, the lighting department sent down a lavender shade that lit up the whole keyboard. As my hands moved they left indigo shadows following just behind. I was so entranced by it that I played a blooper or two and the teacher stopped me outright.

"So, Webb . . . do you call that music?"

I did, sort of.

"Well, I'm not going to hold you back; be an idiot then!"

He wrote my name on a clipboard and I was in the talent show by way of a kind of vengeful default. Come the day of the show he had a good portion of crow to devour as I unsteadily but relentlessly improvised my way to a chorus of screams from the female students. I knew in that instant there was no turning back. It was my first acknowledgment of any kind from the opposite sex.

The closest I had ever come to going to a real dance had been an after-school sock hop in the gym at Stonewall. When my father found out about it he made a special trip over there to complain about dances at school. Glen Campbell used to ask: "Do you know why Baptists don't make love standing up?"

(Nope. Can't say as I do.)

"Because they're afraid people will think they're *dancing!*"

The social lives of the five Webb children were pretty much ruined for life by this nonsense. It made us outsiders and squares but it was the official doctrine of the Southern Baptist Convention. The Lord was more merciful to the Methodists, who were allowed to hold civilized dances inside their actual church. Most Baptists thought the Methodists were just a tad shy of going to hell anyway.

1969

At Cotchford Farm I had a momentary impression of a thatched roof cottage out of a Constable painting and a crusting of new snow under my leather soles, and then was bustled into a cozy interior by Terry and the houseman. My leather case was promptly brought in and I had time only to dispatch Terry Naylor and the hired Phantom V back to London before Richard appeared at the front door, tousled hair to the shoulders and a few brandies to the advantage. He greeted me with a quick hug and beckoned me into the Hobbit-scaled rooms. Both of us, well over six feet, had to duck to gain passage under the doorways so that after a bump or two I complained, "Okay, where's the real house?"

"They were smaller then, Jimmywebb!" Richard retorted.

"Who? When?" I asked.

"People were smaller three hundred years ago, my overfed American friend!" He speared me with a stern expression and his unearthly blue eyes. We sat down in front of the fire. He poured me a brandy straight and said, "Here, have a look at these." He tossed over a stack of photos and I caught them in my lap. Rolls-Royce limousines in gay profusion. On top was a Silver Ghost cabriolet, the kind where the driver sits exposed to the weather out front. An oldie with wire wheels. I feigned interest and looked at a few shots. "You're lookin' knackered, Jimmywebb!" He always called me Jimmywebb, in one clipped flourish.

"While you yourself appear as fresh as a dew-covered blooming rose." I smiled back. He laughed. We were still friends then, but the excitement we had felt for each other, the electricity that it takes to grab the world by the scruff of the neck and shake it . . . that might have been lacking. I had some new songs for him, and we ended up playing a few demos on a battered old stereo as there was no piano.

"This place is haunted, Jimmywebb," he said at one point and nodded toward a row of leaded glass windows behind his chair. "Brian Jones died out there." Everyone knew that Brian Jones had quit, or been forced out of, the Rolling Stones. It was common knowledge that within a matter of weeks he had drowned in a swimming pool. I fought my way up and out of my chintz armchair and looked out through the glass panes. All was white. No sign of a swimming pool or errant ghost.

"Yeah, I heard about it. I think I'm going to pack it in, Rich," I said, polishing off the dregs from a brandy snifter and standing up.

"All right then." He led the way back toward the front door and a cramped flight of stairs. "Come up here then." He grabbed my cowhide bag and led me up and through the first door at the top of the stairs. The door was about five feet tall. I stooped and entered a small room with antique lace curtains, a single bed, and quilted coverlet.

Richard crouched in the doorway as I sat down and prodded the down mattress.

"Y'know, Jimmywebb, that you're sittin' on Christopher Robin's bed now."

"What? Are you putting me on?"

"Not at all." He sprang the surprise he'd been hinting at. "This is A. A. Milne's house, you illiterate youth!"

I was speechless. So this night I was to sleep in Christopher Robin's bedroom on a tiny child's bed. I wondered if Winnie-the-Pooh might be stopping by. It was the kind of magic we had once reveled in. At least Richard was still trying.

"Good night then, lad." And he was gone. The cottage grew quiet and dark and colder around me as I quickly donned pajamas, doused the one bedside lamp, and slid deep into the downy cocoon of English linen. After the flight and the brandy I dreamed of nothing.

"Will ye take yer breakfast, Jimmywebb? I have an appointment in London I must attend!" Richard spoke from somewhere, impossibly loud. I raised myself enough to peer over the top of the duvet and discern him leaning through the doorway, hair long and reddish blond, if a little thinner than when we had first met in 1967.

I rolled off the bed, shocked by the cold floor, and donned some thick woolen socks out of my case. Downstairs the elfin kitchen was all copper, brass, and cast iron. An ancient carved rectory table was laden with two English breakfasts: poached eggs, plump sausages, broiled tomatoes, fried mushrooms, sautéed potatoes, and hot brown beans with sides of muffins, toast, and jars of country jam and farm-churned butter. Whatever shortcomings generally ascribed to English cuisine, breakfast could not be faulted.

We both tucked in and between bites I opened a discussion.

"So I understand you have some problems with Canopy, royalty statements and such," I said.

"Lippman has been in the till," he said brusquely. "Rupert says so."

I was no huge fan of Harvey Lippman and had reasons of my own to suspect him of financial shenanigans. He was a year gone then, had passed on in a particularly unpleasant way, and honestly I hadn't really thought of him much. He was, however, in the thick of things when "MacArthur Park" had been at the top of the charts.

"Well, Richard, he might have done something." Rupert was one of the most respected figures in British management and he lent considerable weight to the allegation. "In which case we've both been cheated. I will go over the royalty statements with Howard, and we will put it right if it's been tampered with."

"If?" he barked across the table. "*If* is it?" His indignation manifested itself in the narrowing of his icy blue eyes and the thrust of his magnificent beak.

I dropped my cutlery on my plate with a great clank. "Listen, Rich, while we're on this tack let's just forget the Rolls-Royce, can we? I was excited about having *your* Rolls because I care about *you*! Not this array of antiquity!" I gestured at the photos of Rollers casually left on the table by my plate.

"Array of antiquity, is it, Jimmywebb?" he raged. He dropped his own knife and fork and quickly gathered a huge woolen coat and his papers. He went out the front door, turning to say, "We'll have a word on this when I return from the city!" Outside he disappeared into an idling Daimler limo and left me there to finish my breakfast.

I took a hot bath and dressed, sobered by the exchange. There wasn't much to do in the cottage except listen to the ticking clocks, so after a couple of hours of reading I dressed warmly and stepped outside. A valiant sun was making futile attempts to pierce a low-flying stratification. I wandered around to the back of the house where a small swimming pool was staked down tight under a tarpaulin marbled with eddies of wind and frost. So Brian Jones really did cash it here. I stood in reverent silence for a minute.

I called up Terry Naylor and had him pick me back up in the Phantom V and take me to the Dorchester in London, accommodations with modern man-sized doorframes. Evie was still in town and in good spirits, hanging out with David Hemmings, who had played the villain Mordred in *Camelot* alongside Richard and Vanessa Redgrave. He was a perfectly charming hard drinker and relentless skirt jockey. The three of us went out on a Wagnerian pub crawl, laughing our way through three fashionable bars and almost as many bottles of Dom Pérignon. It was my send-off party for Dickie Harris. We wouldn't speak again for almost twenty years.

1958

At school, along with the usual curricular fare, I was enrolled in Dale Storey's drafting class. His grinning facade of a face comes to memory without effort.

On our first day in class he made things clear. "Now in this class"—he swaggered in his short-sleeved white shirt and thin black tie—"we don't make mistakes. Girls make mistakes. You don't see any girls, do ya?" We all looked around. He was right. No girls. "In particular, we don't make smudges on our drawings." He paused to fetch down a doublehanded paddle, over four feet long, that hung behind his desk. "For every smudge I see on an assignment paper you put on my desk, you're gonna get a stroke on your rear end from

Ol' Betsy here." He whipped her through a half circle with both hands, producing an ominous whistle. "Well, why don't I just show you? Get up." He pointed the weapon at a blond kid in the first row. The kid got up with a kind of half grin on his face. "Bend over and grab your ankles," Dale said, smiling back.

"What? I haven't done . . ."

"If you don't want to fail the class, do it."

Reluctantly the kid bent over and grabbed his ankles, raising his hindquarters high in the air. Storey rocked back and swung through, hitting his victim in the ass so hard it popped like a Christmas cracker. The kid staggered, white-faced.

"Class dismissed!" Storey smiled.

I was ever so careful not to put a single smudge on any of my drawings. Every once in a while some poor sod would drool on his paper and blur a letter in his title box. He would be invited up front, where he would dutifully clutch his ankles so Dale could take batting practice on his ass.

One day I was sitting at my desk, work done, daydreaming out the window. I was reading Ray Bradbury's *The Martian Chronicles* in the evenings and couldn't wait to get home and cocoon myself in another time and space.

"Mr. Webb!"

Startled into a conscious state I found myself staring at Dale Storey and his four-foot long paddle.

"Can you come up to the front please?

Oh no. It just couldn't be. I was sure there was no smudge on my paper.

"Get on with it, Mr. Webb."

From somewhere outside my body I observed myself getting to my feet and stumbling through the waiting class. A great weariness came over me as I bent over in front of his desk and took hold of my white socks. I had a rush of knowing all as Ol' Betsy and my butt hurtled toward our inevitable intimacy. This is what Dale Storey had come to teach us: futility.

When the blow came it made my father's flailings with his thin leather belt seem amateurish. My knees buckled slightly as the blush of shame spread over my neck and shoulders. My classmates couldn't look me in the eye. Everybody in that room knew I was nothing if not the smallest, most inoffensive prey on the menu.

Storey's class was the last of the day, thank God, as I was having trouble sitting in my chair. A cursory examination revealed welts and blisters forming with mathematical precision. Listlessly, I gingerly walked home without even a pencil, cheeks spread apart, down the old cracked and shifting plates of the sidewalk. It was twelve long prairie blocks back to my house and I went as though in a dream. "Hey Preach!" The terrorists were waiting at the first corner to rub it in. I strolled past them and they fell silent. I reached home and looked up from the backyard into my bedroom window, then turned and walked the twelve blocks back to school. I turned and walked back home again, exploring the dimensions of a completely futile and meaningless act. At the Dairy Queen, people stopped slurping their double malts and stared at me as I walked past for the second time. Eyes straight ahead, gait calm and measured.

The second time around I went inside my house, climbed the stairs, and closed my bedroom door. Plastic models hung from the ceiling, my pride and joy, unseen.

A week later my parents were concerned enough to bring in a psychiatrist. I refused conversation with him. He scratched his head and left. I remember watching the sun track through Mother's handmade curtains and across the hardwood floors as more days passed.

Jimmy Webb and Suzy Horton. *(Courtesy of Suzy Horton Ronstadt)*

CHAPTER FOUR

With Sticky Fingers turned up real loud
We flirted with catastrophe
We were doin' everything that's not allowed
Life didn't come with a warranty for you and me . . .
—JLW, "Too Young to Die," 1993

1969

My stepbrother Garth had a full race Camaro that he built up from speed parts I'd given him for Christmas the year before. He was a genius with anything mechanical or electronic and he'd come up with a mill that would turn around five hundred horses on the dynamometer. He installed a four-speed Hurst shifter and 4:11 rear end.

Tommy, my younger sibling, was visiting from Oklahoma and we all went up to Topanga to Fred Tackett's pad for New Year's Eve. The house perched on the side of a hill in a quaintly bucolic section of the canyon where public thoroughfares had not yet received the benefits of paved roads. There were lots of people around, and joints of homegrown weed were passed, which were potent as hell. There was a lot of beer and a few drinks of hard liquor and of course wine. You cannot attend a party in California and not find barrels of the stuff.

Lowell George and Bill Payne of Little Feat were there. Fred was crazy for Little Feat and we were listening to their songs and talking about label stuff. The Feat were working on their first album for Warner Bros. We were labelmates at Warner Bros. (though technically I was on Reprise) with Randy Newman, Van Dyke Parks, Leon Russell, and other odds and ends. It was not a particularly crazy party and broke up early for California. Somehow Garth ended up riding in the Cobra, and since he was frequently with me I didn't give too much thought to what had happened to his car. I suppose I assumed he was good and stoned and wanted to leave it at Fred's for a while.

We started down the hill. Topanga Canyon Road writhes like a serpent crossing an asphalt road in August. It is a long series of S-bends with an occasional short straight.

Before too long I picked up the headlights of another vehicle behind us coming fast. I edged the throttle open a bit and started driving a little tighter in the turns. The stranger came on. Interesting, because most people didn't go very fast on Topanga Canyon Road. It was a hazardous route at any speed. In the passing lane, a thoughtless error with the steering wheel and the driver would be unceremoniously launched off the side of the mountain. In the right lane, a sheer rock wall demarcated the road. Colliding with such a rough-hewn barrier would demolish the car and might well bounce a driver off into an abyss.

The mystery car made a run at my rear end and swung over to pass. We went into a short chute and ran side by side long enough for me to get my foot in it. I picked out the unmistakable silhou-

ette of a Camaro. I pulled slightly away as we entered another series of S-bends, and I yelled at Garth, "Who the hell is that guy?"
He shrugged. I was now in a street race.

Down the precarious mountain the two cars ran. My challenger
got around me on the high side with a gutsy surge of speed. I
couldn't believe or tolerate that and at the next chance I showed
him what seven hundred horses could do. The flames flared angrily
out of the open headers of the Super Snake. All was forgotten except beating that uppity bastard to Ventura Boulevard. Down we
plunged, dicing on the narrow road, first one and then the other
gaining a temporary advantage. Going airborne and then hitting the
ground in the Cobra was not a viable option. We would burn alive.
I concentrated fiercely on not making a mistake with the wheel or
the throttle on the maddening road, braking into the turns, but not
too much, accelerating like hell while judging the next bend. We
flirted on the edge of an inky abyss. Toward the bottom it straightened out and we went down side by side and pedal to the metal.
We were cowl to cowl even as the Mulholland Drive traffic signal
at the bottom of the hill came into view. It glowed an ironic red.

Both cars entered the intersection with engines maxed out, neck
and neck. I didn't dare risk breaking my concentration to even look
at the maniac next to me in the Camaro. We were entering a resi-
dential neighborhood with engines howling.

With houses on both sides of the street, the Cobra suddenly began to rotate through a series of 360s in a straight line as it hit
standing water in the intersection. I could have taken my hands off
the wheel for all the good it was doing me. I caught a glimpse of
Garth's tight white face as we hydroplaned, spinning smooth as a
pinwheel. Once around, twice around, the third time we slammed
ass first into a fat oak tree, with a resounding smash that echoed up
the quiet street. Not another car in sight.

I sat there for maybe one second, surprised that we weren't already on fire as gasoline was running all over the back of the car.
The forty-gallon tank had ruptured. I yelled at Garth, "Get out of
this motherfucker!" He was pulling and wrenching at the quick release on his harness.

"It's stuck!" he yelled.

"Like hell!" I protested and started working on his treacherous quick release. It had chosen the worst moment in a lifetime of mechanical perfection to dysfunction. I had never before seen one fail. I heard something crackle under the car and opened the door and looked underneath. Little monsters with tongues of blue flame swarmed on the grass underneath the car, writhing and propagating like baby snakes on a sea of burnt grass and gasoline.

"I'm out!" Garth yelled, bursting through his door. I was glad because there was no way I would have left him there to burn alone.

What was next, wait for the cops? Suddenly, like some malevolent ghost, I saw the hated Camaro of my adversary idling to a stop at the curb across the street. Unbelieving, I saw what I took to be my brother Tommy's wicked grin and big ears poking out of the window at me. It all came home: I had been racing my brother Tommy, who was driving Garth's souped-up Camaro!

"Get in, get in, get in!" Tommy laughed as I slid into the backseat with Garth. Doors slammed and the Camaro slid quickly onto a backstreet.

"Get down!" Tommy yelled. "You guys stay down." He drove slowly, never over forty, and stayed on backstreets all the way to Encino. We heard no explosion. We never once ventured onto Ventura Boulevard and arrived at Campo de Encino by many a stealthy twist and turn, all of us subdued by the insanity of the escapade, thinking of how much worse it could have been.

I walked straight into the house and called the Van Nuys Police. I informed them that my car had just been stolen by persons unknown. They took the report in that laconic "So what else is new?" monotone common to the overladen Valley police.

The next day they called me and told me that indeed my car had been found and they were afraid that "those bastards messed it up pretty good, Mr. Webb." My insurance went up. The car went directly to Mike Fennell's restoration shop out in Simi Valley because I didn't want to see it again until it was stone-cold perfect. When Mike had it on hand, I called and told him I had a request that had to remain between the two of us: I wanted gold metal flake added into the paint color, to make the finish glitter and flash as though it were radioactive. And I wanted him to use real gold.

1970

The sixties went out like a supernova that reached its maximum expansion in just ten short years. Now, the seventies waited for the swift hand of fate to write what wonders or horrors?

Success was biting me right on the ass. I was loath to be pigeonholed yet unable to leave the old craft and traditions behind.

Peter Pan, the film, after much hoopla and a lot of grueling writing on my part, seemed to be bogging down in the inevitable morass of "development." Producer Mel Ferrer, tall, urbane, and charming to a fault—he'd been married to Audrey Hepburn—clocked countless trips to London and other places, producing, casting, and scouting. The four-star hotel bills went straight onto the project's tab, though to me it seemed we were mostly treading water. I had a couple of decidedly disturbing telephone conversations with Mia Farrow. She had begun to consider that we were on the wrong track with *Pan*. In spite of the eccentric English tradition, wherein women assumed the role, Mia wondered if the part shouldn't be played by, well, a young boy. James Barrie would roll over in his grave, but she wasn't dissuaded. She even had a casting idea. In December of '69 she had seen a young boy performing on the *Ed Sullivan Show* with the Jackson Five. His name was Michael. He would make a perfect Pan. There was only one thing wrong with this line of thinking: it was going to derail the whole aerial ballet and put both of us out of a job.

Phil Kaufman's television show with the world's tallest hot air balloon started to seem more and more like a sixties idea as the seconds ticked by. Mr. Sinatra was reluctant to appear on such a show. Aretha Franklin had bluntly refused. The wild demands Satan and I had attached to our contract could rise up to haunt us. Like a pyramid scheme, tomorrow's greater success must follow today's success quickly at Universal—there was no middle ground.

My manager Sandy Gallin, a gentle person and second-generation Hollywood Super heir to an old Hollywood fortune, was becoming frustrated with my constant demands to do everything. I wanted to score a picture, I wanted to release an album, I wanted to write a Broadway show. He arranged for me to meet with David Geffen, a manager and entrepreneur who had a way of sorting odd people into profitable roles.

The Shelby Cobra showed up, fully restored, on a flatbed hydraulic truck. The paint job was so over the top it was blinding. Powder blue, deep gloss, hand-rubbed ocean of at least fifteen or twenty coats. Floating in the deep candied paint was a uniform level of tiny gold metal flake. I couldn't wait to mount up and drive a maiden test lap.

On the corner of Sunset was the famous Schwab's Drug Store, where countless actors and actresses had been discovered. I hung a left, and crowds of pedestrians gawked at the outrageous roadster, restored to perfection. I drove up Sunset, past the Cinerama Dome and Columbia Studios, where Simon and Garfunkel had launched hit after hit from Studio A. I passed the old Disney studio where, in 1966, I had watched Tony Martin record "By the Time I Get to Phoenix."

I cruised on, past the hookers dotting both sides of the street, the Chateau Marmont, the Pink Pussycat, and the Whiskey a Go Go, birthplace of the Johnny Rivers legend. Finally I passed my office, Canopy Productions, and then reached my destination, the Cock'n Bull on Sunset and Doheny Drive. The hour was late, the parking lot virtually empty, and I found a dimly lit space to conceal my ostentatious transportation.

What a whizzer of a pub it was, several small rooms with a low, carved beam ceiling waiting to shelter a buffeted poetic soul. I stumbled into the cozy little hideaway, only realizing at the last possible second it was occupied. I wasn't inclined to awkwardly back out; I could already see a pretty young woman with long, dark hair smiling at me as though I was an immensely entertaining and curious object. Her companion had his back to me. I slid into a small booth and looked at the back of his head, and was suddenly one hundred percent sure it was Johnny Rivers, who lived nearby in the Hollywood Hills.

"Hey, Johnny," I said, crossing the room in one stride. He turned and looked up at me and he was another person entirely. I recognized him as a member of the currently popular group the Grass Roots. His dark-haired beauty laughed hysterically, squarely in my face, as I fumbled my apologies and introduced myself. I asked her name: Rosemarie.

Once she stifled her amusement at my clumsy entrance, I noticed her blue eyes shone with a secret and her hair was mussed up. She was wearing slippers. Her companion was flushed, a just-finished-a-workout look. The truth of the situation dawned on me, and Rosemarie watched that ephiphany. They were fresh out of bed. She pursed her lips and guffawed into hoots of uncontrollable laughter. I fled into the night, blushing deeply and laughing.

I took my place in the wind and noise at the helm of the Cobra and decided to concentrate on something I could control. I could make a record. I could build the best concert sound system in the world. I could have my own band and hit the road. I could write songs and play tough and try to figure out how Elvis got such a grip on his audience.

I could see what might pan out with this fellow David Geffen.

1960

Dad had gotten the wanderlust again. Far from Oklahoma City, or anything else for that matter, lay a small petroleum boomtown called Laverne. On a clear day you could stand on Highway 149, look west, and see the horizon fifty miles away with the naked eye. Before we ripped it from them and lost our last shred of decency as a treaty nation, the land had belonged to the Cheyenne and other tribes of the Sioux Nation. A lot of people would stare off into the heat shimmer of the badlands and wonder why we hadn't just let them keep it.

Laverne boasted one traffic signal at the main intersection. If you hung a left at the red light toward New Mexico and the badlands, the Baptist parsonage, a two-story Victorian surrounded by towering cottonwoods, would appear on the right. A few houses dotted both sides of the street in a more or less decaying section of town. If one continued west, Laverne High School, a one-story modern structure of yellow brick, sprawled to the left, with a football stadium and practice field to the right; and a mile out from that the refinery, the last sign of human habitation for a hundred miles.

We settled in and I started freshman year. Same old nauseating feeling of being dropped off a cliff into a sea of new faces. Some of them friendly, many hostile, most downright indifferent.

I would be playing the organ at First Baptist Laverne. It was a Hammond B-3 with an elaborate start-up cycle akin to firing up a jet plane, and the preset black keys to the far left on the manuals. A clever system of bars of different colors allowed these stops to be preprogrammed with sounds of one's own devising; an elemental synthesizer. A system of tiny veined turbines spun at high speed by a motor to produce the actual pitches. A cable as thick as my wrist led from the keyboard to a Leslie speaker, which was also motorized so as to create a slow majestic chorus sound or at faster speed a less-impressive skating rink effect. It was a gadget. A big, heavy electric gadget that could only ever have been built in America and indeed was destined to achieve its greatest fame in the hands of Jimmy Smith, James Booker, Booker T., and other American jazz artists.

My room on the second floor in the two-story parsonage was the first private area I had ever known. Though a little cramped, I had my own sink and bathtub. In that little bathroom I would learn to shave. I can still remember the smell of my first bottle of Aqua Velva reeking in the close quarters.

From my sister's room next door came the sounds of Ricky Nelson singing "Do You Know What It Means to Miss New Orleans?" (w. Eddie DeLange and Louis Alter), warm and comforting on the other side of the wall. Janice had a record player, an RCA 45 changer, but I had no records and therefore no need of it. My musical solace was "Another Saturday Night" (w. Sam Cooke) on the radio. I was enthralled when that track suffused the balmy summer nights from the concealed radio under my bed.

The old house had a root cellar and a stout shed for the car. Dad had done right; it was the best thing we had ever seen.

1970

David Geffen called and asked me to come over to his place in the Hollywood Hills. Harry Nilsson was over there and he wanted to talk to me. He was pissed. I drove up to Van Nuys, made a right, and went up over the hill, following his directions, yet realizing the closer I got to the house the more familiar the neighborhood seemed. When I finally pulled up to the gate with the little push-button phone box it was anticlimactic. This was once Johnny Rivers's house. While a contract writer at Johnny Rivers Music I had sheltered there for a year.

Once inside the gate every detail was familiar. Terra-cotta roof, long front porch in the Spanish style with supports every few feet. It had gotten a paint job along the way but this was the place where it had all started.

Geffen greeted me on the porch. He was skinny, with very curly black hair. His Hollywood smile was all-purpose, which is to pay no disrespect. He was quite well adapted to his environment. His eyes glowed as though he knew exactly what you were about to say, considering your mental capacity.

I was impressed. He handled Joni Mitchell and Laura Nyro. That was enough for me.

"Harry's down at the pool waiting for you," he said. And his smile said, *Man, are you in for it.*

"Oh, great," I said as casually as I could muster. "I've always wanted to meet him."

David laughed and I knew I was definitely in some kind of trouble, though I couldn't imagine what it was. I started thinking as I strolled down to the pool area that it might have something to do with the "B.N." (Before Nilsson) I had attached to a lyric on the Richard Harris album cover of *The Yard Went On Forever.*

Briefly, this was the bone of contention: My line was "skipping like a stone through the garden" ("Gayla" *w.* JLW). The line I had reference to was Fred Neil's "skipping over the ocean like a stone" from "Everybody's Talkin'." My original intent was merely to say, "Beg pardon, Mr. Nilsson, wasn't copying from your huge hit as my lyric was written first and wasn't a deliberate rip-off."

When I arrived at the pool Nilsson was shooting a small basketball into a poolside goal. He put three right through the net before he said a word. He turned around, a beanpole with tousled blond hair, a nose going to red, and a scowl on his hawkish features.

"What's with the B.N.?" he demanded. "Or should I say B.S.?"

I choked, knowing exactly why I had been summoned.

"Hey, no offense intended . . ." I was chopped off at the knees.

"Listen, I didn't even write the song! Fred Neil wrote the song!" he complained while his face reddened.

"Hey, I just meant, in deference to your song, that I was not deliberately cribbing a great line like that!" I protested.

"I just think you were being a prick!" He slammed a shot off the backboard and through the net.

"Hey, stop shooting! Listen, let's say I *was* being a prick and I was just trying to get your attention because I'm such a huge fan."

"Are you sure about your motivations on that?" he challenged again.

We stood there face-to-face for thirty seconds before signs of amusement began to break on his face. I smiled back. He tossed me the ball and I put a jump shot through the hoop.

"Hey, you're pretty good, you know that?" Harry grinned and a lifetime friendship began.

We talked by the pool for a bit. He was of a philosophical bent, more so than your average pothead. As we walked back up to the house and traded phone numbers he said to me, "Don't be afraid of death; it's only the first moment in your life that takes place without you." That sort of whipped my head around.

Mission accomplished, he departed in an oddly shaped German army vehicle. I walked, slightly dazed from the encounter, from the driveway up to the front door, where David answered. His eyebrows asked me an unspoken question.

"We're cool," I said as I walked into the large living room with the cathedral ceiling and the familiar rough stone fireplace. A grand piano sat in the corner. It was eerie; it sat in exactly the same spot as Johnny Rivers's grand piano had done. The colors had changed a little, but it could almost be the same room where Rivers and I had taken acid and listened to *Sgt. Pepper's Lonely Hearts Club Band*.

A young man sat cross-legged on the floor cradling an acoustic guitar. "I want you to meet someone," David invited, and we sat down on the rug. "This is Jackson Browne."

Jackson looked up from the guitar and met my gaze with brown eyes that were like large pools of emotion. He was finely made with long fingers, longer straight hair, and a lean frame. The chords he toyed with under his fingers were well crafted as well, displaying a flair for dissonance and alternate basses.

"Jackson, play 'Opening Farewell,'" suggested David.

Jackson sang and played the elegiac, beautifully constructed song about impending and seemingly inevitable separation. To my mind it conjured up an unmistakable portrait of a woman, and yet she wasn't mentioned, only summoned. After this unforgettable moment Jackson took me back through the kitchen and showed me his room.

"I know this is going to be hard for you to believe, Jackson, but this used to be my room!" I laughed as we walked in. The whole day had taken on a surreal character.

I sat with David out on the porch and we finally got down to the reason for my visit. He had a different smile, a business smile that was closer held and higher on the right side of his face.

"So what do you want?" he asked me. I reeled for a second under the implications of that question. Even in his infancy as an executive and manager, David was famous as a man who could make careers. I thought carefully before answering.

"I want to be an artist," I said fervently.

He smiled blandly. "I thought you were just some guy who liked to play Las Vegas and hang out with Connie Stevens."

So here it was. The bias against traditional venues and artists and presentation.

"You can't play Vegas," he continued.

"Hey, she's a friend of mine and a hell of a nice girl!" I protested.

"Jimmy, it's business. I can do some things for you, maybe turn things around a little, but most of it is up to you."

I explained to him that I had just turned down a lot of money in Vegas. I told him my favorite contemporary writer was Joni Mitchell. I told him I was being typecast by the artists who recorded my music and I wanted to sing certain songs for myself. Even today this seems crazy to me. Should I have been unhappy when Liza Minnelli or Tony Bennett recorded one of my songs? But there it was. I was squarely in the generation gap, musically, and I hadn't done much to help myself. Though when I'd appeared on Liza's network special, there was Randy Newman (alternative music's crown prince) playing piano right beside me in a singer/songwriter segment. In the show's finale, "Tradition" from *Fiddler on the Roof,* Randy and I stood side by side for the inevitable curtain bow. The whole cast was supposed to hold hands and raise our arms overhead singing "Tradition! Tradition! Tradition!" Randy refused to raise his arms or sing "Tradition!" I'd raised one arm.

David agreed, in essence, to act as my manager for an undetermined period, and felt he could get me on track for an album release and—dare I write these horrific words—an "image change." He encouraged me to take voice lessons and to take a band on the road in order to introduce "the real me" to a rightfully bewildered public. He would become a friend and advisor. He would introduce me to Joni Mitchell. He would do everything in his considerable power to create a consumable out of me. Someone who could be welcomed to the ranks of rock 'n' rollers and socially sensitive artists everywhere. I drove away, head spinning with the options that had been so suddenly laid on my table. The confrontation with Harry almost served to underscore David's insistence that I think more clearly about my actions.

When I got home there was a message lying on the kitchen table: "Call Susan Horton's mother!" Susan had been the closest thing I ever had to a childhood sweetheart. She had been a cheerleader and homecoming queen at Colton High School the year I graduated. She was the quintessential California blonde with a stunning figure, large blue eyes, and a sweet smile. Her steady had been a junior college all-American quarterback named Eddie Groves from San Bernardino Valley College. He was handsome and physically imposing. Of course they would be together. That is, if you discount the potency of music and art on the psyche of young romantically inclined females, and to do so would be a mistake. Suffice to say that both of us lost her. She married a schoolteacher named John and they had been tweaking their relationship for several years. It was an unstable union for the most part because she was a dancer and constantly going on the road for various engagements. The one thing she loved more than all of us put together was dancing. In the interval I had written countless songs for her—"By the Time I Get to Phoenix," "Wichita Lineman," and "MacArthur Park," to mention three. This bothered her and it was a devastating and constant psychological weapon on the radio.

I called her mother frequently to see how she was. I never deliberately messed with her marriage. I didn't know John well enough to say anything bad about him; I just knew he wasn't making her happy. I read her mother's phone number off the paper and punched it into one of the newfangled maize-colored push-button phones. Her mother answered and told me Susan and John were separated again, and her daughter was dancing in Omaha. John, the mercurial husband, had embarked to destinations unknown. A wave of lust and longing tugged me off my feet and swept me into an emotional riptide. What separated us except a few hundred miles of empty space and a good deal of unhappiness that had come—in my mind—from being apart for too many years?

I chartered a Learjet to Omaha, arriving late at night but still in time to see Susan in the *Tickle Your Fancy Review* at a nameless casino. I was on fire to see her but I played it as cool as I could manage. I had loved her since high school but my slumbering passion had been quickened by some real life experiences. I wasn't afraid, or even shy, about claiming her.

Six girls and a couple of guys worked their way through some rather thin routines with a small orchestra. It seems there was a comedian, too, but I wasn't paying attention. I was watching the one to whom I had devoted thousands of hours of unrequited love. The one who, in spite of every velvet contrivance, had gotten away.

After the show I took all the dancing girls out to the airport in a limousine for a ride in the jet. There was so much youth, so much beauty, in that plane it was like riding in a giant corsage at five hundred miles per hour.

The next day I brought Susan back to Campo de Encino with me. She laughingly refers to it as a "kidnapping" and remembers lots of crying and protestation on her part. I don't remember it that way. I remember her insisting she was flying back to Omaha as soon as she could get another plane, and I offered to pay for the ticket. Was I heavy-handed? More than usual or perhaps more than ever— that I admit. I gave her some time to think about it while I showed her the house and grounds. She was given her own room, a delightful affair, all done up in lilac, with windows overlooking the pool. She calmed down. I sent Garth out with her on a shopping trip to buy "anything and everything she wants." I was extremely happy just knowing she was in the house.

At this precise moment David Geffen called, which was his habit almost every afternoon, to ask me what I was doing. (Oh, nothing much, just kidnapped my girlfriend and dragged her across four state lines.) I told him about my reunion with my long-lost sweetheart.

"Oh, that's fantastic!" he replied. "You should come with me to Kauai! I'm leaving tomorrow. I know the most beautiful place. Have you ever been?"

No, I confessed, I had never been to Kauai, which unlike today's Kauai was then an obscure hangout of island connoisseurs carrying gold American Express cards and a yen for the local psilocybin, which grew in almost any cow pasture.

"David, that's so generous of you, but I couldn't leave Susan behind, especially right now."

"No, no!" he protested. "You will both be my guests! It'll be perfect!" He went on to describe the plantation at Hanalei Bay where an impressive list of movies had been filmed, including *South Pa-*

cific. I confess that a person only has to say "beautiful South Seas island" once to get my attention. What better place to take Susan than a brand-new island to get things started with perfection?

"David," I responded with a burst of enthusiasm, "we'll come! I can't wait!"

The phone immediately rang again. It was the D-e-v-i-l. "What's up?" he asked.

"Really?" I asked.

"Really," he replied.

"Well, I just went to Omaha and kidnapped Susan and now I'm going to re-kidnap her and take her to Hawaii with David Geffen."

"It sounds like your sex life is getting complicated." He chortled. "I need a place to stay. How about your place for a while?"

"Sure, I could put you up for a while. You can watch the place while I'm away."

"Thanks, Bud," he said as he hung up. And somewhere in the high belfry of the exoverse, great black bells chimed anti-tonal and dispersed a low beating of sub-eternal defibrillation throughout all of space, changing the course of time.

1961

The basketball coach at Laverne was an alpha male named E. G. Pete Jayroe. He could have played the sheriff in any Western epic that Hollywood could conjure. His daughter Jayne was a sophomore like me and was hands down the prettiest girl in Laverne. History would eventually show that she was also the prettiest girl in Oklahoma and then all of America in rapid succession. She was famous in our school because she could sing like blazes, and she was the star of every choral event held in the cavernous gymnasium.

I would loiter shamelessly in the school cafeteria at lunchtime and play the quavering spinet, lots of "Blue Moon" and "Let It Be Me" and Floyd Cramer's "Last Date." There would be catcalls and coyote howls from the jocks but sometimes a girl would pause and flutter to a landing on a nearby folding chair.

Eventually the day came when it was Jayne who passed by and paused, and then sat down with a smile. As long as I would sit there and play she would listen and sing along. I took to visiting over at the Jayroes' and playing the piano for Jayne to sing whatever and whenever she wanted.

The coach said to me one day when he opened the front door, "Every time I look up around here I see *you!*" But he never turned me away.

Jayne and I became great pals and started dreaming of one day going to Oklahoma City and making a record. I had created some of my first original songs; one I still remember was "Gray Skies Are Better Than Blue." It was a tune David Hemmings years later would call "real crapola," but Jayne liked it. I stone flat-out loved her, but I was doing an unusually fine job of screwing that up, as I had created such a platonic friendship that I was in no position to ask her out on a date.

Hawaii, 1970

On the North Shore of Kauai was a small road that wound a half mile off the highway to the old Hanalei Plantation, a venerable watering hole and hideout for movie stars and other celebs since the forties. This string of native-style huts was bordered to the west by the idyllic and placid Hanalei River flowing serenely into Hanalei Bay. To the east lay postcard beach called Pu'u Poa. Each little hut had an unobstructed view of the ocean and beach area below. The walk up and down the mountain required a medium to strenuous effort and occasionally an overweight *haole* tourist would collapse on the way up and either pass over immediately or be transported to the hospital in Lihue. In Hawaii there existed a bizarre duality that has amazed me since I first traveled there. Side by side with the serene and deep peace of an ancient and benign natural beauty existed the possibility of a sudden, banal, or even comical death. So it must always have been.

David, Susan, and I were ensconced in adjoining tiki huts.

David presented the staggering view of the Pacific Ocean as though it were his own personal production, smile beaming at maximum wattage. Susan's eyes were as big as eggs. Forty-eight hours earlier she had been in Omaha getting ready to tap dance.

We dined together in what amounted to a large crow's nest hung on the edge of a cliff that served as the resort's restaurant. David was rightfully curious as to what celestial orb Susan had descended from. She was a perfect little California doll with cornflower blue eyes and long blond hair that gave the impression she was a shampoo model. We had mai tais, endured a seemingly endless serenade of lachrymose Hawaiian ballads performed by the usual trio in flowered shirts, and as candles blossomed all over the restaurant and the trails were lit by Malibu lights, we made our way to bed. David went to his hut and Susan and I went to ours. Before the sun's last bashful blush on the western horizon, two reunited lovers were holding hands fast asleep.

The next morning David came in bubbling with plans. He thought to ease into the trip we should just take sandwiches down to Pu'u Poa where there was a beautiful old banyan tree and have lunch, perhaps swim a little bit, and then drop some acid.

By this time in my life I had been high on weed and had learned to drink a little bit but had only taken acid that one time with Johnny Rivers. I had no idea what Susan's reaction would be to any mention of LSD. She thought I was half crazy already.

The three of us headed down the steep hillside on the well-worn trail until we emerged from a small grove of wood rose and cedar onto a narrow beach of fine, slightly pink sand. A half mile away, roughly in the center of the beach, stood a singular tree, an old banyan with a patch of grass and a small boulder close by.

After we had pitched our minimal camp under the banyan tree Geffen took out the clear glass bottle with little orange pills inside.

"Acid anyone?" He beamed.

"Okay, I'll have one," I said, as though this was the usual sort of thing. I quickly added, "Susan . . . you don't have to do this."

Her dancing eyes smiled and she said, "I'm going along!"

David shook three tabs out on to the palm of his hand and then

we didst partake of Osley's sacrament, what Derek Taylor elo-
quently called "the old dreaded heaven and hell." For perhaps five
minutes it seemed as though nothing at all happened, but when one
abruptly realizes that one has been staring at the fractal edge of a
cloud for twenty minutes or more, watching individual water mol-
ecules split off the main body and dissipate into the ethos one par-
ticle at a time, then one knows that alternate realities aren't just
fairy tales.

Unknown time passed. I looked for Susan and she was gone.
Even in my highly stoned condition this was a matter of concern.
At the far end of the beach I could see her climbing the lower
flank of the mountain that led back to something vaguely remembered as normalcy. Suddenly my love for her flooded my being with
a comber of longing so powerful that I was weeping to see her
going away. I plowed through the water, the coral, crossed a great
deal of beach, and ran shoeless into a patch of lava rock. My feet
were bleeding at every step.

I came into the hotel room sweaty, bloody, and emotionally
charged. Susan washed my feet and we held each other, sitting and
leaning against the wall. When I had caught my breath I went over
to my cassette player and slid Bach's Brandenburg Concerto No. 5
into the slot. We sat with our arms around each other as the sun
passed overhead, as the planets and the moons reconfigured, as
the notes of Bach, a man two hundred years in his tomb, danced
around us in liquid silver droplets of sound.

Hours went by and the sun buried itself in purple and indigo,
froth and spray. We made love deeply, until there was no reason to
ever make love again.

We had found ourselves. In a storm of counterbalanced proba-
bility, after years of Laurel and Hardy flimflam, here in this cli-
chéd honeymoon location, in the middle of a hallucination, we
had actually made the connection.

Cottonwood Farm, Jimmy in foreground, white shirt. *(Courtesy of the author)*

CHAPTER FIVE

How many more times will you remember a certain
afternoon of your childhood, some afternoon that's so
deeply a part of your being that you can't even conceive
of your life without it? Perhaps four or five times more.
Perhaps not even that.
—Paul Bowles, *The Sheltering Sky,* 1949

1970

Upon our return from Hawaii, I gathered a rhythm section for
my first foray into the world of the singer/songwriter. There was
Fred Tackett of Arkansas. He was a North Texas School of Music
alumnus, a trumpet major, who played, for our band, the electric

guitar. His appearance was not unlike one of Little Dixie's moonshiners.

Our bass player was Elton "Skip" Moser, a star at Cal Poly and an intellectual who had stepped away from covert projects in the aerospace industry for a spot with the band. Earlier Skip and I had played together in a quartet called Four More and had made a dozen or so uneven demos. He played bass with a metronomic precision, but understood music like no mere pickup musician. He doubled on flute, a virtuoso.

Freddy had brought our drummer, lean, curly haired, red-faced Ray Rich out of Oklahoma. He was anything but quiet. A collector of one-liners, e.g., "It's so nice out! (pause) I think I'll leave it out!" (Rim Shot!) Ray had come out of the Midwestern club circuit with a lot of experience.

We began to work every night on songs Freddy and I had been rehearsing for my first album, *Words and Music*. It was our intention to perform all this music, some quite complicated, on stage. From this humble goal grew a great ambition: to reproduce the records on stage for the audience exactly as they were heard on the disc. To extrapolate: If we had on stage what amounted to a complete recording studio, we could record our orchestral accompaniment on Studer 16-track (multitrack) machines—those machines would be on stage as well—and we would be able to perform in sync flawlessly with prerecorded strings and horns.

Today, technological gimmickry is common on stage. But at the time, no one had done this before. Brian Wilson had pushed studio technology to the forefront on his universally admired *Pet Sounds* album, which inspired The Beatles' *Sgt. Pepper's Lonely Hearts Club Band*. The Beatles declined to attempt performing *Sgt. Pepper's* tracks live on stage, partly because they thought it would not be possible. I thought otherwise. A change of course was dictated for Brian Ingoldsby, slaving away on the construction of our monstrous sound system in a deserted '30s dance palace known as the Aragon Ballroom in Santa Monica. So it would add a good many thousand dollars, but could we have our own recording and playback system incorporated into the P.A. design?

A lot of effects that we had created for the album in the studio would automatically click in where they were supposed to under the watchful eye of the balance engineer. Susan Webb—my sister—and Suzy Horton—my long lost love—had spent hundreds of hours recording harmonies just *so*, and these would magically appear, without waver or false start. The whole thing would be mixed in a lovely stereophonic bowl with all its attendant echoes and effects. The audience would be stunned.

The live component of the band would sing and play in the flesh. It's just that we also wanted to bring the recording studio, all that technological flash, into the concert hall with us. Very little thought was given to a plan B. It would have been a nice moment, for instance, for the Great Satan to step in and say, "Umm, you guys are losing it all over the place." But he didn't. I began to rely on him more and more for managerial advice and one day I said, "Shit, you know you just ought to be my personal manager. I'm getting ready to go out on the road for a long time. I'm going to need someone to look out for the Camp, look after Susan while I'm gone, and tell me what the fuck I should be doing!" He became a permanent fixture around the house.

We burned through January and into February with an all-important concert date looming over our heads. It was our plan to debut *Words and Music* on February 20 at the Dorothy Chandler Pavilion, L.A.'s answer to Lincoln Center in New York. A high-powered publicity firm had already invited the A-list. Zsa Zsa Gabor was coming, for Christ's sake!

Sure, it was a dicey plan. The one thing that would save us was the brilliant and diabolical *machine,* which would be lit up like something from *Doctor Who* and would take the place of all those pesky musicians and all those hours of rehearsal.

I can hear you saying, "Aren't we getting ahead of ourselves?" You bet your ass we are! The musician's union had strict rules demanding the use of live musicians on stage. A contingent of lawyers and managers went off with Satan to have a meeting with Local 47, of which I was a proud member, to explain to them the brilliance of our plans. We were offering to pay each member of the original recording orchestra double scale for the use of the tape at Dorothy Chandler, plus the same amount for every use of the tape in a live setting into perpetuity, a generous offer that involved no labor of any kind on their part. In our minds it was an offer they couldn't refuse. Later that day Satan and Howard Golden and my dad, along with some other guys in suits came into the Aragon Ballroom where we were running a full dress rehearsal. They saw magic in motion: a whole recording studio set up on risers so that all the parts could be seen, lights blinking, tape spinning so "the music comes out here." It could change the way music would be performed for the next hundred years.

One close look at my suit guys was enough for me to know the meeting with Local 47 had not been a successful one. We sat on the risers and I looked at the glum faces.

"Well, I've got good news and bad news," said Howard Golden, with the only smile in the bunch.

"Let's hear it," I shot back. I figured it was now going to cost more money, possibly a lot more money. But I was prepared for some negotiation.

"You can't use the machine," Howard said, his smile never wavering.

I blew up. It wasn't a pretty sight and I take no pleasure in describing the cussing, stomping fit to which I subjected the others. After a string of obscenities that was only brought to a close by a caution from my father was I settled enough to ask, "So what's the good news then?"

"Well," Howard replied, flustered by my reaction, his eyes darting from side to side. "Local 47 is prepared to offer you their complete cooperation in scheduling rehearsals to accommodate you on such short notice, and brought it to my attention that you don't have to pay double scale for live musicians!"

The rehearsal disintegrated. My dad filled me in as we put our instruments away and gathered our belongings. "Son, we are dealing with some very rough people here. They don't want to know any more about this contraption than they already do," he said, gesturing at the huge set and a quarter of a million dollars' worth of worthless junk.

As though to disclaim this assertion two big bruisers in blue suits came ambling into the old dance hall, all but cracking their knuckles. They were wearing hats. Nobody had worn a hat since the Kennedy assassination! They came up to me as all of our personnel disbanded and dribbled out of the room.

"Duh, uh, so okay, is this the gadget?" the bigger muscle-bound brute asked me, jerking his thumb at the mobile studio. I asked him who he was and why he was concerned. He informed me he worked for Local 47 and was investigating a possible infringement of union rules.

Howard came over and whispered in my ear, "We need to get this shit out of here. I don't like the look of this."

The enforcers walked all over the set and pried into every nook and technological cranny with the clumsiness that advertises total ignorance of the subject. With their inspection finished they tipped the crowns of their Borsalinos and bid us a cordial evening. Still, the consensus among leadership was to put the equipment back on the truck. It was torn down and back on the road before midnight.

Two nights later, the old deserted Aragon Ballroom caught fire and burned to the ground in flaming Art Deco splendor.

I felt like a fool. I had worked with the union for years and had benefited from a system that most heartily discouraged technical inroads of any kind on the traditional canon of union regulations. Sadly this creed of respect for the abilities and welfare of professional musicians has eroded over time into a hodgepodge of compromises. In this day and age, pretty much anything in the world of tracking, syncing, doubling, sampling, and outright stealing goes on unmolested. Though now such matters are mundane, I would be the first to admit, I had inadvertently wandered to the dark side. At the time, my fury and contempt for the union was boundless.

I talked with Howard and my managers about how best to proceed. My first idea, and one in retrospect I should have seized like a pit bull, was to cancel the concert. But I was learning the First Commandment of live performing: The show must go on. If one thinks there's anything faintly amusing about that notion then one just hasn't been there.

I sucked it up and started thinking about what needed to be done. We could cancel the show and pretty much ruin the record release, or we could play live with the Los Angeles Philharmonic. We would need to get the band accustomed to playing with an orchestra. It would be just three vocalists, two girls and me, which was going to be thin. A person in their right mind would try to sweeten that up a little bit, bring in Ginger Blake and Clydie King and Herb Pedersen on backgrounds. But no. We were off in this "purity of the garage band" mentality where it was just our little family against the world. That the audience wouldn't give a flying burrito about anything except *the sound* was a concept that had yet to gain traction with me.

We launched into a hurried series of rehearsals with the L.A. Philharmonic. We found that we could just barely manage to play what was mainly rock music all the way through with the orchestra. No thought was given to lighting, presentation, or staging. We had no feel for the immensity and sheer spatial volume of a symphonic concert hall, with its ranks of balconies and parking lot–sized stage and peculiar acoustic responses.

I toyed with a new black leather outfit that was supposed to make me look mean and Jaggerish. I had decided not to play the piano but to perform standing up, something that I had never done in my life. I was a non-dancer, had no moves, no charisma, nor one noticeable iota of physical grace. About all I had going for me was that great leather outfit.

It was about this time news broke that Epic Records was releasing the first solo album by wunderkind Jimmy Webb, called, with razor sharp wit, *Jim Webb Sings Jim Webb*. (At this point in the narrative the sinking *Titanic* breaks completely in half and the band strikes up "Londonderry Air.")

When I was a greenhorn and driving up to L.A. habitually in search of studios where I could record for nothing, I had traded the rights to many songs for studio time without hesitation. In other words, I would trade the performance rights or publishing share, amounting to 50 percent of the income for a given song, to a recording studio owner for a few hours of precious studio time. This was a sacrifice I made in order to hone and refine my songs, make rough records with my buddies, and explore the parameters of studio craft. In a word: education.

I had signed a deal with Bob Ross Music Service to use their studio to record a band called Four More. Skip Moser, so it happens, was the bass player. I was lead vocalist, never a strong spot for me, but we figured if Mick Jagger and the Rolling Stones could cut hit records, then anything was possible.

My rise to fame had not gone unnoticed at Bob Ross Music. The fact that the company was in possession of eleven or twelve unknown Webb songs with some passable basic tracks and demo vocals by yours truly loomed as an inviting source of income for them. If they came out with the very first Jimmy Webb solo album they would make a killing. Quietly they went about their plan. An obscure producer named Hank Levine was brought in. As far as I was concerned, he was barely competent. But what did that matter? The material at hand was very close to unusable so the components would be complementary.

They (Bob and Hank) began by overdubbing huge "MacArthur Park"–sized orchestras on every track. The arranging was desultory if not criminally negligent. Mixed with the Rolling Stones soundalike knockoff tracks and my out-of-tune vocal song demos from 1965 and engineered by one of the B-string talents of the technical world, the results sounded like a collision between Royal Albert Hall and a tour bus full of Deadheads. They sent me a copy of the record and a polite letter stating that since they owned the rights, and since the masters also belonged to them, that they would like to have my blessing in releasing it.

I called Bob and told him it was in no way acceptable. I told him it was a bald-faced scheme to take advantage of a notoriety that his recordings had in no way created. I told him I would make an *entirely new record for him and pay for it myself* if he would desist in his apparent determination to ruin my entire career for the sake of a few thousand quick dollars. He was immovable. He professed to believe *Jim Webb Sings Jim Webb* was a work of genius! An album way ahead of its time. (In the sense that any time would be too soon I suppose

I agreed.) Desperate, I explained about the Dorothy Chandler concert and my contract with Reprise records. About my pending record release. About the betrayal—intended or not—that was inherent in their scheme. They were as immovable as Local 47. From their point of view, the griddle was hot and it was time to sell pancakes.

They released it. It was sent to every radio station in the United States. As far as I know the only reaction to it was loathing. I never heard it played on the air. It was unmentionable in my circle. If somebody really wanted to get under my skin and make an enemy for life they could bring it out for an autograph.

The harm that it did me was incalculable. I can hear some voices out there from the back of the bar saying, "Well, it couldn't have done you any more damage than the album that you actually put out!" There is, regrettably, ample room for argument on that point, but at least my album, mistakes and all, was something I did myself. The first impression broadcasters received of my voice from *Jim Webb Sings Jim Webb* was indelible. This was no singer. It was a sixteen-year-old kid screaming and carrying on in a cheap imitation of Mick. As a lead-up to my actual debut album nothing could have served as a more ominous precursor.

What was there for us to do except carry on? We stumbled toward the February 20 Dorothy Chandler date and even managed to work up a little excitement, a trace of esprit de corps. By God, we would go out there and in spite of all we would make it a hit! The two thousand–odd seats were packed from orchestra to chandelier. Rather than attempt to list the A-listers and B-listers who packed every cranny it's easier to say that Paul McCartney was not there. A few others were absent, but not many.

At five to eight I came out on stage in my rough trade black outfit with my sister and Susan Horton as backup singers, and the band. We settled ourselves self-consciously and when all seemed ready I counted off the first number. There was immediate shock in the audience. This wasn't Glen Campbell or anything like it! This wasn't the soaring high string passages of "MacArthur Park." This was rock 'n' roll. The opening number was a raucous and direct assault on, of all things, *critics* in the ill-tempered quatrains of "Dorothy Chandler Blues." Anticipating that the assembled critics would hate my departure from the center of the road, I rashly decided I would attack first.

The self-destructive energy of this tactic waxed as the first act progressed. Rarely were the live musicians and the band in the same place. With no conductor, the playing frequently turned into a musical free-for-all. Fred Tackett commented sagely afterward that the music had an enthusiastic "Ivesian" quality, which is about the most that could be said for it (Ives's *Three Places in New England* included a sonic collision between two marching bands).

Even though there is no way to suppose the audience had any idea what had just transpired on stage, they arose as one and gave us a consoling grand ovation, after which they stampeded to their limousines and probably emptied their respective car bars before they reached Beverly Hills. Most of the backstage visitors had little to say, other than to pass along the obligatory pitying praise or condolences in whatever guise.

"Webb's theory that a writer can sing his own works better than anyone else, even if he is not a real singer, was destroyed," Leonard Feather, jazz critic for the *L.A. Times*, summed up. On a lone upbeat grace note, the expensive sound system had performed flawlessly.

1961

In Laverne, Oklahoma, Alma Jo Lotspeich was the hot tamale. She was a divorcée, which—right there for starters—put her on a planet far away from dour, Calvinist Laverne. She drove a dark gold '57 Limited Edition Cadillac Biarvitz and wore red dresses to match her flaming red hair and reveled, it seemed, in the stir that followed her wherever she went. She was twenty-something, and the best-looking woman within five hundred miles of Laverne, except maybe for Jayne, who was not yet sixteen.

Sometimes, to my father's chagrin, Alma Jo would take me for a ride in her Cadillac after Sunday morning services and treat me to a cherry Coke. I indulged in telling her of my dream of making a trip to Oklahoma City to record some of my new songs. She was fascinated by my skill at the keyboard and more than ready for an assault on show business. She encouraged an expedition to Oklahoma City, to visit all the major television studios and also make a recording. I somewhat hesitantly broached the subject of such a trip to Jayne Jayroe, fearing that Pete would put a screeching stop to any such shenanigans. I misjudged him seriously. He knew his daughter; she was capable of behaving like a lady in any foreign country.

I fantasized about some sort of encounter with Alma Jo and made the mistake of committing some lyrics to paper about her one day. My father found them and hit the ceiling, all his suspicions confirmed. Dad thought I needed a proper job to keep me busy, and fixed me up with a farmer a few miles outside of town who wanted the stubble of his wheat crop turned over so he could start some "winter" wheat, a year-round source of income in some parts of Oklahoma. The tractors that accomplished this were on an industrial scale and complicated, but I've never been scared of a machine.

Farmer Ballard was a right enough fellow and I started in with him, driving Dad's old '57 Plymouth Fury to work and taking my lunch in a paper sack. I had a green plastic transistor radio that dangled from the tractor's umbrella. Radio in those days was a mélange of styles comprising the "top forty." It might include an R&B number followed by the Weavers, then "Still" by "Whispering Bill" Anderson, a Bobby Vinton ballad, then Bert Kaempfert with a trumpet instrumental, Mitch Miller maybe, Ricky Nelson, Ferrante and Teicher (piano players), and maybe Elvis. It was anything goes, and it was good for America!

One day close to the end of my shift, I got the tractor out to the end of Ballard's field and stopped. I pushed the lever that lifted a thousand pounds of shiny curved plows out of the ground simultaneously until they were clear of obstruction and ready to be transported. I started up the road to the house and the barn a quarter mile away. A song came on the radio. My ears snapped to attention; I had never heard such a mellow gold singer. It was contemporary but sounded as though it had been pulled from the furnace of folk standards and then blown into a glossy glass bubble:

*"There is someone walking behind you, turn around look at me
There is someone watching your footsteps, turn around look
    at me . . ."*

I heard the splintering scream of raw metal and felt warm hydraulic fluid on my back. In my music daze I had turned the wrong way, with the plow stuck in the ground, and now I couldn't get the machine to stop. All of the threads on the lift mechanism stripped simultaneously, dropping the big plow into the graded road in front of the farmer's house. I bulldozed onward for about twenty feet, creating a gigantic furrow where a duck pond and flower beds had once been. I finally just turned the ignition off, ending up near the front porch where Farmer Ballard was reading his newspaper. We looked at each other, unmoving, shocked, as the transistor radio swung back and forth, blaring idiotically.

The lovely song had finished during this cacophony and the DJ was saying, "That was red-hot wax 'Turn Around Look at Me' from newcomer Glen Campbell. Keep your ear on 'im. . . ." I had just heard the most beautiful record I ever heard in my young life: song, singer, and arrangement in perfect balance. At the same instant I had totaled a $20,000 plow and tractor into a smoldering misshapen wreck and transformed Mrs. Ballard's flower garden into a landfill.

I lost my job on the spot.

That night, after facing my mortified father, I kneeled beside my bed. My prayer arose from one of the most isolated, underpopulated corners of a huge busy earth, rich in peoples and prayers, rife with hopes, troubles, needs, demands, cries for mercy, and even prayers for death itself.

"Dear Lord, if it be your will, one day would you help me to write a song half as good as 'Turn Around Look at Me.' And Lord if you could work it in, someday could I be fortunate enough to have Mr. Campbell record one of my songs? Thank you, Lord. Amen."

The Lord was listening to a hopeful boy in Oklahoma that night. My musical destiny—and perhaps even Glen's—was codified and put into action by the mysterious workings of the universe. During my career I would write at least a hundred songs half as good as "Turn Around Look at Me." And within four years, I would have a hit on the charts with Glen Campbell himself.

1970

The diabolical recording machine was moved lock, stock, and barrel into Campo de Encino. Phil Harris's gigantic cedar closet, built to house a half-thousand expensive suits, became a more than adequate professional studio control room. Now the band was able to rehearse and listen to ourselves. I still have two of the Voice of the Theater speakers from the original setup that looked and sounded so elegant on stage. Huge monsters, but absolutely useless around the house.

Meanwhile we had a tour booked. It combined a few flying segments with a lot of time on the bus. We were to play colleges, concert halls, and some of the larger clubs. "The Circuit," as it was known to some, consisted of Doug Weston's Troubadour in Los Angeles, Marvelous Marv's in Denver, the Main Point in Philadelphia, the Cellar Door in Georgetown. And in New York the funkiest hole of them all, the Bitter End. In between were one-nighters in far-flung, out-of-the-way places such as North Dakota, Montana, Sioux Falls, and so forth. The bus itself was not any luxury coach with a portrait of Jimmy Webb painted on the side. It was rather more of a school bus with some double bunks nailed to the floor, a chemical toilet in the back, and a handful of passenger seats just behind the driver.

I prepared to say my good-byes at Campo de Encino. The Devil assured me he had everything in hand. Susan was not happy about the separation but also not keen to share a chemical toilet with a bunch of musicians. More than once it occurred to me: Why am I doing this? I could just stay home and write songs. The planets would still follow their courses. I have this wonderful girl to love. I have many enchanted spindrift lyrics that I can set swinging on strains of stardust melody. But I had set my heart orbiting around this idea of being a singer. In my mind there was no reason it should or could be denied me. I kissed Susan good-bye and shook the Devil's hand with a mutual nod meant to transfer responsibility for the castle into his hands. I turned my back on Vegas and the easy buck, determined to be part of my generation and relevant to my time.

When our tatty bus arrived in front of the Main Point in Philadelphia, it was raining buckets. There was a real marquee out there and I was headlined in Roman block font: JIMMY WEBB. Right underneath were my supporting acts, FEATURING MAURY MULHAUSEN WITH JUDY SILL. A line snaked around the corner. Overcoated, muffled figures stood in the rain buying tickets. We were raucous on stage, the four of us. We could make more noise than three bands our size. That night in Philly I got irritated with Skip and Fred, but especially with Ray. I turned around on my piano bench and said something like "Goddamn it, you guys have to turn it down!" Eventually this caused me to add Show Business Rule #2. Rule #1, as I had learned the hard way, is "Don't write rude songs about the critics and then sing them to the critics in front of an audience." Rule #2 is "Don't chew out the band on the stand in front of an audience."

As I was walking out of the Main Point's stage door, angry at myself and my band, she was there. A tall, willowy figure with a waterfall of black hair, thick and rich, her face a pale, moonstone complexion. Thin as a rail, her height was such that she could look me directly in the eyes. It made me look at her feet. She was wearing motorcycle boots and a gang jacket. As I drew closer to her I could see not the battered and burned-out features of a motorcycle moll, but a delicate poem in moonlight and shadow.

"Hi," she said. "How ya' doin?"

Even if she was a vicious vampire, I was going to take the whole ride.

"I hope I've had better nights, but right now I'm not so sure," I said, drawing closer, aroused by the size of her, swayed by the power of her chakra.

"I thought you did pretty well." She put her arms around me and kissed me on the mouth and the chemicals ran wild. It was a long kiss. We had our arms around each other.

"Wanna go for a ride?" She leaned back on a Harley-Davidson Sportster, waiting on its kickstand.

"Do I get to know your name first?" I asked, slinging my leather gig bag over my shoulder.

She turned around and rolled the motorcycle off its stand like it was a toy. "I'm Linda," she said, kicking her ride to life as I climbed on behind her. "Where are we goin'?"

She rode fast and expertly with no trace of hesitation. We arrived at the Holiday Inn after a couple of shouted directions and went straight up to my room, landing with a crash that provoked yells through the thin walls. There was a terrifying scene of unfettered lust. Leathers went flying all over the room and we pounded the cheap mattress right through the bed and down to the floor.

After, we lay there hands intertwined, keeping pressure on each other's palms.

"Are you by any chance a person who would be known as a Hells Angels chick?" I asked her, teasing.

"Why, am I a little too much for you?" She laughed. "You scared a' me?"

I was a little scared, but not the way she thought.

"Do you want to go to New York?" I asked. "I've got a gig up there for a couple of days."

"I would have to park my bike somewhere and . . ."

"Oh, I'll make sure you get back . . . uh, I mean if you really need to get back."

I don't know what kind of crazy thing it was she did to me but I knew it could get serious in a hurry. Susan? Oh yeah, there was that, too.

"Have you got an old man?" I asked her.

"Doesn't everybody?" she questioned in return. "We're having a fight. He's off with some other piece of trash so I . . ."

"A little revenge?" I finished the thought.

"Anything wrong with that?" she challenged.

Things started up again.

The next morning, while she went to stash her bike, I called up the Devil. A rough transcription would read, "Wow, you can't believe the chick I ran into out here! She rides her own Harley. Get this, she tears the thing down and does all this manly shit. But listen, she's pretty. She's pretty like nobody I've ever seen." He wanted me to lay it all out for him, all the details. "How's the old fort? How's Susan?" Susan was out shopping but everything was fine. Silky smooth fine.

When I showed up and climbed aboard the bus holding hands with Linda there was absolute stunned silence in the ranks. I was so far into her that the band retreated into a painted backdrop. Was anybody upset with me? I didn't give a shit. Linda and I sat in the back and she told me she had been orphaned into the foster care system when she was thirteen. The first three foster fathers they put her with tried her. None of 'em made it. The last guy, she broke his nose, and went out the bedroom window in her nightgown and ran for the highway. She was hiking it in her bedclothes when the Angels stopped to see if she was okay. Nobody tried to fuck her. They got her some clothes and she explained, "They looked at me like I was some kind of precious thing." Nobody had ever treated her like that before. They became her father and mother and brothers and sisters all at once. They taught her to fight and take care of herself. They bought her a bike. She couldn't wear colors because she was a female but otherwise she was in the family.

They have their own special weddings where girlfriends become "old ladies." When she was eighteen she hooked up with one of the brothers and she had been with him ever since. I wondered what would happen if he ever came looking and found me in a Travelodge with her.

We got to New York and Linda and I promptly retreated to my room until sound check. When I finally showed my face at the club I apologized to the band for criticizing them in front of the audience. I also did my mea culpas for having four perfectly nice customers physically thrown into the street recently at the Cellar Door (Show Business Rule #3: Never throw your fans out of the show).

Things seemed to settle down between us, but the crew kept a wary eye on Linda, who looked like she could take the whole band and stuff it in a garbage can.

The Bitter End was not spectacular to behold, regardless of its preeminent status as a birthplace of folk music. It was a basement in New York City, in August. Huge fans whirled in doorways to no avail. It was a sweatbox. The venue was one storefront wide by three storefronts long, a rough stage flat against one wall down the length of it. Customers entered by a single flight of stairs and paid at the bottom.

Perhaps in an attempt to alleviate the claustrophobic nature of the place, the walls were painted black and subsequently covered with stick figures and graffiti, GEORGE IS A MONOTONE! and so on. We found out quickly that anything other than a moderate volume from the players would drive the audience out onto the street.

The New York gigs ended on Sunday night. That afternoon I shared a cab with Linda to Grand Central. I bought her a ticket for Philly and we sat for a while waiting.

"They'll be looking for me," she said. "I don't want them to sell my bike!" She laughed to take the edge off.

"I don't expect they would let me join up, would they?" I joked and smiled but she stopped laughing and looked at me with one of those "what woulda been, coulda been, shoulda been" looks. She was a woman first.

"Wanna give me your phone number?" I asked her.

She looked at the floor and shook her head as the P.A. announced her train. She took my face in her hands and kissed me, not a tear in sight. She turned and was gone in the crowd, and it was a small death I felt. But there would be no whispering on phones for her, and no tears, and no little white lies.

We played a few more shows, gig-zagging our way west across the country. The band had really melded on the road and we were having fun, though I was looking forward to getting home and starting a new album in my new home recording studio.

I missed Susan. It may sound hollow but there it is. I was looking forward to seeing her at the airport. I walked out of baggage claim with one suitcase and my shoulder bag and saw a glistening burgundy XJ 6 sitting at the curb. I supposed that would be my new car, my

Cobra still laid up. I leaned down to the passenger window and looked in, expecting to see Susan in the passenger seat. Instead I saw it empty. Beyond where I had expected to see her I focused on the Devil himself, southern smile extended like a mainsail.

"Hey, amigo!" he said with genuine enthusiasm.

"Where's Suzy?" I asked.

"Well, I thought when we got home we could talk about that."

"Fuck that, where is she?" I threw my bags in the backseat and got in.

I looked at him and for the first time in our lengthy adventure-filled friendship he looked away. My lips settled in a hard line. I was getting an overwhelming impression of deceit.

"Well, I'm not really sure exactly. She said she needed some space." He commented as though he was only a bystander.

When we got to the house Susan wasn't there and I went crazy looking for her. I called her mother and her friends and every friend of anyone she ever knew. Nobody had an answer. The Deceiver sat calmly in his room upstairs reading Sun Tzu. It took me hours and I had phone ear, but finally I got a bite. She was in Lake Tahoe. I went upstairs.

"I'm going up there to get her and if you're still in my house when we get back you are going to be answering some questions!" I barked, furious.

I rented a Learjet for a quick flight to Tahoe, where Susan was sheltering with friends. I knew one thing for sure: She had been hurt. In a couple of hours I was there.

"How could you do it?" Susan wanted to know through tears. How could I sleep with a big fat Hells Angels woman with pierced nipples and tattoos all over her?

It was a highly decorated and enlarged version of my encounter with sylph-like Linda. And the damning story could have only come from one place, from someone who liked to say he was my best friend. I told her the basic story was true. I met a girl who rode a motorcycle. I intended to choose my own time and place for this revelation, but that was over the dam.

We flew back home, tentative with each other, but she was still part of my world for the time being. When we got into the house there was hell to pay.

"You son of a bitch," I told him. "You slept with my girl while I was out working, you bastard you! You lied to me! You lied to her! (He had told her she was in danger; he had personally put her on the plane to Tahoe; had invoked terror tales of STDs, of violence and retribution from the Hells Angels, etc.) There was no outright and swift denial of these grave charges from him. To paraphrase Mose Allison he looked at me as if to say, "You knew damn well I was a snake before you took me in!" I told him to go far and fast.

The Serpent left by the kitchen door without even a suitcase. Even now I am boggled by the immensity of the insult he had offered me. The armor-plated, wicked confidence that took him out to the airport to pick me up. He had planned to keep us both: her on the outside and me as a ticket to ride.

Susan and I sat in silence for a while and then she started crying.

"Come on," I said, "you look like hell."

Her face was swollen and she had good reason to be pissed at him and me both. I took her upstairs and we lay down on the gold velvet bed and watched the TV in the ceiling. I reached out and took her hand. She didn't pull hers away.

I now remembered what Freddy had whispered to me when I had walked onto the bus with Linda in Philly. "What happens on the road stays on the road." This canon was moved to the top of my show business rules list.

1962

One rainy, chilly morning toward the end of October we left town at first light in Alma Jo's gold and brown Caddy. We were hysterically happy. We listened to rock 'n' roll loud and with impunity. We rehearsed my songs that we intended to record: "Gray Skies Are Better Than Blue" and "Just Excuse the Slip," among others. We performed for fellow travelers in other autos at the risk of their lives and our limbs.

It took five hours to drive from Laverne to the city but no one complained or got tired. Once there, we stopped for breakfast and then went over to WKY-TV to audition for the *Tom Paxton Show.* I played, Jayne sang, the producers rolled their eyes. We heard our first industry song and dance, "We don't need anyone just now, but please come back and try again!"

We retreated to the sacred premises of a decrepit recording studio in the aging redbrick part of town. Inside, every vertical and horizontal surface was covered with the tang and yellow brown wheeze of old tobacco smoke. Still, we looked in wide-eyed wonder at the technological mystery of the glowing recording desk with its circular "pots" and jiggling analog needles on dials. The engineer regarded us with dubious enthusiasm as he set up a vocal mike and I tested for the very first time what had been described to me as a "grand" piano. Our financier and manager Alma smiled through the glass as we made our way through a couple of songs. The chain-smoking engineer grunted monosyllabic encouragement through the talk back from time to time. We learned that each version of the song was called a "take" and we picked the two we liked best. He then crouched over an old recording lathe, an instrument that carved the music into an acetate material called a blank. As the music went from the tape onto the record a fine curl of black acetate hissed into a vacuum hose and was carried away. The finished product was an elegant disc of finely wrought grooves that smelled faintly of formaldehyde. And in those grooves was the music. Jayne and I were in awe at the thought that we could take this item home and play it on a real record player.

"Well!" Alma Jo shouted after we exited the dark little room. "Which recording star would like a malt?"

We sat in a Sonic and ate hot dogs and slurped up malts, as excited and happy as if we had just played the *Ed Sullivan Show.* Then, somewhat sadly, we entered our fine and fancy transportation. Jayne succumbed to fatigue in the backseat, and Alma Jo and I watched the lines march past us in the middle of the highway. She, perhaps musing on the life she had imagined before her marriage hit the rocks, and me, certain that I had finally found something worth all my energy and concentration.

"It will be all right, honey," Alma said softly, reaching over to squeeze my hand. "You kids will show them a thing or two before it's over."

1970

Susan and I settled into something a little more like a conventional relationship. The mutual episodes of infidelity, along with any discussion of the Devil himself, were put behind us.

On the other side of the house, in the home studio, the band and I wasted no time mourning over past mistakes but plunged into a new album project. When I sat down like a punter and listened to *Words and Music* alongside any of the newer Beatles albums, my record withered by comparison. Trying to put this misstep of a record behind me, along with the betrayals and tinhorn amateurism of my first tour, and the "studio on the stage" disaster, I decided to call the second album *And So: On*.

Anyone who has ever owned a home recording facility will attest to the fact that there is a constant demand for studio time, mostly for free, by friends and associates who are likely to stop by at any hour, bearing wampum and a new song or riff. Iggy Pop cut a solo album right there underneath my nose. I saw Iggy around the house a few times and found him affable and smart, but I had no clue he was making an album. I left scheduling to my stepbrother Garth, who divided his time between my digs and an actual job at the Record Plant in Hollywood.

Harry Nilsson visited often. We cut a duet of Felice and Boudleaux Bryant's "Love Hurts." Harry just wailed on the thing, shuffling around his repertoire of goofy sounds, masterful high chops, and inimitable ornamentations. No take was ever the same. The duet never made it on my album, for a simple reason: I didn't want to be perceived as hitching a ride on Harry's coattails.

Ringo Starr was a regular visitor to the home studio, most often with Harry. Mal Evans, another refugee from The Beatles meltdown, showed up often, seeking advice on songwriting. A huge, gentle bear of a guy, Mal had been The Beatles' road manager. Songs were difficult for him: He had specialized in Beatles crowd control with a minor in gophering. He made agonizing but steady progress as a songwriter. I helped him as much as I could.

The pulse of Hollywood was vigorous and rapid and it throbbed through my home. I went one night to Doug Weston's Troubadour to catch Randy Newman live. After the show I sought Randy out in his dressing room. He was bespectacled Lennon style, with a pile of tousled, curly hair and a perpetually concerned expression. I asked him to come out to the Camp for a beer and a game of pool. P. F. Sloan, the master songwriter from Dunhill Records, came in behind me and I invited him along, too.

Randy looked worried. "Listen," he said. "If I come out there, cause I would like to come out there, but you aren't going to play me any songs or anything like that, are you? No live music, right?" He looked at P.F. and back at me.

"Hey, we just play eight ball and drink Coors, so I think you should be okay." I laughed. I didn't blame Randy. There was always some doper hanging out and playing all of his songs, as though that was what other songwriters would want to listen to. We ended up in a convoy, with Randy right behind me, and behind him P. F. Sloan. Somewhere along the way Sloan must have missed a turn because when Randy and I arrived at Campo de Encino, he was M.I.A. As promised, Randy and I played pool and had a few beers, and nobody played any live music.

At the big house in the oak trees, we partied, we recorded, and the humiliation of Dorothy Chandler and the missteps of the previous year were mostly forgotten. I focused on *And So: On*. Many of my early hits had been written for Susan, so I continued in that vein. It was soppy going. A reviewer in a fashionable magazine wrote that the only thing that would empty a room quicker than a Leonard Cohen album was a Jimmy Webb record. Harry Nilsson suggested that if I tried hard and did some simple exercises, I might be able to work up a sense of humor.

Freddy and I were keen to involve the great Larry Coryell, a globally famous jazz influence of the rock fusion era, and concentrate more on the sound of each instrument. One night Larry, small and dark with his crow-black hair in a curl, a fixed smirk on his well-made face, came into the studio and blasted a backward guitar solo that will forever stand favorably in comparison to McCartney, Clapton, or John McLaughlin. Afterward, Larry walked into the kitchen of Campo de Encino and threw a little folded white paper packet onto the countertop.

"This," he announced with conviction and a wide grin, "is gonna change your life!"

Truer words have never been spoken. Inside the bundle was a white, shiny substance called cocaine.

Cocaine's impact on the music business was of a unique and comprehensive social nature. The whole process of record making, the late hours, the expected garrulous sociability of the workplace combined with the egos of people who more likely than not were egging one another on in the display of outrageous behavior; these almost begged the advent of "marching powder," some outside influence that would keep the party and the session and the ostentation running at full speed. I took to it like a fish to water.

1962

As I prepared for my senior year at Laverne High, my father did something entirely unprecedented in the history of our uneasy relationship. I walked out the front door to meet him returning from a trip to Oklahoma City and he pulled into the driveway at the wheel of a shiny two-tone '56 Oldsmobile 98. It was a light tomato cream over the midline and below the chrome, a boisterous brick color. It sported immaculate whitewall tires. He exited the spot-less late-model two-door coupe and smiled at me.

"Wh . . . what's this?" I sputtered.

"It's your new car, son," he said, laughing.

In Laverne most of the rich kids had motorcycles or cars. Tommy Van Meter, one of my hangout buddies, a kid who also wore glasses, drove a '57 Chevrolet convertible. His father owned the dealership. As I slid in behind the thin diameter ridged wheel and wriggled my butt into the leather-upholstered frontseat I realized that I, too, had arrived in the top of the class automotive-wise.

Pop proudly pointed out each luxurious feature from the pas-senger seat. The 98 had power windows, brakes, and steering, a signal-seeking radio with a foot switch on the floor for changing stations, an electric eye that automatically dimmed the lights when an oncoming vehicle approached, and it was the first factory air-conditioned automobile I had ever seen. It had an automatic trans-mission and the mighty 324-cubic-inch General Motors V8 that powered the Cadillacs and Pontiacs as well. This particular mark was the epitome of '50s rocketship styling, each fender swelling, then tapering at the rear end in imitation of two gigantic thrusters and the red teardrop of each taillight lens emulating the open flame of a spaceship's engine. Notwithstanding its luxurious trappings and solidity, the two-door coupe was a hot rod.

I was set free. In half an hour every stud and cheerleader in town knew that four-eyed Preach was inexplicably in the most elegant car, driving around with the beautiful Jayne Jayroe. I was in a state of utter delirium and disbelief. My father did love me.

It was about then—when things were beginning to get so good—that I heard rumors about moving to California. It started with my parents breaking off intimate conversations as I entered the room. It ended with my father announcing from the pulpit his intention of leaving First Church Laverne and moving Mom, myself, Janice, Tommy, and my little sisters, Sylvia and Susan, to Colton, Califor-nia, to pastor in yet another faraway place. All of this was poised for midsummer, just in time for me to miss my senior year with my hard-won classmates. I was stunned, completely outraged. The allure of California, its proximity to all things important to my success as a songwriter, were momentarily forgotten. I saw treachery in my father as he explained to me I wouldn't be able to take my Oldsmobile to the Golden State. He intended to sell it for moving expenses. I hated him all over. His pattern of nomadism and upward mobility had worked unerringly for him, and his lifelong dream of living in California was there for the taking. He would move us stoically, against all protest, as he had so many times before.

1970

A party was on at Campo de Encino. Fred and Patricia Tackett were temporarily in residence in the guesthouse and Patricia's penchant for Isadora Duncan-ism had manifested itself in a grand idea for a divertissement: a nude chamber music concert. One might ask why I would sign up for this insane idea, not understanding the passion I had for erasing my middle-of-the-road-Donny-Osmond image and replacing it with a profile more worldly and intellectual.

I woke that morning and fumbled at my Levi's, only to be interrupted by the apparition of a shockingly nude Patricia coming up my stairway.

"No, no, no!" she cautioned, wagging her finger at me.

Susan wasn't looking forward to the Nude Concert in the Park and came out of her bathroom wearing a pair of panties with her long blond hair combed down in two tresses that neatly covered her generous bosom.

"You're cheating," I pointed out.

She went to the kitchen and disguised her panties with a serving tray. For the rest of the day she was the ideal, attentive, and ever-present serving wench, tray perfectly positioned to conceal the desired region, and up top her hair lightly sprayed into a delicate camouflage.

Members of the L.A. Philharmonic began to arrive at the gate down below only to be met by Patricia.

"No! No! No!" I could hear her saying again and again. Among the players was a pregnant cellist who was granted the only garment from Patricia, even though from the baby up she was au naturel.

From my hiding place behind one of the supporting posts on the front porch I was doing my best to keep a smiling face on things and greet some of the fellas I worked with in the studio as they hauled their instruments up the driveway in the nude and tried to wave casually as though this was just another gig. I was learning quickly: There is a big difference between mankind in black tie and the animal itself crawling up out of the Greater Rift.

The phone rang. Susan came immediately with her serving tray.

"I think it's David Geffen on the phone for you," she whispered, turning to smile and offer the brass section some cheese and crackers and a view of her derriere as they arrived on the scene, wearing only their instrument cases.

I ran for the kitchen phone, delighted to be even temporarily out of the limelight. "Hello, David, hey! What's up! . . . The party . . . yes, there is a party here . . . you wanna come? You *do* wanna come! . . . uh-huh . . . yeah . . . Joni Mitchell . . . you've got Joni Mitchell . . . *You've got Joni Mitchell?* No . . . no problem . . . are you kidding? What a delight . . . well, we have a couple of dress code things here . . . no I'm not joking. No, not jacket and tie. Just come as you are . . . no worries . . . yeah, really that's fine. Okay . . . okay . . . see you in a few. All right now, bye."

Patricia made an entrance. "Where do we put the orchestra?" she demanded. She was loving this.

My mind raced.

"Only outdoors," she elucidated. "All the activities must be outdoors, otherwise what's the point in taking our clothes off?"

Even after a couple of hits on a joint I was able—just barely—to follow the thin line of logic in her reasoning.

"The orchard," I said. "We will do the Mozart French horn concerto in the orchard up on the hill."

This was a decision I had not thought through completely, as it did not occur to me at the time that this would place a rather large group of naked musicians in full view of numerous surrounding residences.

The party was beginning to gain momentum as sangria appeared in huge pitchers and joints were discreetly passed among the self-conscious throng. The pool was crowded with naked people whooping and hollering, casting away their last threads of reserve. Overhead, the Van Nuys airborne police unit hovered watchfully as usual. They would finally see what they had been looking for.

I placed myself on a chaise longue and casually draped a towel over my imposing instrument as a chamber group, sheltered in the shade of an overhanging oak, struck up one of Haydn's lovely quintets. All over the property music started up, the occasional soloist noodling as well as trios and quartets. On the front porch came the sound of an oboist warming up, rehearsing lines from a Mozart sonata.

The party was getting noisier. The concert grand thundered to life inside the house. *Nude Concert Musicians on Drug Bender in Encino*: The lead for the evening news flitted through my brain as Susan appeared, offering me a sangria from her tray and bending down to whisper, "David and Joni are in the kitchen."

My heart leaped into my throat. To this bedlam would now be added celebrity. Patricia and I arrived in the kitchen almost simultaneously so that I was able to hear her cheerful Mary Poppins–like greeting, "No! No! No!"

I threw myself into the breach.

"Joni," I said, facing her and bending slightly at the waist, turning to hug David. "Well, as you can see, we have a situation here."

Geffen was unfazed and even droll as he flashed a big smile. "So what do we do?" he asked, laughing at my beet-red face.

"Well, the dress code is *no* dress code I'm afraid, so would you like to change in here? Oh, my God, I can't stand this!"

I bolted through the swinging door to peals of laughter from David.

They both disrobed calmly in the kitchen and came out on the front porch chatting amiably with Fred and Patricia. Joni greeted a couple of musicians she knew with stunning sangfroid and a dazzling smile and wasn't it all just perfectly ordinary and weren't we all just the coolest?

We stood in a little group, Fred, Patricia, Joni, David, and myself, and listened to the Mozart oboe sonata. It was then we all noticed something peculiar that would not be seen at any ordinary chamber music concert. It takes almost superhuman abdominal strength to support the embouchure of an oboist playing the infamous instrument. This contraction of the lower torso was for the first time in my experience revealed in the flesh as well as the bouncing testicle that accompanied each note and beat of the composition. Pity the poor musician as the audience struggled to retain their composure in the face of such distraction, but to his credit he played on bravely and brought the piece to its conclusion.

The climactic tour de force of the event was the Mozart French horn concerto, and everyone gathered in the orchard after a couple of hours. A chamber orchestra of about twenty musicians was sitting among the trees in folding chairs awaiting the downbeat as skin, accustomed to the concert hall, reddened under the hot sun and the bites of unseen insects. All reticence, all embarrassment had fled. This was a serene group of professional musicians with but one purpose at the forefront of their concern: The Performance.

Mickey Newbury of the Mermaid Tavern took the baton in hand and they went at it, pregnant cellist and all. The clear, haunting tones of the French horn rang out over the neighborhood and echoed from its hillsides to the reservoir high above. The neighbors came out of their houses, arrayed in a kind of impromptu outdoor amphitheater, their view of the players unobstructed. Was this the part, I wondered, where we would be arrested? But the onlookers stood, entranced by the glory of the music and perhaps even somewhat amused by the novelty of the nude orchestra, a spectacle of the once-in-a-lifetime variety, until the last notes of Mozart's masterpiece echoed from the hillsides and faded into silence. Our neighbors ventured a smattering of applause and a couple of cheers before returning to the saner world inside their houses. We had done it. For the first time in recorded history a symphony orchestra had played a naked concert in public and had not gone to jail.

Jimmy Webb and The Contessas. *(Courtesy of Suzy Horton Ronstadt)*

CHAPTER SIX

When I die I don't want to go to heaven
I just want to drive my beautiful machine
Up north on some Sonoma country road
With Jimmy Dean and Steve McQueen
—JLW, "Too Young to Die," 1993

1970

My television special was barely breathing at Universal. We were working for ways around Sinatra and Aretha Franklin as these were essential artists from the Black Tower perspective. I know for certain that later when Mr. Sinatra and I were closer friends and even mutual admirers he would not have hesitated to do me this favor. Aretha, who I did not know and with whom I had no recording history, was an almost mysterious choice from my point of view. This game is often played in the halls of Hollywood. Universal could not deliver her. They were leveraging me in hopes that I would be desperate enough to somehow get her to do it. I called her and had an inconclusive conversation.

While these frustrations and exertions played out they sent me to scout locations. It was odd beyond measure to be sent to Oklahoma to survey farms as a setting for parts of the show. There was a juxtaposing of realities as I landed at the Oklahoma City airport on my mission. This mad ride had started with me driving a tractor on one of those checkerboards down there looking up into the sky, trying to devise a scheme to somehow escape. Now, a handful of years later, I was flying back to look down and rediscover that starting point.

A Bell Jet Ranger picked me up at the private air terminal and I directed the pilot west and south toward Beckham County and the fertile farm country that had birthed my parents. In ten minutes we were in sight of Sayre, a town that could have served as a model for George Lucas's *American Graffiti* with its pretty red-and-white brick courthouse and cupola. We circled the courthouse and the main street, the single traffic light, the Stovall Theatre where I had first seen *20,000 Leagues Under the Sea* as an eight-year-old. I gestured to the pilot further west and a little more north, in the direction of the very farm where most of my young life had unreeled, Buffalo, Oklahoma, home of the Webbs and the Killingsworths.

"Just a little farther and look for a cemetery on a hill," I told the pilot, and he nodded. He banked sharply and the landscape tilted to one side as a little white clapboard church lurched into view, surrounded by only a few unkempt tombstones peeking from the tall grasses and wildflowers bending to the will of the unceasing wind. For one, surreal second, I saw a new pink marble gravestone; it could be no other. The disconsolate snapshot swept by suddenly and the small, seasonal Cimarron River snaked into view a mile away.

Nestled up against the trickling stream were forty acres of prime cotton land, plants well along, hunter green against the noticeably red color of the bottomland. I held out my hand palm down in a stabilizing gesture and the pilot pulled us up into a hover at about five hundred feet. There was the serpentine brook shielded and overshadowed by giant cottonwoods.

From where the helicopter hovered I could see my granddad, clad in his overalls and sky blue denim shirt, driving his tractor, the same old patched-up Allis Chalmers, away down the length of the field towing a cultivator. He was an apparition, an anachronism, and yet a familiar fixture all at once in his worn straw hat. I knew, without being close enough to discern this detail, that a toothpick would be clenched in the corner of his mouth. His back was to us. His tractor made enough noise to mask our presence so I decided to arrange a little surprise for him.

While Granddad was turning around and shifting his aching frame behind the large radius of the tractor wheel, he saw a black and turquoise jet-powered helicopter land right in front of him, just five hundred yards away. The red dust and noise were cataclysmic. He never opened his mouth, shifted his gaze, or blinked for that matter. He bore straight toward us as though he hadn't seen a bloody thing.

I sat with the pilot as the RPM spooled off the turbine and the main blades and tail rotor wound down, watching the old man drive the tractor, right up to the edge of the field. He no doubt assumed we were some representation of authority, at the very least an unwarranted intrusion by a surveyor or some such meddler. He looked right at me through the Plexiglas, took off his battered straw hat, and dried his face and neck with a red bandana. He put his hat back on and began turning the plow. Once it was straight and ready he dropped the blades into the topsoil, engaged the engine with the clutch, and proceeded on his way right back in the opposite direction.

The pilot looked at me and shrugged. "Friendly fella," he said.

I grinned to myself. It was just my granddad. He plowed all the way up to the other end and made his elaborate turn yet again. How many thousands of hours had he spent here all by himself in the middle of this cotton patch? Eventually he came rolling up to us, using the hydraulic lift to pull the plow out of the ground and slowly, painfully it would seem, crabbed his way off the propane-powered Chalmers.

He took a tentative step in our direction and I bailed out of the chopper.

"Granddaddy! It's Jimmy!" I shouted as I ran up to him and grabbed his hand. It was the only time in my life I ever saw him truly surprised. By God, he was even smiling!

"I got you, didn't I?" I was laughing, too. He broke down and let me hug him. "Your grandmother will want to see you," he said in that high, quiet, seldom-used voice. We walked up to the house and cleaned our feet on the foot scraper.

"What is going on out there, for heaven's sake?" Maggie asked, turning around from the kitchen stove, flailing at some biscuit dough in a mixing bowl. She freezes there in my memory, as though caught in a strobe flash, mouth completely open, round eyed, and brows arched behind her bifocals in complete surprise.

"Jimmy Layne, why goodness gracious alive! How did you get here, for heaven's sake?"

I remember her plain country short-sleeved dress and the pattern of tiny faded flowers run amok. I hugged her and puffed flour all down the front of my jeans and on my shirtfront. She was highly strung, and while I'm sure she was glad to see me she was plainly unnerved. That would be my fault. It had been at least three years since I had seen or spoke with them.

We sat in the kitchen for a while and had sandwiches: white bread and bologna, mayonnaise, and some beat-down iceberg lettuce. Iced tea with lots of sugar and lemon juice. We talked about the rain and the milk cows, not as many as there used to be, he explained. I tried to describe what I did for a living, which seemed to be elusive to them.

"And you use a helicopter?" Grandmother asked incredulously.

I could tell she thought I had taken leave of my senses. I was a mystery to them. I had come down out of the sky telling strange stories.

After I burned through a thousand dollars or so of the studio's money I looked at my watch and prepared to take my inevitable leave.

"Would you like to go flying in the helicopter?" I asked my grandmother.

"Oh no, good Lord almighty, no thank you, I'm sure. I think I'll just watch you take off," she said. In our whole encounter she smiled just that once.

Granddad and I walked down past the barn and followed the cow trail, deeply etched in the rough pasture, across the creek onto the Webb side.

I asked him if everything was okay and if he needed anything. "Nope, don't need anything," he said with finality, as we climbed up the rise toward the tractor and the futuristic flying dart. It is hard to imagine two conveyances more different in appearance or purpose. Or two people for that matter.

From the chopper I saw him remount the steel leviathan and turn it 180 degrees to resume his task. The turbine spun up and the great blades became a solid shining circle. He never gawked at the helicopter or even looked up. The flying machine ascended as he became once more a tiny farmer on a toy tractor. I marveled at him. At his singularity and strength. At his determination to force a living out of this land. Perhaps on the surface we were different. Deep down inside, however, we shared something indistinguishable: Neither one of us would ever be anybody else's man.

1963

The family exited the San Bernardino Freeway in our Plymouth Fury and rode in silence through the postwar chicken wire and plaster mishmash of modern Colton, California. I was flabbergasted. On all the billboards and in the movies and magazines California was a lush landscape of exotic flora, green grass, swimming pools, and palm trees. Colton was more like the movie *Inferno*. A few hardy palm trees sprouted here and there but the area's hifalutin moniker, "The Inland Empire," hardly seemed deserved.

On Jeryl Avenue, a side street in a beautiful grove of old oak and eucalyptus trees, we pulled up in front of a stylish house, lushly surrounded by an irrigated lawn and landscaping. A bougainvillea bloomed outrageously at one corner of the low brick structure. After the long hot reaches of Route 66 it looked shady and inviting. Maybe it wouldn't be so bad here.

I was lying on my bed one afternoon in my new room, '30s-style industrial metal windows cranked open, when I was hypnotized by the sound of unsynchronized sprinklers at work all over the quiet neighborhood. Joni Mitchell would call it "the hissing of summer lawns." As my eyes closed, I heard a song floating through the garden.

"There's a world where I can go and tell my secrets to,
In my room, in my room."
—Brian Wilson

I went out the back door as though in a dream, and followed the sound across to the neighbor's fence. A teenager, stripped down to his shorts at the back of his driveway, was soaping down a dirty van in the shade. On top of the vehicle were a couple of long shapes I vaguely recognized as surfboards.

"Hey!" I said to the stranger, who jumped and turned to face me. "What's that?"

"What's what?" he challenged.

"What's that song?"

"Dude, are you puttin' me on?"

"I'm new around here."

"No shit." His tanned and freckled face broke into a sawtooth grin. "That's the Beach Boys, man. The Beach Boys?"

"Oh. Yeah." I bluffed.

"Wanna come inside?" He walked over to the fence. "They've gotta coupla albums out."

California slipped it to me somewhere about halfway through my first Beach Boys album. I caught a case of California and I would be deliriously ill for a long, long time.

In a couple of short weeks Janice, Tommy, and I were back at the schoolhouse standing in long lines and facing for the umpteenth time the ice-water glances of total strangers who thought our twangy accents betrayed innate ignorance. However, by this stage we knew a whole hell of a lot more about getting along with others than most kids we encountered. Even so, the masses of students astounded me. It was a hundred times more populated than Laverne High.

The only class I remember taking was P.E., and the only memory I have of P.E. is doing jumping jacks on the football pitch in my gray sweats. At the other end of the field I saw the cheerleader corps in their short gold-and-white pleated skirts and cuddly sweaters. California girls. But as pretty as they all were, one stood out. She was shapely, blond, and had a personality that made her the center of attention.

I asked my nameless P.E. mate about the cheerleaders. "Who's that one in front? There! She just jumped halfway over the bleachers!"

"Uh-huh," he grunted. "That's Suzy Horton. She's just about the most bitchin' girl in school."

He had that right. But Suzy Horton might as well have been on the moon as far as I was concerned.

I went out for marching band, as it was a tremendous organization at Colton High, winning awards all over Southern California. Since the cheerleaders went along on the competitions, Susan and I met without too much drama. She was choreographing steps for the whole band—a new thing in those days. As a non-dancer I didn't feel conspicuous spending extra time with her. When she would touch my arm to adjust my position my whole body would freeze into a grooming trance. She would laugh and say, "Hey, loosen up!"

During this time I wrote songs in a frenzy. I would listen to records by major artists like Little Anthony and the Imperials or the Four Tops, and then attempt to write my own version. My parents were so distracted by my incessant caterwauling that they moved the family piano into the garage, up against the wall beside the car. On those fall nights I would back the car out into the driveway and open the garage door wide. Neighbors would crack their windows and yell, "Keep it down!" I had my first fans.

I gave only an occasional thought to what Jayne Jayroe and the rest of my former classmates might be doing. I wrote Jayne from time to time and followed her growing success in the world of beauty pageants, but the rest seemed to fade away quickly. California moved into my head with a sense of its own importance. It had its own fashion, its own music, and even its own language. It also held out the chance, however small, of some fragment of fame and fortune. Hollywood beckoned, only an hour's drive away from Colton High School.

With all this, the best thing California had going for it was still Suzy Horton. I had emboldened myself to talk to her a couple of times in the cafeteria and persuaded her to sit down on a piano bench and I barraged her with original material. She was only a little impressed. Still, I had managed to develop a connection, even though she wore the ring of a Junior College All-American from San Bernardino Valley College. Eddie Groves knew about me and we even crossed paths in her front yard a couple of times. He glowered at me. Easy, big fella.

I invited Suzy out to the hills in Grand Terrace nearby, where there was some decent rock climbing, and as the weather warmed up, so did we. The orange blossoms bloomed in the vast, pungent groves that encircled the region. There was a boulder there, near the top of the hill, where I kissed her for the first time and she kissed me back. I had been in love with her for months. I had already written songs for her. I began hanging around her like a wasp haunts a mint julep. I would walk three miles down El Rancho from Johnston Street to Latham Street, and knock on her door at night. She wouldn't let me in, but she would direct me around the side of the house and she would come out to the porch swing in the back. We would sit in the dark and talk softly, the way young men and women have talked for millennia. The night-blooming jasmine would fill our nostrils. There would be a few tender kisses. Some talk about Eddie and what the hell we were going to do with him. The harmonies of the Lettermen would drift softly from the house. There was a lot of ambivalence. After all, it was only a first love.

1971

I was giving an interview to a *Rolling Stone* reporter at Campo de Encino. It was one of a series of interviews with different publications that all seemed to be asking the same question: "What the fuck is a Jimmy Webb?" This made me all the more anxious to reinforce my left-wing credentials, the fact that I played at the Monterey Pop Festival and loved the Rolling Stones above all. Yes, I hated the war in Vietnam and the Mike Curb Congregation. No, I wasn't on the same Orange County Republican bandwagon with Glen Campbell and Bob Hope and John Wayne. When Johnny Mercer had called me up and asked me to organize a library of my favorite recordings for the White House (for the warmonger Richard Nixon), I turned him down, explaining I didn't think the Nixons would appreciate Frank Zappa's *Live at the Fillmore East*, or Little Feat's *Sailin' Shoes,* or *Sticky Fingers* by the Rolling Stones.

The political orientation phase of the interview continued with a question about gun control. I assured my interviewer I was against violence of any type but that I, in fact, owned my very own handgun, strictly because the extensive grounds of Campo de Encino invited nocturnal visitors and my chosen career encouraged rumors of caches of cash and drug stashes. My reporter's eyes widened. He had just interviewed Neil Young and Neil had lots of guns! I relaxed a little. Could he see *my* gun? Sensing no pitfall I went into my bathroom and reached up on the top shelf of the closet to retrieve my Colt 1911 .45 in matte black.

I brought it into the bedroom and laid it on the table. It effused menace and my interviewer seemed unable to take his eyes off it.

"Here, you want to hold it?" I asked, adding, "Have you ever handled a gun?"

"No, I haven't," he said, staring with undisguised fascination.

"Well, first thing is safety, you know," I said, and popped the full clip out into the palm of my hand. I jacked the weapon open routinely and no cartridge was ejected so I closed the breech, flipped on the safety, and handed it to him. He held it up and squinted through the sights.

"So if I took off the safety I could pull the trigger right now, right?" he asked.

"Sure," I said, and watched him do it.

With a tremendous roar the firearm bucked and discharged. A

forty-five slug penetrated the floor of the bedroom. Later I dug it out of the back wall inside one of the kitchen cabinets below.

The young white-faced reporter dropped the gun onto the table shaking like a leaf. I wasn't feeling that good myself. There was no mention of the incident in the very upbeat article that appeared in *RS*.

1964

My mother fell over a piece of furniture in the front room of the house in early April. She and Dad laughed over it and later she came out on the patio with a glass of iced tea. I noticed she was closing her right eye against the bright spring sunshine. I remember teasing her about that squint because she looked like a baby, shading her eye with her hand.

Soon after she began to complain of headaches and pain in her eye. Her medications were adjusted, her condition improved, and for the next few weeks she seemed her old self. However, her sensitivity to light grew and she wore sunglasses most of the time. By June her condition caused her to be admitted to the hospital. There was a dreadful gnawing apprehension in my gut. I graduated high school. Mom missed the ceremony. It seemed like something that was happening to someone else in another room.

Her brother, Joe Verne, arrived with my aunt Jean and stayed for a couple of weeks. By July my mother's sister, Joy, was there for a week and then just as suddenly she too was gone. I was smart enough to know that these brothers and sisters had come to say good-bye. Dad gathered all the kids into the car and drove us over to St. John's Hospital to see our mother. The habit-clad nuns surrounded us in the corridors and shepherded us to the perpetually dark room where our mother was kept.

My eyes strained to adjust to the reduced lighting in the hospital room but I could see that Mother was transfixed by tubes and needles, her head slightly raised so she could see in front of her, a smile on her face and her blue eyes clear and loving.

"Ann," my father said to her as he sat down by her side and took her hand. "Do you remember who this is?"

Her smile widened to see me. "That's my Jimmy Layne," she said.

My eyes opened like the floodgates on a dam. "Mom, I love you," I said through the tears. She didn't cry. How could she be so radiant in such darkness? We had come in our childish way to comfort her only to find that she was—as always—the ultimate comforter. Even in this. One by one the children said good-bye.

After an exploratory surgery the following day our mother died of complications resulting from an inoperable brain tumor. She was thirty-six years old.

Twin funerals were held first in Colton, California, and then Oklahoma, at the First Baptist Church in Sayre, the latter being her final resting place. Before the first funeral, Dad called all us children into his pastoral study just off the sanctuary. We all lined up in front of his desk, little Sylvia and Susan seated, Janice, Tommy, and I standing.

"Now, kids," he said, "I don't want to hear a lot of blubbering and bawling out there today. We don't want to make a spectacle of ourselves." He paused. "Let's go out there and show them how the Webbs bury their dead."

He needn't have worried. We were catatonic. I was excused from playing the organ for the day. The sermons, the sentiments, the favored hymns and remembrances all wash away in a breaking wave of grief, smeared across the neurons of my brain in a muddled stain.

Dad was strong, almost superhuman, and handled everything with the same aplomb with which he conducted a Sunday service. No onlooker could have guessed how deeply shaken he was, how apprehensive he was about carrying on without her, or least of all that his belief system was in dire jeopardy. He continued to preach on Sundays; at times it seemed with as much fire as ever. However, at nightfall he would sink into an armchair in the living room, not much interested in dinner, "Blue Eyes Crying in the Rain" (w. Fred Rose) in constant rotation.

The family had a difficult time generating much excitement or joy for anything in my mother's absence. My oldest sister, Janice, took refuge with her boyfriend Dennis Linnens and spent at least half her time with him and his family. My brother Tommy, always a tall kid, went out for freshman football. His smile became a rare thing. Susan and Sylvia, only seven and five, retreated in on themselves.

I, on the other hand, turned my back on the horror of it. I found a high lonely place where a secret door led to my room with the impervious walls. I enveloped myself in the radio and hits of the day: "You Don't Have to Say You Love Me" by Dusty Springfield (w. Vicki Wickham, Simon Napier-Bell, Pino Donaggio, and Vito Pallavicini), "Baby I Need Your Loving" by the Four Tops (w. Brian Holland, Lamont Dozier, and Edward Holland, Jr.), and "Goin' Out of My Head" by Little Anthony and the Imperials (w. Teddy Randazzo and Bobby Weinstein). I was fascinated by the superimposition of string orchestras over rock 'n' roll tracks. The best example of this was Ben E. King's "Stand By Me" (w. Ben E. King, Jerry Leiber, and Moke Stoller) The string arrangement by Stan Applebaum was nothing less than a classical masterpiece.

I started calling up radio stations and talking to disc jockeys. I focused all my energy into music, and organized an all-female group: The Contessas. Suzanne Weir, Alyce Wheaton, Sharon Johnston, and Susan Horton. All blondes, all gorgeous, and all inspired with the idea of making a splash in the suddenly preeminent music business, heady with promise at the high tide of the British Invasion. We began rehearsing in the garage at night with the door open. Dad no longer yelled about the noise or came out to restore order. He continued preaching with, to my ear, a subtle lack of conviction, as though he were trying to persuade himself as much as his listeners. Lachrymose Ray Charles and Hank Williams dominated the home hi-fi.

A Sunday or two later my father calmly surmounted the dais at the Laurel Church and delivered a sturdy sermon. Afterward he announced his intentions to resign his post in Colton and return to his homeland; the better to weather the storm that God in his wisdom had loosed upon his family. My father was a much-beloved figure by many in that church and there were members weeping openly at the end of the service. In spite of his stratagems to cut his losses, to fall back and regroup, there was yet one small trauma for him to endure.

I had started classes at San Bernardino Valley College as summer ended and moved in with the Penyak twins, Mickey and Billy. They were identical, good-looking guys with lots of hair. They would have made a great recording act. I was slowly moving my stuff out of the house and over to the Penyaks' apartment as Dad sold everything that wasn't nailed down. A truck headed east down the long curling of Route 66 loaded with clothing, Mom's old piano, and other major items. Dad told me to get ready to leave, that he would meet me over by the Sunset Palms Motel, near the college, and he would load my few possessions for the trip back home. I met him there. His station wagon looked like something from *The Grapes of Wrath*, loaded to the gills with odds and ends tied on the luggage rack on top. Inside were my brother and sisters.

"Where is your stuff?" Dad asked. "I've saved a place up top here."

I looked at him in silence for a moment.

"Dad, I'm not going with you."

"Don't talk stupid, son, of course you're coming with me," he growled.

"Dad, I'm in too deep here. I want to write songs. I'm where people write songs and . . ."

"This songwriting thing is just going to break your heart, son," he pronounced with finality.

We stood there looking at each other for a long minute, neither wavering.

"Jimmy, this is the hardest thing I've ever done in my life," he said at last.

He dug into his pocket and pulled out a battered, slick wallet. He took two twenties out.

"This is all I've got, son. I wish I could do better." He turned and walked back to the wagon, beaten. He got inside and slammed the door. He looked at me one more time as the starter squealed and the engine started. The neon palm trees blinked and buzzed above my head and a stained California half-moon navigated through the smog and the San Bernardino mountains in the distance. The adrenaline rush of confronting him was ebbing and turning into something like grief with a tinge of fear. He drove away.

Jimmy Webb in a hot air balloon. *(Courtesy of Garth Sadler)*

CHAPTER SEVEN

I'm a skywriter, rebel without a cause,
 drifter without a name
And I can't seem to give up this flying game
I'm a wing walker, working without a net
 That's all I've ever been
And I wonder if I'm ever coming down again
 —JLW, "Skywriter," 1993

1964

Disc jockeys were as popular as most of the recording stars of the day. On the radio is where I first heard the Devil Himself, doing his top-rated drive-time show. He was glib and fast, and so border-line obscene you had to love him. I would telephone the overnight jock at two in the morning when no other living creature could possibly be listening to his show and ask him about the Devil.

"Well, kid, he puts his pants on one leg at a time just like the rest of us," he would intone in a pretend plaintive wail. "You can call him up and talk to him as easy as me." Before the end of the call I would ask him to dedicate the Four Tops' "Baby I Need Your Loving" to Susan and he would always do it. Finally one afternoon I called up the Demon himself. He was a charmer.

Professionally there were good omens on the horizon. A local entrepreneur, a tall blond kid named George Clements, had seen the Contessas perform, and whether impressed by their considerable talent or good looks, he was prepared to put up some money to start his own record company. I was commuting to Hollywood, visiting Dick Glasser at Warner Bros., where I landed a couple of Everly Brothers cuts. I had struck up friendships at Jobete, the publishing arm of Motown Records, and they offered me a songwriting contract. Next door at Bob Ross they were offering me studio time in exchange for publishing rights. The trip back and forth to Hollywood was expensive and time-consuming. As for college, my grades were abysmal. I was failing music theory and harmony and musicianship, mostly because I was always late. I would slink into the back of Russell C. Baldwin's—the dean of music—classroom, and he would survey me with one dour eye.

"Recalcitrant again this morning, Mr. Webb?" he would drily muse. I had to look up "recalcitrant." Seemed fitting.

I had two songs I wanted to record with the Contessas. As it happens I had never written parts for an orchestra but this was a minor problem that could be surmounted once we had a decent-looking logo for George's label. We came up with a white "E" on a Grecian pedestal rampant on a red field. "E" Records for "E" Street San Bernardino. George, a kid my age, was now prepared to invest his entire inheritance in the prospect. The sum was not insignificant for the time, approximately $3,500. He was given approval of the songs and allowed as much input as was practical, but I don't think George ever fully realized the ephemeral nature of money in the delicate and chancy environment of the music business. Possibly I could have been more emphatic in warning him of the danger.

Instead, we plunged ahead. We set a date for our first recording session at Bob Ross's studio. On the back of George's inheritance, we were able to book the world-famous Wrecking Crew for the rhythm session.

I knew the intricacies of orchestration involved transposing for some instruments, such as the French horn, clarinets, trumpets, and others. In some cases instruments called for special clefs and an arranger needed to have a precise understanding of the ranges of all the different instruments. I had a general idea about some of these limitations, but with a recording session coming up in a few days I had no time for in-depth study. My solution was pragmatic. I decided to write only for instruments all played in the same key. Violins, violas, celli, and basses all played in "C" or "concert" key. Among the brass instruments I had trombones. In the woodwind section there were the flutes. Aha! Almost forgot the harp! And all the percussion keyboards like vibraphone, orchestra bells, and even timpani. Voilà! I had my ideal orchestra.

Before the day of the session I had copied parts for every musician in amateurish blue ballpoint pen on lined notebook paper.

I showed up at the little studio that day, my Contessas in tow and my heart in my throat. Technicians were running the spaghetti factory of wiring that was necessary to capture a whole orchestra, tripping over earphone boxes and cue lines that linked all the players into a single organism. The musicians jabbered in a completely dispassionate way about their lawns, their wives, their instruments, or the damn union in a huge chorus that threatened to engulf me and push me back into the earth.

I walked into the booth as pale as a white grape and went to where Bob Ross and the guys from Motown sat coolly behind the console. "What do I do?" I asked plaintively. Bob walked me out into the studio where the A-list players were poking and squinting suspiciously at the primitively copied parts with hand-drawn staves on their stands.

"Are these the real parts?" someone bellowed conspicuously. Several huge guffaws followed.

Bob and I stood on a two-inch-high podium with a music stand sitting on it.

"Uh, fellas, let's show a little courtesy here. This is our arranger and conductor Mr. Jimmy Webb." I was a nobody, a seventeen-year-old kid.

There were a few polite little taps of bows against the stands. I looked back into the rhythm section and got a big smile and encouraging nod from the great Hal Blaine. He flourished his sticks and said, "Mr. Webb, do I need to count this off for you? Where do you want this, looks like a ballad, right?" He clicked his sticks together in a moderate tempo and I seized this life ring with a passion.

"Has everybody got 'This Is Where I Came In' on the stand?" I asked in my first coherent sentence of the day. Uh-uh. Yup. Everybody had it.

"Yes. Well, uh . . . then Hal you could give us four counts . . . and, uh, we could start."

The four clicks came like a metronome and the rhythm section came in as one man, all in tune, playing the way I always imagined a band could play: Joe Osborn with his head down concentrating on the bass strings, Larry Knechtel as casual as a rag doll with his long blond hair and movie star good looks playing an exploratory and rock solid piano. Tommy Tedesco with a sunburst Gibson jazz guitar. They were all playing the chords exactly right the very first time.

My heart leaped as halfway through the verse the vibraphone joined in. They could do it! They could read my homemade manuscript. As we approached the big chorus where the Contessas sang "So this is where you're gonna leave me," Hal played a nice drum lead-in, something I hadn't bothered to write, and then, in a feeling that must have been a little bit like that of a skydiver seeing his parachute open the very first time, the strings, twenty strong, and the three big trombones came in right after a harp glissando. It was gorgeous. There was a smile on every face in that room. I looked to the control room; The Contessas were there, faces pressed against the double-paned glass with huge smiles and gigantic blue eyes.

Gil, the record promotion guy for Motown, came out on the floor at the end of the take and said, "It's a fuckin' hit!" George Clements had to be scraped off the ceiling. For the rest of my life there would be no thrill remotely approaching the high of hearing a professional orchestra perform one of my arrangements. I still get that narcotic buzz every single time it happens.

After the session, Hal Blaine motioned me over.

"Hey, Jim. This is your first time arranging, right?"

"Yes, sir," I said.

"You need to stick with this. This is a good thing for you, 'kay?"

He looked at all the guys in the control room glad-handing one another and making deals.

"I know this is all confusing, but you just stick with the music, 'kay?" His kind dark brown eyes lingered on mine. He smiled and walked away and just left that great big drum set sitting there. Imagine that. He didn't even stick around to load his own drums.

1971

It is hard to convey how instantly pervasive cocaine became in the corridors of Hollywood office buildings, recording studios, movie soundstages, and private homes. With blinding speed, it became a universal pass code for a generation of people who came from nice families and didn't necessarily think of themselves as drug addicts.

My dealer was an aging beatnik named Dope Danny. He approached the subject of drugs with a spiritual reverence. Even in his seventies he always sported a tastefully dressed young woman on his arm. Cocaine seemed respectable, and its use, a pursuit of refined inside people. It was infamously, cruelly expensive. A hundred dollars at least for a gram, which might last an evening. Top commercial-grade was usually made in the Columbian jungle and then cut with something like novocaine, or a laxative.

In short order it became de rigueur to have a gram, a small bottle of the powder, in one's pocket when heading out for an evening's entertainment. Tiny silver coke spoons for the nose, worn on platinum chains, became fashionable neckwear. More commonly, lines were laid on coffee tables or small mirrors. Banknotes were rolled into compact tubes and used to inhale the powder through the nose and into the sinuses. It was considered cool to use a high-denomination bill.

There is a terrible symbiosis between cocaine and firearms. Garth and I added a couple AK-47s, two Browning fourteen-shot 9mm automatics, crossbows, and Bowie knives to our arsenal. It all went together in the world of coke-logic. We patrolled our six acres at night with binoculars, armed to the teeth. A limb cracking down in the dead of night from a towering eucalyptus would cause a wide-awake state of alarm in our house.

When I went to bed, I prayed that some crazy hippies would come over and try to kill us, or just anyone actually. It was Elvis behavior: the paranoia, the surfeit of weapons, new drugs, and Cad-illacs. Elvis was right. You couldn't trust anybody.

1965

Otto Mielenz was conducting Johann Sebastian Bach's "Jesu, Joy of Man's Desiring" with the San Bernardino Valley College mixed chorus. He stood on the podium in front of us emoting with his hands as the stirring polyphonic masterpiece burst from fifty passionate throats. The music was strong. It was redolent of sacrifice, death, and dedication. Tears sprang from Otto's eyes as the theme and subthemes crossed and intertwined on their almost painful journey to salvation. Sympathetic aquifers sprang from the eyes of most of Otto's singing acolytes. This was no ordinary choir. This was Otto's fraternity, drinking club, and cult. As the piece ended, choir members embraced one another and the divine tension evaporated in laughter. The young women dashed out to fix their makeup and the men gathered around Otto, the font of all our inspiration.

"Well, boys, is it time for a beer?" He laughed with a smile that meandered like a river.

Otto was that one teacher that a student has to meet at some point during his or her education for all the pieces to come together. He taught us that blowing air through our pipes and following a score wasn't singing. Singing could only take place if the soul was engaged. This philosophy was directly connected to the works of the great master J. S. Bach, who had stated without equivocation that his music was an extension of the voice of the creator.

My roommates, Mickey and Billy Penyak, were such identical twins I wasn't able to tell them apart for years, and then only by their quirks of personality. We were starving most of the time. I remember the three of us crouched forlornly over the last slice of pizza in the box, all of us hungry but unwilling to take the last piece from our mates.

I played gigs with drummer Jimmy Stotler, a phenomenal musician named Elton "Skip" Moser who played electric bass and flute, and Greg Waitman, brought in on electric guitar. For lack of a better name we called the band Four More. Immediately we started making pretty good money on one-nighters and began driving the hour and a half into Hollywood for sessions at Bob Ross's little clapboard studio. Just across the way was the biggest music store in L.A., Wallichs Music City. Miles of vinyl records lined the aisles.

One sunny afternoon I was driving to Newport Beach to meet some acquaintances from college, a stack of vinyl on the passenger seat of my trusty VW, and a tune began to circulate in my head. I hummed it, and because I had nothing to write the notes on, I concentrated fiercely to fix it in my head. I began adding lyrics. They seemed good enough that I was loath to have them fly out of the open window to be left on the shoulder of the Santa Ana Freeway. Over and over I sang the simple two-verse song to myself:

This time we almost made the pieces fit, didn't we?
This time we almost made some sense of it, didn't we?
This time I had the answer right here in my hand,
Then I touched it and
It had turned to sand

This time we almost sang our song in tune, didn't we?
This time we almost made it to the moon, didn't we?
This time we almost made our poem rhyme
This time we almost made that long hard climb
Didn't we almost make it this time?
—JLW, "Didn't We?"

I walked into Betty Wall's house and went straight to a piano, with a face screwed into an expression of concentration. I sat down and sang "Didn't We?" in one smooth motion, front to back. When I finished I turned around to see the owner of the house, and several of her guests, standing there dumbfounded, mouths hanging open. I never had written a song on the fly like that and never did again.

I was halfway across the Rubicon as far as going pro was concerned and it made life difficult. It was about this time that I met the Devil.

One day he drove his metallic green Mustang coupe over to the music department and parked outside the administration building. I called and pestered him so much while he was on the air that he finally given and agreed to come see me and find out what all the fuss was about. He was wearing tight jeans, a cowboy shirt, and a rodeo belt buckle. His smile unfurled as wide as a four-lane highway and his teeth were white and predatory. He was slightly bandy legged, and this effect was accentuated by his stitched cowboy boots. I had never seen anybody quite like him. We went to one of the practice rooms and I started to rip through songs, talking and singing at the same time about the Contessas, and Four More, and this guy George Clements who wanted to put up some money for a record. I was trying my best to impress him. Finally after ten or fourteen songs he said, "Hey, I tell you what. I'm on my way to kind of a cool thing. You want to go?"

Hell, yes, I wanted to go, and the next thing I knew I was in his special edition green Mustang with a big engine and leather upholstery and all that. I was babbling about how much I loved his show and my favorite records and did he really think The Beatles were here to stay? He looked at me occasionally with a bemused smile. He had seen my kind of youthful enthusiasm before.

We pulled up in front of a hot dog stand that was bedecked with all sorts of horrid, yellow plastic flags and a big sign that said FREE HOT DOGS! And another one that said FREE BALLOON RIDES!

"Wanna go for a balloon ride, Jimmy?" he asked me as we got out of the car.

I didn't even know it was possible to go for a balloon ride but I said sure and I started lookin' around, the adrenaline pounding in my veins because this was the guy who could put me on the radio.

"I don't see any balloon," I said. I held my hands out in a gesture of futility and he grinned politely and pointed upward, and sure enough, up there in the sky there was a great big beautiful balloon. He explained it was a "tethered" balloon and would soon come back to earth. I stared up into the cathedral-like interior of the huge inverted pear shape with awe. The alternating panels of blue and red reflected sunlight on the inside like stained glass windows. A woven wicker basket swung underneath as it ascended to a height of perhaps fifty or sixty feet. I could see people looking over the edge of the basket and chomping on their free hot dogs.

In due time the balloon descended and Belial and I cut in line because it was a radio station promotion event and I was with the big-time jock. We climbed inside and up we went for an adventure that was anticlimactic. Tethered ballooning is not exactly a high-adrenaline thrill ride. On the long ascent he told me about his idea.

"You know these beach movies with Frankie Avalon and Annette Funicello?" he asked.

"Yeah, sure."

"Well, I've got this idea for a screenplay about balloons. All these kids are out in the desert, no ocean or surfboards. They're making out around campfires, riding horses, and singing rock songs and shit like that, you know what I mean?"

"Yeah, I'm getting it," I said, trying to be cool.

"Instead of riding surfboards, they are getting into balloon races, and falling in love and fucking in balloons. They are crashing and getting into storms and, you know, all the detail stuff like that, I can work it out. We get some great-looking chicks in bikinis. We've got to keep the bikinis, and some old rock stars who will work cheap and it's a fucking hit, man. What we need is a song."

"A song?" I was momentarily confused.

"Before the beach blanket movies there were the Beach Boys and hit songs about surfing and shit, right? We need a hit song about balloons and then we can make the balloon blanket movies!"

He was excited and his enthusiasm was contagious.

"Can you write me a song about balloons?"

"Hey, it's a great theme. It's a happy idea," I said, staring up into the dizzying architecture of the giant balloon.

"Check it out," he said, staring up. "Look at those curves, the colors. This is the next big thing, Jimmy!"

By the time he dropped me back at Valley College he had me convinced I should write a song about a balloon. As I watched him drive away I was sure I had found my guru, the show business insider who was going to pave the way for me.

There wasn't a soul in the music wing except for a couple of piano majors down in the practice rooms slaving away on Chopin. I had the rehearsal room on the ground floor right outside Otto's office all to myself. I sat down at the brown Steinway and started slamming out the opening chords to my new song about balloons.

An hour and a half later I had a finished version of "Up, Up and Away." The phrase was familiar in the American vernacular because in the original *Superman* radio show of the forties it had been the man of steel's stock exit line. Song titles are happily (or sadly depending on your point of view) *not* subject to copyright. Theoretically there is nothing preventing a writer from creating a new song called "White Christmas." Nothing, that is, except the contempt and disdain of every other songwriter.

So the Devil and I became acquaintances, companions, and eventually best friends. He never wrote a script for the balloon movie, which I found disappointing, but I was soon to learn he had a tendency to leap at an idea with a burst of energy and verbalize it without being prepared to dig in. I added the bouncy little song to my portfolio and in the short term set about rearranging my domestic situation.

As much as I loved the choir and worshipped Otto Mielenz, my presence at the college had become mostly symbolic. In harmony and musicianship I was hanging on with a D. One day my professor Russell C. called me in to tell me I had earned an A on the final, which consisted of an original composition. Notwithstanding my final grade, he informed me I would flunk the course because of a lack of attendance and a very spotty record for turning in homework on time, if ever. Russell C. was a big African American man and I could detect under his crusty exterior an ember of affection for my dreams of becoming the next Irving Berlin. He gave me a brief lecture that day:

"Mr. Webb. We don't enjoy your presence at our institution any more than you enjoy being here. If you want to go to Hollywood and be a goddamn songwriter, then why the hell don't you *go* to Hollywood and *be* a goddamn songwriter!"

He politely held his office door open in order to facilitate my exit. It was the most useful thing any of my many teachers had ever said to me in my journey through the educational system.

Jimmy Webb in his Schweizer. *(Courtesy of Henry Diltz)*

CHAPTER EIGHT

All truth is a tale I'm telling myself.
—Brion Gysin, 1970

1971

And So: On was released and recognized as Record of the Year by *Stereo Review* magazine, the gold standard of the audiophile. I went on a support tour for *And So: On* as the weather began to turn cold all over the country. We played many of the familiar gymnasiums and coffeehouses. We played Doug Weston's Troubadour, which was becoming famous as a nightspot where a person could become immediately famous. Joni Mitchell for one. Elton John for another. I, however, did not immediately become famous. I did find a carving on the dressing room wall, which certain informers attributed to Tom Waits: JIMMY WEBB PLAYS GOOD CASH REGISTER. In the present era money is all anyone cares about, but in those days of supposed utopian equanimity (All you need is love!), I was embarrassed and a little guilty about the influx of unceasing cash. I deliberately dressed down. I went to extraordinary lengths to prove my collar was blue and my politics were pink. Meanwhile Mr. Sinatra was playing "Didn't We?" at Royal Festival Hall in London and giving me a shout-out from the stage. Glen Campbell sang "Wichita Lineman" on Johnny Cash's television show. The "Wichita Lineman" album had been a "stone cold smash" as the promo guys liked to say in that ancient time. Is the reader tracking the dichotomy between the world I lived in and the world my music lived in?

On November 17, I was booked on the *Dick Cavett Show*. I surmised I was there to explain some of the inconsistencies in my career, my appearance, my politics, "MacArthur Park," and my private life. I was rumored to be a drug user. My reaction to this was: "Hot damn! Now we're getting somewhere!" I found out once I got on the set that I was merely the opening act. I played a couple of tunes; I don't recall exactly which ones. I chatted with Dick perfunctorily as he couldn't have been any less interested in me had I turned out to be an expert on parking space management. Once we negotiated the fifteen-minute segment with an interview that was not a high point of either career, Dick moved to the reason he had shown up for work.

His special guest that evening was an alleged murderer, ex–army officer, and doctor, Jeffrey MacDonald. I perched on the couch and watched this devastatingly charming man in the hot chair deny that he had killed his wife and three little girls and then faked the scene to make it appear as though Manson sympathizers had done the killing. The crime scene had been painted in blood with messages such as "Kill the pigs!" This interview consumed the rest of the show and I found out everything I needed to know about the army's relentless persecution of Jeff MacDonald. The mysterious woman in the yellow hat, the impossibility of certain crime scene details occurring without interference of the police (i.e., it was a big setup and he was being sent down the river). A blond refugee from a *GQ* cover with a nice gold watch, fashionable jacket, and good shoes, MacDonald looked more like Michael Douglas than a murderer. After the show I went over to him under the influence of some inexplicable impulse to shake his hand. I suppose I thought if I shook his hand I would know; something would tell me if that hand had throttled three little babies.

He greeted me with a huge smile and automatically took my hand.

"Hey, man, I love your music. Thanks for listening," he greeted me.

I believed him. His energy, his deportment, and the look in his eyes did not suggest any culpability in murder. I followed MacDonald's travails for years after that. He was in and out of prison, he had new trials, and he appealed incessantly and with inevitable futility. He never escaped the ambiguity of whatever actually did happen.

Cavett himself found MacDonald to be a poseur and insufficiently convincing. "His affect is wrong, totally wrong," Cavett said years later after viewing footage of the interview.

1965

The Contessas tapped their college funds, I gathered together the small bills and smaller change I made off band gigs and tips, and we put it all together and moved to Hollywood. We shared our first apartment: a twin bedroom and kitchenette two-floor affair. I slept on an air mattress in the dining room downstairs. The atmosphere was redolent of hair spray, perfume, and a mixture of all the ointments, permanent treatments, creams, poisons, and spells that are necessary to epitomize the female persona times four. There was an occasional spat, but considering five people were living in a space designed fastidiously for two, we got along. Because it was my goal to keep "the group" together, it fell to me to referee and organize peace summits from time to time. All the group members had to be treated with painstaking equanimity. So Susan's and my relationship, or lack of one, was put on permanent ice, pending the outcome of the group's fortunes.

I was damned proud of those women when they were turned out. They had good taste in clothes; their platinum blond tresses were immaculately styled and maintained. They labored tirelessly on their routines and harmonies. Suzanne Weir, a very pretty woman and the lead singer, was like a lot of overly trained classical musicians: not finicky about pitch at times. I would take them over to Motown to see if Frank and Hal could rub some "soul" into her; however, "soul" is a hellaciously difficult thing to teach. There were white singers in the pool who could sing "soulfully": the Righteous Brothers, the Walker Brothers, Joe Cocker, Tom Jones, Felix Cavaliere, or Janis Joplin. Sometimes white folk could decorate their singing with the correct artifacts and affectations to sound soulful, but "white soul" was truly a rare thing.

I hoped Motown might want to sign them. Their record had just been released on "E" Records and the ladies would dress up in identical blue gingham "farmer's daughter" dresses with blue ribbons in their hair. Into Motown West we would troop, through the oversize door. Immediately Suzanne Weir would find a way to get into Hal Davis's lap. Frank Wilson would be there with his almost impossibly handsome face and soft voice, often with George Clements, our producer, and sometimes Gil the promotion man. Tapes from Detroit would manifest from locked cabinet doors and I remember one night hearing "My Girl" (Smokey Robinson and Ronald White) for the first time, long before it hit the airwaves. I knew as soon as I heard the opening bass line and verse that it would be one of the biggest records of the era.

Meanwhile the Contessas flirted, insinuated, and enchanted the office like a well-trained machine, knowing instinctively what was required and precisely when to ease off on the throttle to avoid any suggestion of entanglement. This is something I never coached.

There was that much lauded *je ne sais quoi* in the ambience of the office. It was a pulsating excitement that was only just short of something you could put out your hand and touch. Motown was on a roll with the Supremes. They had released five or six number-one records in a row with Diana, Mary, and Florence, and the Contessas were blatantly motivated to be a white version of that.

The girls made one major promotional assault at a San Bernardino radio station. They invaded the station one afternoon and went into their full-on flirt mode, sitting on laps, posing for photos and pretend-smooching, but this time it was disconcerting and I felt slightly queasy. A Top 40 radio station was where the rubber met the road. The Devil had already recounted to me several anecdotes about major recording stars handing over sex right on the premises, in the control room or in a car outside; anything to get their record played. Jocks were accustomed to these kinds of favors without having to ask. It was a perk of the job. Female artists were under subtle but steady pressure because so many artists were vying for a limited number of slots on that chart. In other words I knew the girls were teasing but the jocks didn't or, maybe to put a more accurate read on it, didn't care. I felt like a hockey goalie fending off a hat trick.

We had reached a critical juncture, but I wasn't ready to tell the ladies if they wanted airplay and if they wanted to crack key stations they might have to do some unladylike things. So far it had been good fun. No one had gotten hurt. I crossed my fingers and prayed for the indefinable mojo that would turn our first record into a hit.

The Contessas' single "This Time Last Summer," backed with "Keep On Keepin' On," fluttered unsteadily toward the sky and rock 'n' roll heaven in the summer of '65 and came up short, plunging to earth after a few short weeks. Still, the ladies had created enough excitement that West Coast president Marc Gordon offered them a recording contract at Motown. It was exactly as I had pictured it, and then, unaccountably, the Contessas began to talk about breaking up. Almost simultaneously Marc Gordon resigned or was canned at the label. I found myself superfluous and Jobete let me out of my songwriting contract. I had written forty-five songs for them. They were generous and returned many of my copyrights, including "By the Time I Get to Phoenix," and "Up, Up and Away." I left behind an album cut with the Supremes called "My Christmas Tree" and a Billy Eckstine single "I Did It All for You," and some other bits and pieces.

Sharon went back to Colton and married guitarist Greg Waitman. Alyce went home as well, and enrolled in classes with the intention of pursuing her dancing aspirations. Suzanne Weir threw up her hands at the unpredictability of show business and headed back toward academic circles. Susan Horton ended up at an insurance desk, installed in an imposing skyscraper that stood just west of MacArthur Park near Wilshire Boulevard. George Clements somewhat bitterly wrote off his investment in "E" Records with the suggestion that I probably should have paid my share.

Well, he had paid his money; he took the ride and had his fun. Four More, Jim Stotler, Skip Moser, Greg Waitman, and I went our separate ways as well. The Vietnamese Conflict was revving up and the draft was a growing concern for all of us. Jim and Greg suddenly joined the Marines and thankfully spent the duration stateside. Skip graduated from Cal Tech and went to work on helicopter blades for a secret military project.

There was a sense that I'd had my ride on the carousel and the ring had somehow slipped from my grasp and was now rolling away like an errant coin. I set about finding myself a niche somewhere in "the star maker machinery behind the popular song" (*J. Mitchell*). I had no money. No income. I had borrowed money from Betty Wall in Newport Beach to purchase an old battered Volkswagen. I began a sojourn on the meaner side of the Hollywood streets.

1971

And So: On was a sensation with the critics. *Rolling Stone*'s reviewer wrote that the album was "another impressive step in [Webb's] conspiracy to recover his identity from the housewives of America and rightfully install him at the forefront of contemporary composers/performers." This was, incidentally, back when what *Rolling Stone* said about records meant a hell of a lot in the marketplace. Still, sales were tepid. Radio stations were nervous about my image, unsure where to place me in the starting grid. Warner Bros. sent me out on the road with a seasoned promotion man named Walt Calloway as a buffer, a grizzled pioneer of the airwaves, who looked the part with his white mane of hair and matching mustache. Walt walked me into every Top 40 station in America with a copy of *Rolling Stone* magazine and a big "Why not?"

Top 40 jocks ruled the world in those days and if you weren't someone they took seriously they would leave you cooling your heels in the waiting room while they got around to your inevitable pitch. I was sitting in the anteroom of a small station somewhere out in the provinces for almost an hour and chanced to look up at the same time as the guy sitting opposite me who had been there since before I sat down. It was Jim Croce.

Walt would have me stay over for dinner with a program director and his wife and friends as a guest to be slightly poked and prodded like a dodgy bit of food, gingerly examined, one might say. I remember one night in an Italian restaurant sitting across from a P.D.'s wife. She was all gussied up in a low-cut gown and kept looking at me like some exhibit from a museum. Finally she wrinkled up her pretty little face and asked, "When are you going to write another 'MacArthur Park'?"

This translates pretty much straight across as "When are you going to write another hit?"

"Never," I said. "I'll never write another 'MacArthur Park.'"

When I got home I sat at my kitchen table, contemplative and angry. The *LA Times* was open to the entertainment section and something caught my eye. A sailplane, a sleek facsimile of a modern fighter aircraft, complete with the transparent bubble canopy and aerodynamically smooth shape. It differed primarily and significantly from a small jet in the fact that it used no engine to achieve flight. Nor did it have a "delta" or V-shaped wing, but instead an unbelievably long and tapered span that met the fuselage at ninety degrees. After a bit of reading I learned it was no mere "glider" but a "soaring plane," a sophisticated machine that was designed to ride air currents and was made with a highly efficient airfoil and lightweight materials.

I decided immediately I was going to fly one.

That weekend I drove my XJ6 out the Ventura Freeway to Highway 14 and ascended into the high desert. The San Gabriels rose ruggedly, with their crests of pine, on the right. I merged onto the

Pearblossom Highway, a potholed two-laner that was a shortcut to Vegas if you were ornery enough. Truckers dominated this ominous track at high speed, reaching seventy or eighty miles an hour as they met automobiles also making up time. Occasionally two of these missiles would come together at 160 miles an hour. Steel tore apart like paper. Arms and legs would fly.

I had a little trouble finding the turnoff, but spotted a few small aircraft fairly close to the ground out my window and turned that way. A half mile up the road, virtually in the shadow of majestic snow-covered Mount Baden-Powell, was a hand-painted sign: GREAT WESTERN SOARING SCHOOL.

The scene that greeted me through the windshield was one of almost chaotic industry. The dirt runway curving up and down like a roller coaster was packed with gliders and towplanes. The northeastern end of the strip was nose tip to rudder with about twenty gliders waiting to take off. A Super Cub roared at full rpm as it towed an impossibly graceful and eager high-performance sailplane off the deck and slowly out into a wide circle. The two aircraft climbed as one, linked by the towrope. A Piper Ag Cat came whistling over the line of waiting aircraft, coming in for its next pickup, a nylon towrope flailing behind.

With a loud metallic ringing sound, a long towrope was secured to a pelican-looking bird with two people inside. The pilot of the Ag Cat gunned his engine and the towrope came taut, the two craft strained together for a moment, moved forward, and then, effortlessly, the sailplane lifted.

At this moment another ship approached the runway, apparently traveling the wrong way, and a tough-looking cowboy in a tennis hat ran out of the operations trailer, red faced and screaming, "You can't do that, goddamn it!" He ran out on the flight line waving his arms and screaming, "Shut it down, for cryin' out loud, shut it all down!" He stood on a thin strip of tarmac and stared at the glider bearing down on him as though daring the pilot to run him over. "You idiot!" he yelled, shaking his fist. The gawky bird touched down just over the weeds at the far end of the runway, and attempted to make a right turn. He hung his right wingtip in the dirt and the glider circled at high speed toward other ships tied down helplessly at the edge of the field. He skidded within inches of the control trailer and dramatically stopped, nose in the dirt and tail high in the air. The cowboy went about restoring order.

Finally the reverberations of this episode ebbed and I felt emboldened enough to walk up to the cowboy and introduce myself.

"Hi, I'm Jimmy Webb, I called you."

The fierce individual was suddenly all charm.

"Hello, Jimmy, I'm Fred Robinson! Sorry about all the excitement. Some well-meaning journalist put a story in the paper about this old ranch and things have been snafu'd ever since." He grinned and threw up his arms for a second and then dropped them helplessly. "I'm just afraid some idiot is going to get themselves killed out here. It happens, you know!" He snorted. "What can I do for you, Jimmy?"

"I would like you to teach me to fly."

"That's what we do out here," he exhorted "Let me show you our training aircraft."

He walked me out to a temporarily idle kite, one of the ungainly pelicans. "This is our Schweizer 2-33. Thousands of people have learned to fly in this." I glanced at the high wing 33 but my attention was diverted by another design. She was tied down securely next to the trailer and was the exact plane I had seen in the *Times*.

"What about that one?" I gestured toward it.

"That's a Schweizer product as well, a 2-32. But that's a high-performance sailplane. We normally don't teach in that."

"How much is a glider like that?" I asked.

He was surprised. "Uh, about fifteen thousand dollars."

I walked her sleek length, grazing the thin aluminum skin with the tips of my fingers. I looked through the clear glistening canopy at the intriguing world of analog instruments that were clustered on the panel. I took in the big five-point flying harness that secured the pilot to his seat.

I smiled at him. "I'll take it."

"Well, you can't take that one. It belongs to a customer!" he complained.

"How about a brand-new one? Blue trim." He stopped fretting and grinned. He was beginning to get an inkling of my intent.

1965

I got a job at a low-rent music studio as a demo pianist, lead sheet maker, and mostly, a janitor. As an added perk, the studio manager let me sleep in her spare room. There was one bright light in my life. Though the Contessas had scattered to the wind, Susan Horton was unaccountably still living in Los Angeles. We met each other many times at MacArthur Park, a vestige of Wilshire Boulevard's more genteel days. Well-heeled people had lived here and taken their promenades beside the large inviting body of water, lush with palm trees, beneath the quaint, turn-of-the-century streetlamps. Then drug dealers moved in and replaced bright curiosities like paddleboats and mallard ducks. The vivid colors faded under a layer of dust as traffic became a nonstop polluting stream.

Neglect was the word that sprang to mind when Susan and I met for lunch on the grass that summer and watched the old men playing checkers and chess in their last surviving enclave under the trees. We had never even made love. I was an eighteen-year-old virgin, for Christ's sake. Here I am, saving myself for her, and our conversations are drifting into long silences. In her vague, unfocused gaze I could see that the park wasn't even real to her. It was streaked and faded like a watercolor wash and I was dissolving with it like a snowflake on the hot dirty sidewalk. The life was drawn out of me. And yet I loved her. Even as I walked away for the last time and behind me, out of my sight, MacArthur Park melted in the dark.

1971

Harry Nilsson announced he was headed over to London for a while and suggested I consider visiting. In my life Harry and cocaine were hopelessly entwined. When I was with Harry I was probably doing lots of cocaine but that is in no sense his fault. Cocaine was gaining momentum and I always had to have a bottle in my pocket if I went out. Harry, it must be said, went the extra mile.

One night, we were waiting for our drinks at Marconi's, a place packed to the gills with industry types and celebrities. Harry reached inside his suit coat and pulled a gram out of his inner pocket. He took the plastic screw top off the little bottle. Then, elevating his left hand in order to make a level surface, Harry poured a small mountain of cocaine on the back of it. Everyone within eyeshot stopped what they were doing to watch. H, as his intimates called him, shotgunned the coke up both nostrils with a great hooting snort. White powder went all over the place: down his beard and the front of his shirt, into the air where it lazily drifted onto other patron's tables, all over me—it was like setting off a cocaine bomb. The clientele paused for a second and then went back to their steaks and martinis.

"Want some?" Harry offered, with a smile that showed all his teeth.

"Maybe later," I replied softly. Harry's big red nose was decorated with a splotch of white icing.

As we sat there I told him one of my best buds had punched my girl's ticket while I was out on the road. He told me something similar had happened to him recently.

"A close friend?" I asked him.

"They don't get any closer," he responded drily.

It is small confidences such as this that close the distance between two people.

Let me correct any negative impression I may have created about Harry of the great golden heart. Drinker he was. Fatalist he was. Knight in shining armor he also was.

One late night Harry was driving down a lonely stretch of Pico Boulevard, which was not one of East Hollywood's more elegant thoroughfares, when he heard screams. In the middle of a car dealership's abandoned lot, a young woman was being hit in the face by two grimy-looking thugs. Harry hung a 180 and drove directly into the center of the melee, flying out of his German mystery vehicle to tackle the nearest lowlife. This philosopher, this poet, this man with the fine vulnerable voice of a rare canary threw himself bodily into the midst of the fracas. He ended up in the hospital with a bruised spleen, broken bones, and numerous lacerations and contusions about the head and shoulders. Those of us who knew him would back him come hell or high water.

When we got to London, I went to several of the *Nilsson Schmilsson* sessions. My friends Jimmy Keltner and Gordon were on the gig, as well as Klaus Voormann on bass, and many of Elton John's sidemen. Harry was the de facto pianist and always prepared very carefully for recording. We would go to a pub, have a couple of brandies, and then visit the loo and snort coke off the back of our hands. Then we would smoke some hash in the alley and go to the studio. After the session we'd retreat to one of Soho's late-night jazz bars and do straight shots of tequila and snort coke. One had to be more careful in London; one couldn't lay mountains of marching powder out openly on the bar. Not cricket, old boy. Daylight would find us wherever we passed out. Sometimes we would have breakfast; sometimes he would disappear. Sometimes a girl might be seen, but never more than once or twice. Harry's sex life at the time, if any, was circumspect. After all, he was a new dad, and trying to make it work with his wife, Diane.

I came back from London and my late-night hangs with Nilsson, drinking much more heavily and on a steady regimen of cocaine use. None of this hangs in Harry's closet. He never forced anything down my throat—or up my nose for that matter. Harry's unfettered chain-of-consciousness approach to record making had been an epiphany during the creation of *Nilsson Schmilsson*. I started planning some songs and arrangements for my next solo LP, songs I thought would please Harry. Cocaine gave me the energy to stay up all night and create. To my mind, it wasn't affecting my creative touch. I couldn't see that I was making mistakes.

1965

Marc Gordon, formerly of Motown, called and asked me if I would like to take a trip up to Vegas, all expenses paid.

"What's the catch?" I asked.

He explained that Tony Martin, one-time Motown artist and husband of Cyd Charisse, had been asking about me and wanted to hear anything new I might have. He was playing the Riviera Hotel and offered to buy me a plane ticket and put me up for the night in return for a song or two. I grabbed my binder of songs and my one pair of slacks and headed for the airport.

I arrived early, checked into a very decent accommodation and around 6:00 P.M., not being able to contain myself, went down to the stage entrance. I walked backstage unsupervised and gazed in wonder at the soaring proscenium arch and the hundreds of lights suspended in midair, decorated with their festive-colored gels. I wandered into a back corridor carrying my fat score and found myself standing in front of the breakroom, where performers could rest or watch television between shows.

It appeared empty, and I walked in thinking I could wait there until my 7:00 appointment in Mr. Martin's dressing room a few doors away. I found a chair, sat down, and looked around. The room was dimly lit, a towel thrown over the lampshade. A man sat, resting his head on a corner pillow at the end of the couch, apparently napping. He was a black man, fairly small in stature. In one hand he held a trumpet against his chest. His breathing was slow and even. I resolved to leave him in peace and opened my binder, searching through the pages for a suitable offering.

After a few minutes my companion on the couch stirred a bit, and groped in his coat pocket for an old handkerchief. I heard him blow his nose very loud. Then he said, "What you got there?" in a voice like an old scratched record.

"Me?" I squawked, dropping the binder into my lap and looking into his large eyes. He was focused on me now and was probably going to light into me for waking him up.

"Yeh. What you lookin' at so hard there, young man?"

"Oh, this? Oh, this is nothin' much. Just some of my songs for Mr. Martin. Mr. Martin? Mr. Tony?" I sputtered.

"Oh, I know who he is all right. Bring that over here."

I stood up and the binder slid off my lap onto the floor. I scrabbled around on the linoleum gathering up some leaves that had come loose. My hand landed on "Didn't We?"

"That one right there. Bring that one over here," he ordered.

"Uh, this one? Uh, okay . . . It's really not one of the best ones. . . ." I trailed off.

He reached up and whipped the towel off the lamp. In the sudden flood of light I saw the old man's lips, encompassed by a white circular scar. A lifetime of performing was indelibly carved into his face and I recognized him in that instant as Louis Armstrong.

He took the lead sheet from me and scanned the melody, raising one eyebrow slightly and barely humming the tune. Suddenly he raised the battered and bent trumpet and softly blew the opening strain:

This time we almost made the pieces fit, didn't we?
This time we almost made some sense of it, didn't we?

He paused and looked at me, or perhaps down my throat as my mouth hung open like a tailgate on a Ford pickup.

"You gonna stick wid this, right?" he said gently in his gruff voice. My head swirled as I nodded affirmatively.

"Thank you, sir, thank you," I managed to respond.

Out in the hallway someone was knocking and summoning.

"Mr. Armstrong! Five minutes!"

Louis "Satch" Armstrong smiled at me and held on to my hand.

"You stick wid it, kid, you got something," he said as he stood up and headed for the door. He was gone for a second but then he leaned back into the room for a final word and a smile.

"You stick wid it." And then he really was gone.

I stood there with a warm golden glow suffusing my whole body. Eventually I looked at my Timex and realized I was late for Tony Martin. I went down the hall to his dressing room and he treated me like a prince, looking at every single song and highlighting a few for future interest. As curtain time loomed he was immensely preoccupied with his vitamin B1 shot and back brace, his coif and all the makeup and arcane applications of an aging star who still summons the courage to walk on stage and singlehandedly roll back the hands of time. A happy warrior, laughing old age in the face in the dressing room mirror.

1971

I learned to fly in thirty days, give or take.

Once the towrope is released, a sailplane's path upward through the sky is remarkably similar to the circular one that carries hawks and other raptors aloft. The view from the deeply banked glider, through the clear blister, is dizzying.

As I gained experience and confidence with the controls, my lines of flight became more stable and there were fewer jolts and aimless meanderings. The tension level also came down. Ergo I started feeling better and actually enjoyed the occasional look around at the scenery, indulging in a deep breath or two, but such recreation almost always immediately evoked a warning from Fred in the backseat that my nose was dropping, or that I was too slow or dragging a wing. It was a game of precision where an aggregation of tiny mistakes could eventually bring the big bird down to an ignominious plow through an unfortunate farmer's field.

One afternoon we went up routinely, butterflies fluttering in my torso as usual, and Fred had me "box" the towplane and practice recovering from a couple of stalls. After the second recovery he made his first editorial comment since the beginning of instruction.

"You're a born pilot, Jimmy." We landed back at the field and he popped the canopy and got out. He waved at a towplane pilot, who taxied over.

"Time for you to leave the nest and fly solo." Fred grinned wryly as he bent over to secure the towline. I palmed a big red knob with a pull and release that secured the ring to the rope. He didn't actually expect me to fly this turkey by myself, did he? He did. He walked back about thirty feet and stood there with his arms crossed. The tow pilot opened the throttle just a shade and the slack went out of the towline with a slight tug on the airframe. I waggled my rudder to signal the tow pilot that I was ready, my palms sweating on the stick.

I looked out and Fred was running my wingtip. As the two aircraft gained momentum he kept the wings level. The empennage lifted off the deck. The airframe began to float in ground effect. The controls became living extensions of my arms and legs, another instrument for me to learn to play. A feather touch of back stick and the glider was airborne. It was my job to keep it in an imaginary box behind the towplane.

At about three thousand feet I checked my altitude and looked out over the billiard table–flat desert toward the Tehachapi Mountains forty miles to the northeast. I reached forward and pulled the spring-loaded release. There was a metallic thunk as the towline twisted and flailed and the towplane banked hard right and disappeared. My first sensation once I was settled down was loneliness. There was no reaffirming gentle voice right behind my head to tell me what to do.

I started thinking almost immediately about how I was going to get down. As I checked for traffic, "neck on a swivel" as they say in the fraternity, I noticed a strange wisp of cloud southeast of my position and began to witness the formation of a small cumulus cloud. It blossomed like a cotton ball while I watched; a burgeoning animated cauliflower that glowed an unearthly white in the bright sun. Well, this was interesting. Perhaps I was in a position to investigate such a hypnotic unfolding from a new perspective. I drifted over to the vicinity of the cumulus that was now as big as a small skyscraper. The closer I approached, the more absorbed I became by its deepening contours and darkening grays and indigos.

It was a smattering of raindrops across my canopy that brought me back to a sobering reality. I was a fledgling pilot, several miles from my home field and approaching cloud base under a cumulonimbus cloud that suddenly towered in vertical walls far above me.

I flew along the side of the cliff, awed by what my tiny white carnation had become in a matter of minutes. More important, I pointed the nose of the glider at the ground and watched the airspeed wind up to eighty and then eighty-five knots. Against all expectations I continued to gain altitude. I turned away as the cloud moved laterally, trying to pull me in. I ran up to a hundred miles an hour, close to red line, now terrified. It had me.

I was in peril of being sucked into the cloud. This was potentially disastrous, as I would immediately be blind to any external visual reference and would probably stall or go into a spin, providing the enormous vertical shear inside the cloud didn't rip us apart without ceremony. I got a grip on my emotions and resolved, as Robinson had always admonished me, to "never stop flying the glider." I was at ten thousand feet and the cockpit was suddenly frigid. I was shaking. But my teacher had introduced me to artificial emergencies. By using a special sliding lever, slats, whose only function was to spoil lift, could be raised on the upper side of the wings. Hence their nickname, "spoilers."

As I increased my angle of descent by pointing the nose further downward I engaged the spoilers and anxiously scrutinized my instruments. Slowly but surely I began to see altitude spooling off and eventually I approached level flight once again, no sign of the cloud except a light pelleting of raindrops that spattered over the canopy.

I made my approach downwind, flying a base leg that was more of a closed loop. I wanted to get down. I used the dive brake, adjusting the threshold for my touchdown, and when I landed it was no cinematic, slow-motion landing but rather I planted the plane firmly on the X and then, almost in tears, steered and braked the Schweitzer to a stop in front of my tie-down.

Fred Robinson strolled over with a brace of instructors and an ice-cold soda.

"Congratulations, Jimmy!" He beamed from ear to ear in a highly uncharacteristic pose. As I clambered out of the deep cockpit I was clapped on the back as other friends from the field gathered round to add their congratulations.

The flight line was busy and as I gulped at the soda the im-promptu celebration broke up quickly. Normal operations resumed.

Fred looked at me with an appraising stance. "So, how was your solo, Jimmy?"

"I loved it. Er . . . a little scary landing by myself, but I had a good teacher!"

"Did I teach you to stay at least five hundred feet laterally from any cloud at all times?"

"Yes, sir," I bluffed on.

"So that must have been someone else I saw up there clowning around in that big q-nim then." He reached out his hand to shake mine.

"Hands are a little chilly there, Jimmy, and shaking, too."

I stood there looking at the blue patch of sky over the flying field. What untold mysteries floated there in plain sight and yet invisible? It was another world entirely, a place of three-dimensional freedom where a man's senses were elevated far beyond those of the earth crawlers below. I loved it more than anything I had ever known in my life save perhaps music.

The 5th Dimension, Jimmy Webb, and Marc Gordon at the Grammy Awards.
(Courtesy of William Eastabrook and NARAS)

CHAPTER NINE

Would you like to ride in my beautiful balloon?
Would you like to ride in my beautiful balloon?
We could float among the stars together, you and I
For we can fly, we can fly
Up, up and away in my beautiful,
my beautiful balloon
—JLW, "Up, Up and Away," 1967

1966–67

Though he unaccountably remains underrated by the Rock and Roll Hall of Fame, Johnny Rivers had just been selected "Male Entertainer of the Year" for the third year in a row. He would go on to win a fourth time.

Johnny decided to double down on his burgeoning star power and create a record label: Soul City. Again, Marc Gordon put in a good word for me. He brought Johnny by the studio where I was working and I played a few songs. Johnny decided to take me on as a writer, and invited me to stay in his house until I was on my feet. He paid me $100 a week and offered me a new car.

When it comes to the '60s Johnny Rivers lived at ground zero. I was lucky enough to be along for the ride. He brought me on board as a rehearsal pianist for the 5th Dimension, a group Marc Gordon had brought to him after the departure from Motown. The singers consisted of Lamonte McLemore, Ron Townson, Florence LaRue, Billy Davis, and Marilyn McCoo.

I knew Marilyn and Lamonte from my short-lived Motown songwriting tenure; he had been a photographer and she a model. They were dating at the time. Marilyn was a UCLA business school alumna, her father was a doctor, she sang phenomenally well, and she looked like a New York haute couture fashion model.

Billy Davis, one of the finest singers it was ever my privilege to work with, was from East St. Louis, where life had been a little bit different. He had grown up in rough neighborhoods on the fringe of criminality. His feet were well under him and he was as physically hard to move as the bollard of a cruise ship. Not someone to cross, though his eyes often betrayed him as being generally filled with unrestrained mirth.

Florence was a vivacious pinup, bright as a penny, a born organizer and trustee of the ethos of "the group," which was a mystery to me in many ways. They had their own rules, their own means of determining future actions, and a system of rights and entitlements that was codified but never written down. I was never, not even for a second, "in the group."

Ron Townson, a tenor, was a trained opera singer given to a generous avoirdupois and a florid Neapolitan style, which could be blended gorgeously into the group's choral work but seemed a bit out of place at a rock show. Regardless, he had a solo spot on each album, the same as all the other members. One of his favorite routines was to come on stage dressed as a clown and sing *Pagliacci* to a makeup mirror. He was a tough guy. He belonged to the Police Auxiliary and sometimes wore a holstered snub-nosed .38 to rehearsals and recording sessions. He was a loving man, quick to laugh, but his emotional hair trigger could just as easily snap the other way and once pissed off it was a job getting him back on track.

Lamonte the Implacable, the peacemaker, the bass, was a benign imperfection, with a home-styled grit to his voice that may have been one of the 5th Dimension's great secret weapons. He came in at about the same altitude as the listener. His was a street voice, honed and shaded around fiery oil drums on cold winter nights.

At first called "The Versatiles," it didn't take the quintet long to vote for the more trendy "The 5th Dimension." All together, they were simply brilliant.

We gathered for rehearsals huddled around the piano, me wearing a pair of moccasins that had holes worn through the soles. I would sit cross-legged on the bench sometimes, and one day, right in the middle of a vocal run-through I felt one of Billy's fingers wiggling through the hole in my shoe like a snake. I jumped as high as a bullfrog and Billy laughed maniacally and they all teased me, "Jimmy, when are you going to get yourself a new pair of shoes?" When things calmed down we went on, pounding out the notes for each line of every song. "Woodshedding," we would call it. No music paper, no iPads, nothing but our brains.

"Let's try this." Lamonte would jump in and sing a line.

"And then," I would say, "if you guys do that then the girls could do this." I would pound a line out on the piano.

They would stack up the harmonies and Florence would say, "Wouldn't it be better if Ron sung this? We could switch notes with him."

And I would nod and we would have another bar. Painstaking. Note by note. Person by person. Idea on idea. *We loved it into being.* It was the very stuff of our lives. And we could change our lives with this magic stuff.

The biggest American act in the country was the Mamas and the Papas: John and Michelle Phillips, Cass Elliot, and Denny Doherty. "California Dreamin'" was an example of the group at their best.

Johnny pitched us a song written by John Phillips for his group called "Go Where You Wanna Go," a song that had never taken off for them. We began rehearsing parts that sounded remarkably like those of the Mamas and the Papas. It was slightly irritating to me that we would go off in that direction. The 5th were going to be a black version of the Mamas and the Papas? The concept seemed flawed.

Johnny, Marc, and I worked hard on the album, experimenting like mad scientists with any kind of instrument or non-instrument that had a possibility. We were just beginning to realize what could be done with multitrack recorders and the search was on for "new sounds." Multitrack recorders gave the musician access to eight or even sixteen separate tracks on which instruments or voices could be layered. Orchestras and effects could be overdubbed at will in perfect sync with other instruments. Hundreds of instruments could be overdubbed theoretically, by "bouncing" two or more tracks to a single track repeatedly. For the first time, highly technical studios and recorders melded with musicians as an integral part of the creative process.

That was the spirit of the time . . . innovation and the exploitation of new technology. Al Casey played a Japanese guitar called a biwa on "Go Where You Want to Go." The Baldwin Electric Harpsichord was a new invention. We procured a prototype, and Knechtel and I sat side by side combining a plethora of keyboards and organs. We visited the ubiquitous electric sitar, a fad that started with Joe South's "The Games People Play" and ended a month or so later. The studio had been full of gourds, castanets, congas, jawbones, tin cans full of popcorn, Styrofoam cups full of BBs, wind chimes, and thumb harps. Hal Blaine developed a set of tuned tom-toms of different sizes, flared around his perch like a keyboard. Ringo Starr heard about these and asked Hal to come to London and bring a set.

Up, Up and Away was released into a maelstrom of competition from England, Haight-Ashbury, Motown, and Mussel Shoals in April of 1967. The first single? John Phillips's "Go Where You Wanna Go." The 5th Dimension had consulted with a popular costume designer of the day, Boyd Clopton, and the result, while imaginative in the extreme, was a bit of a head scratcher for the unwashed.

Each group member appeared as though they had dressed individually in their street clothes: hats, vests, skirts, pants, blouses, belts, and buckles, and yet the fabrics, velour and velveteen in complementary shades of similar thematic colors, sent a mixed message. That message was "We are individuals but we are wearing some sort of coded uniform." This was in an era when a person's mode of attire was an unambiguous comment on their entire ethical position on all the important questions of the day without portfolio. Traditional performers, such as the Four Tops and Gladys Knight and the Pips, wore identical uniforms. Then came the Rolling Stones apparently wearing on stage whatever they woke up in. The original 5th Dimension costumes were stylistically located on a point midway between these two. It was confusing.

At the same time, with all due respect to John Phillips, "Go Where You Wanna Go" had not come blazing off the launching pad. It had entered the chart in a respectable position but when the public *saw* the 5th Dimension on television in their outfits, singing a track heavily influenced by the Ma's and Pa's, they just didn't know how to identify the product. The record was stalling in the high thirties or low forties when Johnny decided to pull it. Briefly Tim Hardin's "Misty Roses" was in the running but Johnny's choice for the next single was "Up, Up and Away," the Devil's little brainchild from the film that never was. At the same time the 5th dropped the quasi cowboy gear and adapted a more uniform rhythm and blues appearance, embracing the fact they were a vocal singing group with choreography, a recognizable team.

There was a lot of discussion about "Up, Up and Away" before it was given a chance. It was said to be a "show tune." It belonged in a musical, not on a rock 'n' roll radio station. What was that sound anyway, that orchestra stuff? Was that jazz or what? I could see the bend in the river. If the record hit, it would change my life forever. It was more likely by far it would not be a hit (it sounded like nothing else on the radio) and my life would take a random off-ramp into a small town somewhere, where I would burn out in the role of an embittered band director with a plain wife and kids with bad skin.

Stoically, Rivers put the record out in April and it took off like it had a Saturn V strapped to its behind, thanks largely to promotion genius Marty Lippman working it to the bone. It was everywhere, just suddenly "there," always on the airwaves. I would hear "So Happy Together" by the Turtles and then "Up, Up and Away" with no comment whatsoever on it being a weird song, or an old-fashioned song, or any of that. The song went to number seven on the Billboard chart, and the 5th Dimension was launched in a big way. They were an attractive, energetic, and appealing group of bright kids and they grabbed the brass ring with both hands, determined to exact their last full measure of success from this wonderful, unlikely carousel ride. Almost immediately they were playing live in the most posh of venues. As long as the group stayed together it was an unstoppable and beloved American original, and they'd go on to have hits with other notable writers, like Laura Nyro's "Stoned Soul Picnic," Rice and Webber's "Age of Aquarius," and Burt Bacharach and Hal David's "One Less Bell to Answer."

1971

Toward the beginning of the year I did *The Tonight Show Starring Johnny Carson*, a fact unlikely to be verified because of the loss of several years of *Tonight Show* kinescopes in a studio mishap. The producers would occasionally book a "novelty guest" such as a child prodigy who would do complicated math problems and look cute as Carson deadpanned straight at the camera. I was still young enough to be regarded as a wunderkind of sorts and I believe that was what they had in mind.

Carson: So, you decided to write a song that's seven minutes and twenty seconds long?

Cute Kid: Well, my mother used to say the longer the better, sir.

Carson: Deer-in-the-headlights-look right into camera A.

I didn't really play cute kid as much as I projected angry, tortured young man. This was exacerbated by the fact that I wasn't a one-liner virtuoso. For all the real communication or sympathy that was exchanged, I might as well have been talking to a television.

The great man got a few laughs by working around me and then he sent me off to perform "MacArthur Park" with Doc Severinsen and the Tonight Show Orchestra. The band was excited about doing my chart; they relished the challenge of tackling something a bit out of the ordinary.

I sat down in my hippie flowered shirt at the grand piano and played the introduction. Strictly routine. I looked at Doc, who stood with his glittering trumpet and an infectious smile, more bandleader in the traditional sense than conductor. It was easy going as I yodeled through the first verse and chorus and we found ourselves floating in the center section. This was childishly simple, a ballad from the 1930s really, and a matter of no concern. Then came the interlude in 3/8 leading to the allegro and instrumental section. Good. We were chugging along with a great rock beat and . . . but wait, as we entered that second break in the middle of a fast part I felt a couple of horns get out of sync. It seemed impossible, but part of the band was now on the second eighth of each beat and for the present that seemed awkward, but it was still being barely held together. Then we approached the second interlude where there was a drastic change into a slower tempo, the classically flavored stair steps leading up to a crescendo that ended with a last dramatic verse. And here, right now, on *The Tonight Show* ladies and gentlemen, in front of twenty million Americans, the band and I were quickly, inexorably, and inexplicably breaking apart. Confusion and discord were spreading quickly, and then I missed my vocal entrance. I panicked. I did the only thing I knew to fix it.

"Hold it!" I yelled. On live television. "Hold it, guys, hold it!"

Carson, the crowd, the crew, and most of all Doc Severinsen looked at me in horrified surprise. The band came to a ragged stop.

I turned on my bench to face the band. "All right, guys," I yelled, "bar eighty-seven, one, two, three, four!"

The band started up again like a smoothly tuned machine. I sang the last verse and mercifully we reached the end. The trumpets played closing notes so high and perfect they threatened to wipe out my immediate past but I bolted for my dressing room, red-faced and looking for a place to die. Doc caught me in the narrow passage-way behind the set and turned me around.

"Hey, where do you think you're going, genius?" he asked me without a smile. My face must have crumpled. "I don't know what to say," I almost sobbed. "I don't even know what happened!"

"Hey, Jimmy, you're a pro! I couldn't have done better myself." Doc Severinsen was grinning at me. "I just wanted to ask you to write something for the band. You know we play on the weekends."

He patted me on the back and moved on.

Jimmy Webb and Ray Rich at the Royal Albert Hall, London. *(Courtesy of Ray Rich)*

CHAPTER TEN

This is the answer to the letter unsent which
even so arrived some years later
Like a song sometimes written for love long before
it is alive . . .
— JLW, "Simile," 1972

1966

Benny Shapiro bore an uncanny resemblance to Captain Kangaroo.

In the fifties he had started a beatnik club just across the street from the forties nightclub Ciro's. He called it the Renaissance. It became a mecca for the beats and it was where Lenny Bruce got his start. It was also where Miles Davis, Wayne Shorter, and many others had blazed the first trails of modern jazz.

Benny had a house full of kids and a happy wife. The walls of their home were decorated with representations of India's deities and Sanskrit banners, the atmosphere heavy with incense, and wind chimes tinkled softly in the garden. He was Ravi Shankar's manager.

In 1966 Benny had an idea. It was a big, goddam, explosive show business idea. Why not harness the powerful tribal instinct that had kids out in the streets in the thousands, burning vehicles and stoning cops? What about inviting them all to the biggest, ass-kicking-est Battle of the Bands ever staged on the planet? He would start with Ravi and build around him. He chose Monterey, already the site of the Monterey Jazz Festival. It was a nice central location where the Haight-Ashbury scene could drift south. The Sunset Strip, Venice Beach, and Topanga crowd could hitchhike north up the Pacific Coast Highway to one of the most beautiful places on earth. Monterey would be the place.

I remember Benny telling me and Johnny Rivers about it and Johnny getting extremely excited and sharing the idea with mega-producer and founder of Dunhill Records, Lou Adler. Lou involved his attorney Seymour Lazar and inevitably told the Mamas and the Papas about this once-in-a-lifetime event and its nascent opportunity. As the players became more important and influential, other financiers heard of Monterey and became interested. The pressure mounted on Benny, a small-time promoter in the opinion of many. However, Benny had earned himself a place at the table by copywriting the name, and protecting the concept under the banner of the Monterey Pop Festival.

Benny was getting elbowed by some powerful people to take a secondary role or perhaps just walk away, but he was a stubborn guy and wouldn't surrender his brainchild that easily. Through it all he was adamant that it would be a free concert. Lou Adler and John Phillips redoubled their efforts to wrest it away from him. How do I know this? Benny told me.

One idyllic Sunday afternoon while Benny and his wife were at the movies, their house burned to the ground with all the mystic Indian gods and the Sanskrit banners unable to prevent it.

The housekeeper was able to escape safely with the Shapiro's children.

It would be unseemly of me to suggest there could be any possible connection between the fire and the festival; yet not two weeks passed before Benny's fierce handlebar mustache had disappeared from the inner circle where the decisions were being made.

How do I know this? Because my fate and that of the festival were entwined and traveling the same curve through space.

One afternoon, fellow songwriter P. F. Sloan and I and the 5th Dimension were in our garret above the old Imperial Records office, rehearsing parts. Johnny suddenly popped his head through the door and said, "C'mon, kids, let's go for a ride."

He required only the two songwriters to go along so we said farewell to the 5th and wandered out to the parking lot where Johnny's black Buick Riviera was idling, his/our ancient bagman Harvey Lippman lolling in the shotgun seat. The two of us bundled into the back and Johnny drove down La Brea to Sunset and made a right. Twenty minutes later, we were turning into the gates of exclusive Bel Air and soon thereafter found ourselves idling in front of a massive pile I recognized as that of John and Michelle Phillips.

As we waited, Johnny demonstrated his impression of W. C. Fields.

"Well, boys, this is it, yes indeedy, this is the big one." He grinned at us over the backseat. I gave it a seven.

"The big what?" I asked, biting my tongue.

"All will be revealed," said Harv.

Johnny and Harv had their game faces on. We were admitted to the house and found ourselves surrounded by lush Persian rugs, heavy wrought iron sconces, and massive Spanish furnishings, making me feel as if I were in the lair of a seventeenth-century warrior prince.

Lou Adler, producer of the Mamas and the Papas, stood in the foyer, stroking his beard thoughtfully. It was his careful overdubbing of four-part contrapuntal harmonies that was the secret of their sound and success. Years of hunching over faders in the studio had given him an eternally grief-stricken posture and countenance. Cass arrived and then Denny. John and Michelle came downstairs together and joined us as drinks were served. There was microscopic small talk, containing not a clue as to what this was all about. Paul Simon and Art Garfunkel walked in next and my mouth hung open like the village idiot. This wasn't a meeting; this was a *summit*.

The last person through the door was Lou's grim-faced lawyer, Lazar. He was carrying his briefcase, and as soon as he entered two huge iron-bound doors opened into the dining room as though on cue. Harv began shooing the guests into the dining room, except for P. F. Sloan and myself. We were told politely but firmly our presence wasn't required.

Flip and I, a little disappointed, scuffed down the gravel drive to Johnny's Buick Riviera and smoked a reefer in the front seat.

I don't know, and I don't suppose anyone will ever know, exactly what was said around the table that afternoon. I know seed money was raised for the Monterey Pop Festival. Around $40,000 was promised by Johnny, the Phillipses, Lou, Simon, and Garfunkel. It was a hell of a lot of money in those days.

One result of this secretive meeting was obvious. All the performers at that table eventually appeared at Monterey, including Johnny, who was taking a serious beating from snobby rock critics for his middle-of-the-road covers of Motown hits. It is my opinion that Artie and Paul, and Johnny and the Mamas and the Papas, were the nuclear core that attracted a lot of the big-name talent and insured their attendance.

Lou and John came away as the "producers" of Monterey and ended up also shooting the documentary. Lou was *jefe* from then on. A small office was opened, secretaries were hired, and art designers were engaged to produce an official poster and a logo. In one interesting footnote it is said that Lou Adler went to Monterey and had a private meeting with the police chief. Conjecture has held that an agreement was reached by which the heat would be turned down during the festival on recreational drug use.

Johnny continued to make a contribution to many of the details of the concert. Time would reveal it to be a unique, almost perfect idyll in sublime weather. The first and the best of its genre. However, it was destined to end in a particularly surprising way, not at all included in the best-laid plans.

1971

On the surface, Joni Mitchell was a friendly, almost deliberately ordinary Canadian girl with a bright smile and a quick wit. But when it came to music and lyrics she had been blessed with a divine gift. I knew with no envy or jealousy that she was a better writer than I was. I envied her easy conversational phrasing that turned everyday banter into a new kind of song lyric. Her sensual guitar tunings delivered deep, dissonant, yet compelling chords that, to use an expression by Linda Ronstadt, "rubbed." *Play that warm chord.* I would sit with her and watch her hands and listen to her songs in the making, determined to follow, at least for a while, as closely in her shadow as I could. I was especially entranced by her surprising and unheard-of habit of opening the air-sealed titanium housing around her most inner being and letting the whole world gawk at the intricate workings of her complicated, gifted, tormented, soul.

I saw her frequently at my manager Sandy Gallin's soirées in Trousdale, where the objective seemed to be to invite as many famous people as practicable and then, if possible, persuade them to perform for one another. One night Joni excised me from the center of the party where I was playing a medley of my hits at the baby grand. She wanted to talk to me privately. She told me quite a tale.

Back in 1968 when she had first opened at Doug Weston's Troubadour she had not been aware I was in attendance, nor even aware of my existence. The rush of stardom initiated by that engagement perplexed and even frightened her as it came like a tsunami out of years of playing tiny, cheap bars and literally passing the hat among the bitter grounds of the coffeehouse scene. Then in a flash her genius was recognized and she was captured by the nameless millions and swept away. Fortunately, and wisely for her, she was also swept away by mega-managers Elliot Roberts and David Geffen. Years passed. She came to know me and actually liked some of my songs. She found me to be an affable guy and had been fascinated by my nude concert on the grounds of Campo de Encino. It was wonderful that we had become friends, she said.

Recently she had moved house. Her new place in the world called for a proper residence and the old house in the Hollywood Hills where she had lived was a time capsule. The original pre-stardom furniture was there with the cats and the photos and mystery boxes. She set out to clean the place up, discard what she could bear to part with, and carry the remaining treasures to her new digs in Bel Air. Halfway through she and her helpers had decided to move a large, heavy couch in the living room as it was destined for the Salvation Army. As they moved the stubborn couch from its groove, an old piece of paper was liberated and fluttered to the floor. Puzzled, she picked it up and perused: It was a letter from me, from 1968.

June 12, 1968, I was in the Troubadour for no particular reason. I had wanted to meet Doug Weston for a long time and talk about doing some kind of appearance there. It was a large club for folk music with a capacity of about four hundred seats, way too big for me. When Joni started playing I happened to be leaning on the balcony upstairs and watched her come on stage.

There was a center spot on her, displaying her long blond tresses to great advantage, but she was highlighted with that damn train light in her eyes for the whole evening. Nobody moved or even breathed loudly while she was singing. The atmosphere was electromagnetic. Yes, her playing and singing charmed me, especially the repertoire of grainy, almost jazz-based chords on her Martin. I am attracted to the basic dark matter of music wherever I find it. Her soprano was crystal clear with considerably less vibrato than she would come to use later as her career progressed.

My affections turned on a dime at that stage of my life, but this was different. I was fascinated, entranced by her ability to communicate on the deepest level from the outset. After the show and the encores and the immense roar of approval that shook the old house to its foundations and dislodged decades of dust languishing in the beam work high above, I could think of nothing but her.

Years later I would watch Jackson Browne fall in love with her. I remember him coming to me, very nervous, and saying, "So, how should I talk to her?" And I smiled, moved yet deeply amused at the same time.

"You just talk to her like you would talk to . . . a really nice person," I said.

He tried to absorb her through the music and the words and when that failed he inevitably moved toward something more immediate. In more or less the same delicate state I went home that night in 1968 and poured out my bleeding soul on a piece of stationery. It was one of those moments that—twice considered—would never evolve beyond the first crumpled missile aimed in the general direction of the wastebasket. I sent her the letter backstage, hand delivered to her Troubadour dressing room, with twenty-four long-stemmed roses of the most rare and fragrant variety. Years passed without a reply.

Joni smiled at me.

"I just wanted you to know I got your letter."

I blushed deeply trying to remember exactly what I had written in the way one always dreads what one has written.

She laughed.

"It was a very nice letter, and yes, of course I would like to see you for tea or dinner!"

Her blue eyes danced with barely restrained mirth.

"If I'm not too late," she remonstrated.

Sandy Gallin, with his elfin demeanor and ringmaster patois, came through the bedroom door like a fabulous jinni and found us sitting on the bed.

"Am I interrupting? Where in the world are my performers?" He did his impeccable imitation of Kate Smith.

Joni and I became friends. We liked flea markets and stuffy old antique shops. Before Morton's on Robinson became the power restaurant of the Hollywood cognoscenti it had been a fashionable old barn full of antiques run by proprietor Jules Bucheri. We went in one day together and bought a most gorgeous Art Deco chandelier. She insisted I take custody of it. One time in a not-so-subtle hint about my wardrobe she fitted me for a herringbone jacket in a flea market off Melrose. It must have looked a little strange; a man with more hair and beard than John Lennon and Jesus put together posing in an English gentleman's country costume. She insisted it was perfect.

Joni consented to come in and sing "just a little" with my sister Susan on my latest LP *Letters*. A woman of her word she ended up singing just two notes. Two glorious notes. My world was on the surface chaotic and yet beneath the storm, a very well-kept secret: I had things exactly the way I wanted them.

1967

I was beginning to chafe in the role of Johnny's contract writer. Musically I was headed in the direction of Joni Mitchell and James Taylor as well as Randy Newman, Warren Zevon, and Lowell George.

In the studio with John I really should have been content to tread water for a while but there were issues. John and I would be looking at a chord sheet and he would be trying to finger it on his rose-colored Les Paul and he would say: "Why does it have to have those two extra notes, the low one that's a discord and the other one that just sounds weird?"

I would measure my response for a moment. "Well, this second interval is really holding over from the last chord and I just love this 'aug five' move, you know?" I banged it out on the piano: *kachong, kachong*. He would scratch his head for a minute and then reply.

"Well, listen." *Splonk! Splonk!* He would play it on his guitar real loud and pull the corners of his mouth down in a badass grimace as he pumped his guitar.

"Well, I think that's fonkey, just the A chord." *Splonk! Splonk!*

He did his best to collaborate but ultimately he would become frustrated with the musical niceties and revert back to the rocker from Baton Rouge, Louisiana. The guy who used to hang with the late Hank Williams's wife and drive around town in Mrs. Williams's pink Cadillac.

"Let's get down to the real nitty-gritty," he would insist. "Let's make a record, man. Let's put it in the groove. This isn't a symphony." *Splonk! Splonk!*

I kept my mouth shut as we got ready to go to Monterey. Hal Blaine, Larry, Mike Deasy, Joe, me, and our front man Johnny Rivers, who had been carefully grooming a curly kind of Italian Afro along with a painstakingly maintained mustache and goatee.

At rehearsals, I gradually became responsible for playing a concert chime part in Johnny's arrangement of Smokey's "The Tracks of My Tears." I privately thought this belonged further back, in Hal's department. The chimes, a sort of keyboard arrangement, were rolled over to the piano within reach. When the conspicuous four beats of silence rolled around just before the dramatic last verse, "So take a good look at my face . . .," I was expected to pick up a little wooden hammer and whack the A above middle C. It was awkward. I had to stop playing, halfway rising to my feet, and then locate and clobber the correct chime in a nest of silvery tubes that all pretty much looked the same, all this precisely in the middle of a big rest. As summer grew hotter and the day of the Monterey Pop Festival drew nearer, a nagging question persisted at rehearsals: "Are we going to drag all these goddamn chimes to Monterey just so Webb can bang on one note?"

When the plane took off on June 14, 1967, I carried a single chime across my lap.

Johnny had simply walked over to the rack, rented from S.I.R., and without ceremony, detached the A chime and handed it to me. "This is your responsibility," he said grimly. "Whatever you do, Jimmy, don't lose this damn chime!"

In the documentary film Lou Adler created, I can clearly be seen disembarking from the jet and walking down the stairs with a silvery tube under my arm. There was no horde of adoring fans. A half-dozen bored roadies dully watched the nation's number-one male vocalist walk across an empty expanse of cracked concrete.

On the limousine drive to the hotel, Johnny looked out the window at the twisting highway and said a little wistfully, "I wonder where all the hippies are?"

Twenty miles north, a hundred thousand hippies, highwaymen, peasants, and fans slept in fields or vans or standing up, waiting for a moment they could not describe. They would know it when it happened.

For Johnny it was an image crisis. He was clad in hippie apparel, 100 percent. There was the long, curly hair piled up like a helmet, sideburns, goatee, and mustache. He wore the unavoidable leather vest and blue jeans. It was a stark change from the handsome, clean-cut Italian kid with expensive suits and hair by Jay Sebring who had kicked ass at the Whiskey. It was worth trying, breaking the type cast of traditional showbiz, which had become a kind of curse.

Driving toward the venue, traffic slowed to a standstill half a mile out. Here and there stood a perplexed traffic cop, his motorcycle decorated with chains of wildflowers contributed by ladies dressed like Arthurian damsels who danced free-form all around us like Terpsichores.

I could hear distant music like strange thunder. Sometimes bass notes would punch through the din, irrelevant and feeding back. At a snail's pace, gently nudging our way through a human ocean, we found ourselves at a cyclone fence at least seven feet tall with a gate. The stage loomed beyond like twin launching gantries for moon rockets. At the gate several members of the Monterey Police Department and a score of security guys in red MPF T-shirts eyeballed the kaleidoscope of swirling confetti that was the crowd: the hippies milled in random motion, dressed in every color of the rainbow.

Johnny was riding shotgun and opened his window to talk to a meaty patrolman who shouted down at the goateed figure in the Leon Bennett lid. "Who's in there?" bellowed the sweaty, red-faced cop trussed up in his full summer uniform and yet unaccountably not wearing a sidearm.

Johnny looked him right in the eye and deadpanned with aplomb and sincerity, "We've got Paul McCartney in here," in his Louisiana twang.

There was a short pause. The policeman peered through the rising dust and the dirty windows and focused on my babyish and Beatle-coiffed face and my De Voss cotton turtleneck shirt.

"Hot damn!" he yelled as his mouth fell open. "Let these sumbitches through!" Scarcely a minute later we were exiting the limo in the strictly controlled compound behind the stage.

Johnny was laughing with tears in his eyes. "Paul McCartney, whoa!"

Harv met us, looking as usual like he had gotten little or no sleep. Lou joined the powwow in unusually high spirits. Even he was impressed by the noise and the crowd. Somewhere along the way Shapiro's free concert had died. Every skinny-ass had paid to get in. Within seconds we had bright red passes stuck to our jeans that said we could go anywhere and do anything short of walking out on the stage during somebody else's routine.

The first thing I did was to get out of the rarified backstage area with its twenty-four-hour green room, never-ending buffet, and array of private trailers reserved for important artists. I wanted to see my brothers and sisters, the ones who were going to change the world, if we could amass enough love. I walked into a dizzying storm of faces elevated toward the stage, carrying my shining silver chime like a baton. I had sworn to Johnny that I would keep it in my hands.

Our people were embracing one another . . . anybody's other. They sang and clapped their hands. They lay in the hot sunshine and snored. They poured beers over their heads to stay cool. Pretty girls with tan thighs wearing white short shorts perched on the shoulders of college linebackers with "Property of UC Berkeley" stenciled on their bare backs. A lot of the kids had what Jack Nicholson once referred to as "that dreaded bandana look" with calfskin vests and Day-Glo war paint on their cheeks and foreheads. Hair was all over the color spectrum from Kool-Aid red to the ever-popular green, blue, and purple mix. Blacks and whites and Hispanics were fairly evenly represented. Most of the crowd was tripping on anything from Professor Owsley's acid to mescaline, psilocybin, and peyote as well as other substances unknown. The smell of cannabis was sweet and unilateral.

My mind holds on to some indelible impressions of the Monterey Pop Festival.

Johnny's guitarist for the day, Wrecking Crew member Mike Deasy, bearded and in a Robin Hood hat with an eagle feather and hand-laced leather tunic complete with a red velvet swag bag tied around his waist. He walked through the crowd like the Fisher King and the kids made a path for the man with the best costume in his pointy Byzantine slippers with little bells announcing his approach. The kids were a swaying ocean of human waves, congregating and then breaking apart. A dance line would appear and then turn into a giant circle only to fragment a moment later. Some stood alone, eyes closed and swaying to the music. If there was a little open space they would dance, though a lot of the music, strictly speaking, wasn't danceable.

Ravi Shankar on a bright yet cool Sunday afternoon, in the lotus position under a flowered panoply with his tabla player, his fingers singing through the liquid notes of his sitar. All the rockers sat as though at Sunday school, paying careful attention.

Laura Nyro was playing on Saturday night, a shy girl in appearance with large, wide-set and deep brown eyes, long dark hair and dark, old-fashioned, floor-length velvet dress. She looked like a pioneer woman, playing her Martin D-18 and singing her memorable, chantlike songs. All seemed to be going well until she sat at the grand piano, the only solo piano performance at Monterey. The festival-goers callously booed her off the stage and no gallant guitar-playing rock star rushed on to defend her honor. A couple of beer cans flew. Weeping, she walked past me as I stood in the wings and into the arms of a man later pointed out to me as David Geffen. He would reassemble her.

Allen Ginsberg had first defined the meaning of "hip" in the fifties. He was quoted as saying that to be "hip" is an honorific, meaning "innately understanding and all-tolerant." "Hippie" is a designation that was coined from this word "hip." There were a lot of people at Monterey who didn't actually belong to the club.

Our turn came on the very first night, after a long afternoon of carrying that silver tube with me everywhere I went. We performed after British folk musician Beverley Martyn, a personage that I am no more familiar with today than I was that afternoon. The crowd behaved as abominably to her as they did to the emotionally scarred Laura Nyro.

The fact that the crowd was somewhat discourteous didn't intimidate Johnny. "All right, let's rock!" he said to the band as Beverley exited to boos and we took to the boards. I carried my chime and little wooden hammer dutifully to the piano. All of us, Hal, Joe, Larry, Mike, Johnny, and I, stared point-blank into the faces of ten thousand people. My fingers were stuck together as though in preparation for some karate blow. The P.A. shrieked simply "Johnny Rivers!" and Johnny strolled out carrying his beautiful white Stratocaster. We were immediately playing "Help," a cover of The Beatles hit, and the fear was pushed back by the thumping, pulsating rhythm. As long as Johnny rocked, the audience was ecstatic. When he trotted out his Motown covers, such as "Baby I Need Your Loving," their attention ebbed and out came the whistles and catcalls. One had the sensation of playing on the edge of a great abyss where only bona fide ear-busting rock 'n' roll would prevent the whole show from sinking into oblivion. Johnny had plenty of guts. He stuck with the playlist, performing "Poor Side of Town," such a smash, to a listless and distracted audience.

Finally, it was time for "The Tracks of My Tears." I anxiously played the whole song waiting for "My smile is my makeup, I wear since my breakup with you . . ." 2, 3, 4, with one eye on my hammer and one on my chime. The song's rest came. Chime on the second count. I assumed a half crouch, grabbed my little wooden hammer from the top of the grand, and lifted the chime from the floor barely in time to take a mighty swing at the little metal lip that ran around the top. I swung and hit—at best—a grounder. The timid *ka-ping* that issued off the miss-hit chime caused Johnny to shoot me a look straight from Sicily. I sat down suddenly seeking anonymity but I needn't have worried. My big moment didn't register with the crowd. We left the stage after playing "Secret Agent Man," which the audience liked, and we received a warm round of applause.

At the end of the first day, Paul Simon and Artie Garfunkel were just two guys and a guitar after a day of loud, rigorous music. Their perfect two-part harmony drifted into a tired crowd of sunburned and psychic voyagers come to port. Couples hugged each other as the two sang: "Are you going to Scarborough Fair? Remember me to one who lives there . . ." And there we were, we happy few with the luck and the buck to make it to Scarborough Fair. Paul and Artie were a highlight.

The next night, Otis Redding closed. He took the stage and presented probably the most nuclear-powered forty-five minutes in the history of rock 'n' roll. Some would say it was properly rhythm and blues and some would say lines were blurring. It was ironic that after all the costumes, after the Who blew up the whole goddamn stage, after Janis Joplin had torn her voice into a tattered flag, after Springfield and Canned Heat and Quicksilver and Steve Miller, it was the humble and unpretentious man from Dawson, Georgia, who is most remembered when people speak of the festival. The crowd stood and beat their hands raw and screamed themselves hoarse through his entire performance. This was the moment they had been unable to describe, the one they had come for.

The closing slot of the entire festival was reserved for the Mamas and the Papas. Just before their expected triumph a relatively unknown guitarist named Jimi Hendrix was booked with his "Experience." Jimi looked like a suburban housewife's worst nightmare or most exquisite daydream, an avenging wraith, streaming plumes and scarves, the colors of the rainbow, bracelets and breastplate, a warrior poet standing alone in front of a stack of amplifiers that towered several feet over his head, played like a demon. "Purple Haze" reverberated over the Monterey Peninsula and I found myself looking at him in awe. How could one person create so much goddamn sound?

He played guitar like he had four arms. Some of the deep feedback techniques and super chords were created electronically, but live on stage! The show reached a climax of *cacophonia*. It was a tone poem to the apocalypse. Johnny was standing backstage with Lou Adler and a fire marshal in full regalia watching the increasing mania. Pyrotechnics were being routinely detonated on stage and the fire marshal was there to watch for any illegal shenanigans. Hendrix was remarkably accommodating. With his amps turned up to S.E.D. (Serious Ear Damage) he started swinging his Strat over his head and pounding it into the stage. The guitar's destruction was audible in head-rending impacts and shrieks of protest from the pickups and amps. After a few hefty swings there was a pile of kindling and guitar strings in front of him. The crowd was rabid, he had gotten them in the mood, and now *they* wanted to break something.

Jimi kneeled down, took out a can of lighter fluid, and squirted the entire contents onto the remains of the guitar. He took out a matchbook. The fire marshal freaked and started to dive onto the stage yelling, "Shit! He can't do that!" Lou Adler, wily as ever, dared restrain him.

"Hold on, officer, that's just part of the show. That's just his act for cryin' out loud!" The official hesitated a half second. Jimi dropped the lighted match onto the saturated mess, and it exploded into a ball of fire big enough to set flame to the whole festival. Jimi must have taken a gigantic leap as he released the match because he came through unscathed. The crowd lost their chops. They had seen what they came to see. They screamed, they salivated, they pumped fists, they roared like ten thousand lions. This was it. This was the high point. The Monterey Pop Festival was officially over.

If there was ever a moment more inappropriate for a performance by the Mamas and the Papas, Adler and Phillips had managed to create it. So as some of the crowd began to pack up and head for the highway and journalists rushed to meet their deadlines, the remaining crowd heard what the real Mamas and Papas sounded like without the reverb cocktail and three layers of hand-edited vocals.

Johnny Rivers' performance was later omitted entirely from the film *Monterey Pop* by editors John Phillip and Lou Adler. Our world-famous Wrecking Crew was thus ignominiously passed over as well. If this was peace and love then you didn't want to mingle with a less tolerant group of friends.

1972

I was on my way to London to play the Albert Hall. It would be recorded on multitrack and hopefully become an album. The concert was already sold out. This would only be my second attempt at performing with a big orchestra. The Albert Hall was as round and nearly as big as the Roman Colosseum. Derek Taylor had promoted the hell out of the show and Warner Bros. was generously continuing to sponsor me. Derek and Harry met me at Heathrow in a new Daimler limousine, liberally stocked with brandy and cocaine.

We had a week or so to get ready. These preparations consisted primarily of rehearsing the arrangements on at least two occasions with the whole orchestra, a group of some eighty men and women. Sound was checked over and over, the mic-ing of the band and piano accomplished. A run-through of the entire show with lighting cues was preplanned for the day before the performance.

The whole week I was running around like the proverbial headless chicken from BBC II to BBC I radio and television as required. I did a morning talk show on Channel Three and was having a terrible time with my voice because of all the yakking. One of my fellow guests was Twiggy, who fixed me up with her patented vocal cure: tea with honey, nutmeg, and cinnamon. Twiggy was wonderfully sweet and intelligent, and her cure did work somewhat, but it seemed inevitable that I would go into the all-important concert hoarse. I spent light-years in the Tardis booths of BBC Radio talking to Scotland and Wales and Yorkshire, spreading the word that I was in England, and then finally I was done. Any more talking and there would have been no show.

The day of the performance I holed up at my hotel with lots of tea and honey. Harry came over to help me plan the after-concert blowout at my place and insisted we come up with some decent coke because "I think George is coming." He meant George Harrison. Harry had a guy's number and said we could go fifty-fifty on the "girl," a hipster name for coke. "Boy" was heroin. "I could just call the dude and have him drop the girl off at the hotel." I agreed, trying to confine communication to facial expressions, hand motions, and grunts.

Halfway through the afternoon a rakish-looking young ruffian appeared at the door with a very substantial package and I gave him the three hundred pounds Harry and I had put together and closed the door as quickly as possible. I had no interest in drugs for the moment but cracked the wrapper enough to get a finger file inside for a sample. My impromptu analysis of the contents was that it was one part Drano, one part Novocain, and one part Benzedrine. It was one of the most bald-faced frauds I've ever encountered. I put it in the bottom drawer of a dresser in the bedroom where I was sure no one could possibly find it, threw some underwear over it as a further obstacle, and shoved a chair up against the dresser just to make sure it wasn't disturbed. I intended to show it to Harry and insist he get our money back.

One reaches the point where the nerves are trying to climb up through the skin and escape the body. This is stage fright. Usually it gets progressively worse for me, much like stretching a bungee cord, right out to the end where a heart attack is imminent. TV studios were generally where I had stage fright the worst. They were kept so frigid a slight fright could turn into a tremor that would affect my piano playing. I broke down on the *Steve Allen Show* once and stopped playing in the middle of a song, shivering. Steve was a real gentleman about it.

Derek Taylor introduced me in his calm, understated way while this torture was ratcheting up. I stood in the wings shifting my weight from foot to foot. I looked up into the cavernous dome of Albert Hall and around at the crowded seats. The rumor was correct. Derek had covered the stage, every inch of it, with roses, surrounding the orchestra, the band, and the piano player. It was very much like a symphony seated in a garden. "Jimmy Webb!" I heard my name. I nervously walked on to a tidal wave of anticipatory applause.

One thing I remember about the concert, which will be obvious to anyone who has a copy of it, is that I sang no vocal on "Wichita Lineman." This was very near the beginning of the show and I remember the lovely Carol Kaye intro being reproduced by the cellos and the contrabasses, the high plaintive string line by Al De Lory, and I realized that it was certainly almost time for me to sing. For some inexplicable reason I did not.

I determined there was nothing for it but to play an instrumental. Feeling like a deranged goose I sat there, blood rushing to my head and played one of the loveliest instrumentals you will ever hear. I was devastated. When on stage, one mistake has a tendency to procreate. The mind dwells on a small error and on ways to redress the balance and in the process makes another mistake, this one more damaging than the first, and so on. In this case I had gone out and made a monstrous, amateurish, insufferable mistake right off the bat. I was off balance and panicked throughout the whole show. The audience's response was a standing ovation and repeated curtain calls. Nevertheless I was despondent afterward as I made my way through one of the labyrinthine passages of the ancient hall and sought out my dressing room in order to have a proper nervous breakdown.

The dressing tables were covered with gifts of roses. I knew it hadn't been that good. People began arriving to dispense congratulations or condolences or both. My business manager, Jerry Rubinstein, and his wife, Carol, all the way from the United States, were consoling in their praise.

Harry stuck his head in and said, "See you at the hotel." I went over to him and whispered in his ear, "That coke is industrial waste. Don't try to find it. Don't touch it!" He smiled his sly smile.

Officials and fans with programs for signing were attended to in a blur until finally Sandy Gallin came in beaming and spouting, "Was that fantastic? I mean, really, was that fantastic or what?" Meaning: Could have been better but keep smiling.

"I would like to introduce you to someone," he said, and gestured to a lady who stood just behind him. My first impression was of a tall person with beautiful long dark hair burnished to a sheen, wearing a most elegant gown of dark black and magenta, piercing me with green-flecked blue eyes that were large and wide, set over a sweetly shaped mouth and an enticing smile.

Everything on the face of the Earth stopped. I looked at her with sudden recognition. She was the girl in the Cock 'n Bull, tired from frolic and not caring if I knew it, whose husband I had mistaken for Johnny Rivers. Somewhere in the distance Sandy was saying, "This is Rosemarie."

"You were absolutely fantastic, Mr. Webb," Rosemarie reassured, and she meant it.

"Jimmy," I said.

"Mr. Webb, I mean Jimmy, I would like you to meet my friend Dudley Moore."

It was him all right, and the lucky bastard had her on his arm.

"Would you care to join me at my place for Champagne and autopsy?" I asked, staring at her.

"It was a wonderful evening, perhaps we will join you," she said, and took my hand. When she touched me I felt like my hair had been set on fire.

When I got back to the hotel there were already guests in my room. Hors d'oeuvres were being distributed by uniformed waiters. There was a bar with silver buckets of iced Perrier-Jouët. Rosemarie was radiant, dancing with Dudley Moore who responded with hysterical pantomimes of people who can't dance. I seethed with jealousy.

I greeted Jerry and Carol Rubinstein. Jerry was a low-key, highly efficient business manager who also handled Harry and Joni and was quickly becoming the baron of celebrity CPAs. Carol was his attractive brunette partner, New Age before that coinage was even dreamed of. I conveyed my best as I passed them, intent on getting to the action.

"Hello," I said as I approached Dudley and Rosemarie. "I know you're Rosemarie, how could I ever forget? But I didn't catch your last name!" I smiled at her.

"It's Frankland, old boy," Dudley answered for her. He turned to look her up and down theatrically. "Regrettably, interminably married to a lucky sod," Dudley opined, taking a glass of Champagne off a passing tray.

"I see," I murmured, surprised and dismayed. So she was still married. I turned to Dudley. "I'm a great fan of yours and the band of course." I flattered him mercilessly but in truth he was one hell of a keyboard player and a better-than-average composer.

"Oh yah, right, thanks so much, Jim."

Beautiful people smoked cigarettes on the wraparound balcony and as always, a few toked on the foul smelling *gif*. Neil Young's *After the Gold Rush* was wailing on the stereo. Harry was sitting at the round wooden dining table in his shirtsleeves, sweating profusely, his face red as a beet. In spite of my dire warnings he was chopping up the substance that was best qualified as an unknown toxic chemical.

Carol Rubinstein appeared behind him and, no doubt meaning to surprise and delight, slipped her jeweled arms around his neck from behind and bent over him to put her hands over his eyes.

"Oh, Harry, my beautiful genius!" she crowed.

"Get away from me, you fucking bitch!" Harry snarled, leaping to his feet, throwing her backward as he flailed his arms in the air to detach her.

Jerry Rubinstein turned as white as Travertine marble and I saw a hard notion, basic and brutal, form in his normally benign expression. Carol retreated to the lavatory weeping, disgraced and disheveled. The whole room stood silent after witnessing the encounter. I put my arm around Jerry's shoulders, hard as rocks, and walked him out on the side balcony facing the hotel across the street. He was choking, he was gasping, his eyes were tearing up.

"I feel like I have to kill him."

"Listen to me, Jerry," I said quickly. "First, he's a client. Second, he's pretty much out of control on coke right now."

He shrugged me off.

"Just yesterday, Jerry, he told me what a great pal I was, his *best* pal. I seized on the opportunity to ask him to introduce me at the Albert Hall. He turned me down. I mean it was two seconds later. He laughed and said he didn't think it would do him any good."

"I need to look after Carol," he said suddenly.

"Exactly. Don't hate him, Jer. He won't remember it tomorrow."

I could only imagine what those few moments had been like for the couple. Humiliated by a client in full view of an audience of luminaries? Harry was slipping.

The Rubinsteins left and many others followed. The festive spirit of the moment had evaporated. I said good night to Rosemarie, not knowing how or when I would see her again but prescient with confidence that it would be soon. Dudley carried her off with a wink of triumph.

I went on a hunt for Harry intending to give him a little bit of what he had given Carol. I found him and George Harrison in my bedroom, a pile of the dreaded crap from Mordor lying untidily on the end table. George was clutching a handkerchief to his nose that dripped with fresh blood.

"Goddamn it, I told you to stay out of that shit!" I erupted.

George was trying to speak through the handkerchief even as he tried to stuff it up his nose.

"Manks arot Jmmf," he said, apparently to me. They got up and, supporting each other, headed for the door. Harry was past speech. As they opened the door and stumbled into the hall George said one last time as clear as a bell in his Liverpudlian brogue: "Thanks a lot, Jim."

Ah yes, someone would have to take the blame for this debacle. Nevertheless I eventually came to be friends with George. He was a fine man.

I turned out the lights, chuckling in spite of myself, thinking about the accidental instrumental "Wichita Lineman." I went to the piano in the dim and littered salon that looked like that of a suddenly abandoned ship. I played the opening notes for a new song. A song about Rosemarie.

Jimmy Webb conducting the orchestra during "MacArthur Park" recording session.
(Courtesy of Henry Diltz)

CHAPTER ELEVEN

Love is a glass of wine balanced on the side
rail of a ship
Across the sea at midnight comes, It may not
last the daylight comes
And the trip is long, and the waves are strong
But then again it might be up there forever
I've heard of birds that never touch the land
But sleep on the winds . . .
—JLW, "Asleep on the Wind," 1974

1967

When the Monterey Pop Festival was over, the alchemists and fa-
kirs, the princes and wood nymphs, the trolls, fairies, pirates, magi-
cians, troubadours, wood carvers, candlemakers, accountants, and
cameramen faded away as suddenly as they had appeared, ". . . like a

moment's sunlight fading on the grass" (*w.* Chet Powers). Something had happened to change the space-time continuum in those three ecstatic yet conflicted days. The sense of bonding with others of their own kind would hold these rebels in continuing proximity. It was the beginning of a movement and a national outrage over the Vietnam tragedy that would gain momentum and eventually move worlds.

Johnny and I didn't pause to reflect on the possible cosmic reverberations of Monterey. He grabbed me and we jumped on a plane to San Francisco. He wanted to check out Haight-Ashbury and the Fillmore West. He wanted to talk to Bill Graham and more particularly to Janis Joplin. Big Brother and the Holding Company had made a splash at the festival and Johnny was building a record company, so north we went. As we left the hotel a rumor made the rounds that Paul McCartney had paid a secret visit to the festival grounds. Johnny and I were laughing hysterically in the car and he was having me on. "McCartney, we're going to do this," and "McCartney, you should do that." Thankfully the nickname did not stick.

The Fillmore West was dirty, starting with the bathrooms and extending to the debris-strewn floor and air quality. "I hate this fuckin' place," Johnny said. By comparison the Monterey Pop Festival had been a wholesome high school outing. This was a darker vibe. There weren't a lot of wildflowers and circle dancing around the Fillmore. We could smell the sweat of addiction. We threaded our way through the crowd, occasionally pushing off somebody who was temporarily missing from their body.

On stage were Janis Joplin and the Big Brother organization. She was working very strong, singing "Ball and Chain." Her voice was a sawtooth blade that cut through the smoke and boredom. The band was sloppier than hell and I don't mean their state of dress.

We stood by one of the pillars off to the side and listened to several songs. Johnny was excited; Janis was having a very good night. After a quarter of an hour Bill Graham materialized out of the gloom. He was the entrepreneur behind the Fillmore West and its sister venue in New York, Fillmore East. Bill offered to take us backstage as the show ended in a storm of feedback and odd rim shots and shitty drum licks. Sloppy.

"Backstage" is a word I choose euphemistically as it was a flop-house of squalor back there. The band sprawled like a clutch of playhouse dolls thrown into a soapbox. Two or three expression-less women were breastfeeding infants. There were a couple of near-empty bottles of Jack Daniel's sitting on an instrument case that served as a bar and coffee table. The cloying scent of vomit hung nearby.

Graham introduced us to Janis, who was jocular and expansive, articulating a very bluesy patois punctuated with four-letter words. She was down to earth and very soulful. An earth mama. She swigged Jack Daniel's out of the bottle and chain-smoked tobacco while Johnny talked.

Had they ever thought about a record label? John wanted to know. Janis replied that rather than labels and career strategy the Holding Company was more interested in bread. Enough money would do any trick. As for the rest of the band they sat in amiable silence, a collection of knees and elbows and hair.

"Where could we get together and talk it down?" asked John eagerly.

"As soon as we pack up this shit," said Janis, "we'll meet you at Sambo's on the corner."

No problem, everybody knew where Sambo's was.

The two of us left the Fillmore West quite happily, Johnny grumbling as we passed through the door, "Whew, that was fonkey!" When John said "fonkey" with an "o" he meant "less than fastidious" as opposed to "funky" with a "u," which meant "infectious and down to earth." He was very particular about cleanliness, and had all kinds of other provincial Southern traits I admired.

We were sitting in Sambo's a few minutes later when Janis and her boyfriend and their bald-headed lawyer came through the swinging door of the restaurant and plopped into the orange vinyl booth opposite us.

First they told the story about how half the female contingent were either pregnant or had small babies. The band's equipment was shot and one thing wasn't negotiable: bigger amplifiers.

"How much do you think you guys need?" Johnny asked. I looked at the veins on the lawyer's bald head, pulsating. There was tangible suspense.

"Eighty thousand dollars," the attorney said confidently. There was a long silence. Was Johnny thinking? Was he completely shocked into silence?

"Well?" Janis finally asked.

"I can't write you a check right here," said John. "Let me think about it." Faster than you could finish a cup of coffee Big Brother was gone.

We paid the check and walked toward our hired car. "Goddamn," Johnny said, "they must be fucking crazy!"

Now we know Clive Davis gave Janis the $80,000 and more and she eventually made a very good move in dropping the Holding Company and their domestic difficulties, and she became the biggest blues singer in the country since Bessie Smith. She would have been worth millions to Soul City Records.

In the aftermath of Monterey there was little sense of a letdown. Johnny had just released an album called *Changes* that contained both a lovely ballad he had written called "Poor Side of Town" and "By the Time I Get to Phoenix," which he had cherry-picked out of my small catalog as a single.

"I know it's a hit," Johnny said of "Phoenix" at the time. Meanwhile "Poor Side of Town" went screaming up the charts earning a "bullet" (a red dot signifying a hot single) almost every week as it ran straight into the top ten.

Johnny had recorded a song in 1962 called "The Long Black Veil" with a young sideman from Arkansas named Glen Campbell. The cut appeared on the modestly titled album *The Sensational Johnny Rivers* on Imperial Records. Johnny followed Glen's progress as he helped form the Wrecking Crew and appeared on hit single after hit single in every imaginable genre. Among Glen's innumerable accomplishments was the feat of playing the lead electric guitars for the legendary *T.A.M.I.* [Teenage Awards Music International] *Show* movie because many of the live musicians were, bluntly speaking, not up to par. On the grainy video he can be seen in silhouette, just offstage in a folding chair, playing the guitar parts.

More recently he had enjoyed a modest hit with the unabashed war protest song "Universal Soldier" (*w.* Buffy Sainte-Marie), as well as a significant chart appearance featuring John Hartford's brilliant and poetic "Gentle On My Mind" that peaked at thirty-nine on Billboard Hot 100 and thirty on Billboard Hot Country Singles. Glen was a powerhouse. A born showman and brilliant arranger who could improve even great writing into records that would chart.

Johnny started thinking about Glen Campbell and "By the Time I Get to Phoenix." On impulse he placed a phone call to Al De Lory, Glen's producer and string arranger. He told De Lory in no uncertain terms that he had a hit for Glen Campbell.

Al drove over to Johnny's house on Angelo Drive and walked in, probably thinking he was on another wild-goose chase. Johnny walked over to his Macintosh rig and dropped the needle down. De Lory sat there in shock.

"Why would you give us this record?" he asked. "Phoenix" was fully fledged, with Marty Paich's gorgeous strings and Bud Shank playing his elegant jazz-based flute riffs. "This could be a number one for you," Al marveled.

"Al, you can only have one hit at a time," Johnny said. "Run with it."

Johnny remembers hearing it on the radio a couple of weeks later. I had nothing to do with it.

Meanwhile, I moved out of his house and into Laurel Canyon, a nexus of songwriting activity. One night in my little shack on Kirkwood Drive I was watching television and clicked onto the Miss America pageant. They were crowning my Laverne classmate Jayne Jayroe as Miss America. Her familiar radiance warmed me.

It was about this time Johnny and I got a hold of one of the early pressings of *Sgt. Pepper's Lonely Hearts Club Band*. Johnny had just come off the road after a few days and brought the intricately decorated album sleeve into the house like a sacred object. We scored some first-class LSD and lit the living room with candles. John reverentially slipped the ornately covered album out of its Shrink Wrap and turned on the sound system.

A whole generation knows what we heard next. It was a tidal wave of sound on sound, texture on cross texture. The melodies soared and seduced. The lyrics teased and shamed and stirred one's soul. They announced a new creed. They called for a better world. Music had never in its entire history said or done quite so much.

We listened to both sides, the acid kicking into deep-space drive. Even Johnny seemed uncharacteristically at a loss for words. My imagination soared under the inspiration of these Beatles. *Sgt. Pepper* was nothing less than a heroic album. It was as important as any music ever written. What could *I* do? What could *I* accomplish?

Suddenly, in a refutation of all the peace and beauty that suffused the room, there was a deafening blast of horns and sirens. A helicopter swooped low over the house, swinging high-intensity searchlight beams through the windows and into our shocked faces. Outside doors slammed, voices were raised, and the roar of multiple diesel truck engines surrounded us. On the peaking acid our outraged brains amplified this assault of glare and noise.

"It's a bust!" yelled Johnny. "The cops are all over us!" We were running around in circles grabbing up our stash from wherever it had ended up, emptying ashtrays and dumping everything into a trash bag. Outside the noise increased and the helicopter sounded as though it were hovering over the front yard. Johnny made a pass through his bedroom and came back with every single baggie, ready roll, brick, and even some stuff I had never seen before. He dived into the guest bathroom and started flushing madly. Everything went. Just as suddenly as it began all the noise ceased. We looked up at the ceiling as the helicopter seemed to move away. Cautiously Johnny and I crept out through the big double doors onto the front porch. No cops. Out on the street we saw big Beverly Hills Fire Department trucks moving past the gate at a sedate pace. Firemen were yelling at one another.

"It's all over here, boys!"

"Yep, another damn false alarm!"

Police cars were turning off their blinking emergency bars and slamming their doors as the crisis de-escalated and adrenaline subsided.

"We just flushed all . . . *all* of our shit down the john!" Johnny said indignantly.

We both tried to keep a straight face, but couldn't help but laugh, remembering the undignified panic of our late crisis all too well. Shortly thereafter Johnny Rivers stopped using drugs altogether. Too much stress.

1972

The morning after the Albert Hall concert I was awakened by peals of laughter from outside my hotel door at the Inn on the Park. I slipped into my terry-cloth robe and went to the door in search of someone to yell at. Sandy Gallin's room was just across the hall, his door open. It was the pealing of Rosemarie's musical laugh that pulled me across the hall to where I peered inside. Sandy was on the bed doing calisthenics, sit-ups, and what not, and begging a critique from Rosemarie, who stood at the end of the bed.

"What about my glutes? What do you think?" Sandy was asking as he flexed his behind. "Oh, hi, Jimmy."

Rosemarie's only response was to laugh until the tears ran down her face. She was wearing blue jeans decorated with swatches of antique lace around the bell-bottoms. This morning, her hair, with its auburn tinge, was caught up, gathered in a bun and pulled back underneath a wide-brim black hat, her eyes hidden behind designer sunglasses. She was the cutting edge of current rock fashion.

"Oh, hello!" she exclaimed as I dared edge into the room. "Hell's bells, it's Jesus Christ himself!" she taunted.

For the first time my jungle of facial hair discomfited me as well as the waterfall of loose curls that cascaded down far below my shoulders.

"I wonder what you look like under there?" she speculated aloud. "Perhaps you're extremely unattractive and all of that fur is there to hide the fact that you look simply ghastly!"

Her mouth twisted into a funny little challenge as she stood chewing on the inside of her cheek in deep thought.

"Perhaps, you would like to find out," I answered, meeting her frank appraising glance with one of my own. Little sparks flew.

"Now, kids! No fighting and no flirting either!" Sandy stood up on the bed unsteadily, wrapping his bodywork in a white sheet.

"Would you like to come in for some tea?" I directed specifically at Rosemarie.

Her mouth, like a rose, uncurled and she said, "Oh no, darling, it's not going to be as easy as all that. Cuppa and a cuddle? I don't think so." She giggled.

Everything she said was meant to keep me off balance. Sandy stood there with his eyes open wide, knowing something was in progress, perhaps had been in progress for some time.

"How about dinner?" I heard it coming out of my mouth so I must have said it.

"Well, I was waiting for Sandy to ask me but you seem to be a man of action. The only thing is, if I come to dinner, you must promise that we will discuss a means of trimming your beard properly."

"Okay," I said with a wide grin. "Nothing's off the table."

She was gone suddenly, with a couple of tote bags from expensive boutiques, and from somewhere down the hall she called, "Sandy's got my number!"

Sandy and I stood there looking at each other. He was shaking his head.

"This could be the biggest mistake you've ever made," he commented dourly. "Her husband's a great guy. He's in a successful band. You know the song 'love grows where my Rosemary goes and nobody knows but me,' written by the last guy who went down the garden path." (w. Tony Macaulay, Barry Mason, and Sylvan Whittingham)

"Tell me more," I commanded while he pulled his outfit together.

"They're a happy couple, you home-wrecker!" He faked indignation. "She is a former Miss World. She's famous in England. She was in A Hard Day's Night. She's been to Vietnam with Bob Hope repeatedly to buck up the troops, a job for which she seems to be particularly well qualified. She's funny."

Around six o'clock she came by the hotel in a white dress, an intricately embroidered white silk shawl, and white leather platform shoes. Her hair was down and brushed to an iridescent sheen, curling loosely over her shoulders.

We walked out into Hyde Park where the daffodils waved gently as far as the eye could see across the green grass. We didn't hold hands.

"So you're married," I said as we walked.

"Oh, yes," she paused. "Seven years ago we were married on LSD. I love him, he's really a wonderful person," she said as though it was something that needed to be said.

"Why do I encounter so many beautiful English wives living apart from their beloved husbands?" I ventured, a cheeky comment more for my benefit than hers.

"What's the harm?" she asked. "You're not a dangerous person, are you?"

"Extremely dangerous." I made a fierce face at her and she cackled. It really depended on the way one defined danger. I suppose I had every intention of upending her happy life as she knew it, but to do so I would have to know that in some sense she was unfulfilled.

I had the big Phantom V of Terry Naylor pick us up in the park and we went out of the city for dinner, avoiding all the places where it was virtually certain we would be seen. Terry found us an elegant country inn dripping with Jacobean charm. There were no more than three couples cooing in front of the comforting fire. I had venison, she had grouse, both in the English manner: roasted and basted in a savory wine sauce. The sommelier opened a Château Margaux and we lingered over it, talking about music and the life of a rock star's wife. They lived just off Sunset on a little street called Miller Drive. They had been lucky to get a house on the hillside that had once belonged to F. Scott Fitzgerald. As we conversed I watched my hand as it crept across the table toward hers in the flickering firelight. I didn't know what I was going to do with it when it arrived over there but it was moving as though of its own accord. Finally I took a drafty full breath and laid my hand down on hers, mine twice as big.

"Why are you touching a married lady's hand?" Rosemarie asked sternly.

"I am now ready to discuss trimming the beard," I said. She studied me intently for a moment and then locked her fingers through mine.

"All of it must come off. The beard has to go, period. Hair we can talk about later."

"Agreed," I said.

Back at the hotel I stood at the mirror in my bathroom in front of an empty sink with scissors, a new razor, and some blades. I started shearing great hanks of my treasured Leon Russell chin shrubbery into the trash can. The almost forgotten contours of my face began to emerge from the chaos. It took an hour but I whittled it down to within a half inch of my face. I ran the sink full of water as hot as I could stand it. I soaped up a brush in a mug and, when I had a thick lather, saturated my remaining beard with shaving soap and steaming water.

Rosemarie lolled on the bed watching the BBC, patiently waiting for the transformation while she drank red wine. Occasionally she would shout encouragement. "Need a nurse? How's it going in there?"

I started in with the razor and the blades at the base of my whiskers and went to the scissors when needed. A face appeared through the steam. It was still there, though my features were red from scraping and marred by a couple of lacerations. A figure appeared in the doorway behind me.

"Let's have a look then!" she announced, as though she were examining a cabbage at the grocer. I turned around. She walked around me, inspecting me thoroughly. She touched my face and went over my features carefully. She stuck her finger in my ears and swabbed out the excess hair and soap.

Her clothes hit the floor. She reached over and turned on the shower as mist and steam filled the little bathroom. We stepped into the shower together and I was purged of blood, soap, and all the tiny clippings of my once magnanimous beard. She kissed me. She gently coaxed me to the bed. We listened to *After the Gold Rush*. It was the only album I had.

1967

Johnny called and told me about a friend of his, Frank Silvera, a character actor who had played many a Mexican bandito and also ran a nonprofit called the American Theatre of Being. A benefit gala was being planned at the Coronet Theatre on La Cienega. The nights would consist of readings, poems, musical numbers, and scenes, all with a decidedly antiwar message. Johnny wanted me to volunteer for the job of musical director. The theatrical director was an Irishman named Richard Harris. I was familiar with his performance in *Camelot* opposite actress Vanessa Redgrave earlier in the year, and anxious to do something for the cause.

First I would have to meet the director. Richard Harris lived at that moment in a pink and tangerine Italian villa on a hilltop in Bel Air. It sprawled over a six-acre plot of fountains and lush landscaping, and boasted a classic Romanesque bathing pool surrounded by appropriate statuary. When Johnny and I pulled up in front of the house I recall quite specifically that George Harrison was singing "Within You Without You" on the radio. "With our love we could change the world . . ."

Richard met us inside, and enveloped us in huge bear hugs, planting wet kisses on our ears. He rubbed his hands together in anticipation. I was in awe of the sheer size of the man; even onscreen at the Cinerama Dome he didn't appear as large as he did in life.

"Ah, 'tis good of you to help us out," he said in a whispery Irish brogue accompanied by a sly wink and a quick wide smile while he capered with joy like a spiritual pony.

He clapped his hands together as though striking a set.

"You must meet Kathe," he said, gesturing to a pretty blonde, all of nineteen, holding a gut-string classical guitar suspended from a strap around her neck. "Kathe is going to sing in the production," he announced, placing a protective and possessive forearm over her shoulders. She smiled up sweetly, revealing a fawn's large brown eyes and betraying an adoration and trust of this flamboyant figure that was touching to behold.

"Sing us a song, Kathe," he commanded, and she dove immediately into a performance of "Where Is Love?" from the musical *Oliver!* by Lionel Bart. My ears were deceiving me. She was singing exactly like the little boy in the film. Richard delighted in revealing she had actually sung the role of Oliver in the smash film scored by her father, the respected Johnny Green.

We talked a bit about the show and what was expected of us,

which is to say, not very much. It would seem, in the spirit of the times, Richard was going to make this up as he went along.

Johnny and I rehearsed a band of the usual suspects and then showed up for run-throughs a few days later with a half-dozen songs in the sub-genre of war protest. We watched with interest as Richard jumped like a madman from platform to rope to floor and back again, and cajoled, pleaded, cried, and laughed maniacally, as he forged his impromptu cast into a functioning theatrical unit. Walter Pidgeon sang 1922's "Going Home (*w.* Duorzak, Fisher)" from a rocking chair. Edward G. Robinson read masterfully the Alan Seeger poem "I have a rendezvous with Death / At some disputed barricade . . ." He read in a voice cracked with emotion; I wish I had spent a little pride and asked him for his autograph. Among other notables were Faye Dunaway, at the peak of her career, Bobby Morse, Mia Farrow, Robert Mitchum, Elsa Lanchester, Peter Sellers, and Jean Simmons.

I met Mia, wide-eyed and delicate to a point near frailty, looking like a very concerned child of twelve and unnervingly precise with her questions and answers. I had seen her on occasion at the Daisy, where I was sometimes a wallflower. She was in the process of obtaining a divorce from Mr. Sinatra.

It was *after* rehearsal that the situation began to gather steam. Richard had taken a shine to me. We found a tavern somewhere by the wayside with an upright piano and he demanded I play as we drank.

"Come here, Jimmywebb, and give us a song! Play that lovely song 'Didn't We?'" In return he would teach me some of the grand old Irish standards like "Carrickfergus" or "She Moved Through the Fair." He taught me scores of them and I soaked them up like a sponge, finding them to be not unlike some of the more stirring Baptist hymns. He had a much better than average ear when it came to picking a bonny air. His soul was hopelessly wound up with the written word and he wept over Brendan Behan and Dylan Thomas and Cavanaugh. *There are men too gentle to live among wolves . . .*

This was the innocent in Harris, but if someone on the crew made him angry, his face would turn red and he would bellow fiercely, "For fuck's sake!" or "Bollocks! That is bloody bollocks!"

"Bollocks" is an Irish way of saying "balls." He was a profane saint on that stage, calling on the powers of hell to turn back the accursed war. Fighting fire with fire.

The performance came off on June 5 and 6 of '67 if not without a hitch, then with a hell of a lot of good will and camaraderie. I came away with Mia's phone number and thought idly of perhaps taking her out, momentarily forgetting my station in life. On further reflection I came to the conclusion that this might be a good way to end up stuffed into a Dumpster in Palmdale. I decided to wait until the divorce was final.

When Richard and I said good-bye outside the theater, as he was on his way back to London and its rain, he put his big arms around me and gave me one of those snuffling wet man-kisses in the ear. I hadn't been raised in a culture where grown men embraced each other with such abandon but I didn't really see anything wrong with it. I had found a big brother I didn't know I had.

"Ah, Jimmywebb, maybe you'll come over soon and you'll make a recording with me then." He laughed.

"If you ever want to make one let me know," I called after him. He was gone with Kathe close by his side and it was as though someone had removed something without my permission. A wall or an oak tree or a favorite mountain.

1972

I did a lot of joyrides in my Schweizer 32 sailplane with friends and celebrities. People wanted to come out and see what I was doing. I flew Joni Mitchell, who became extremely ill as we circled at low altitude near the airport; Rosemarie, who hated the whole business; and master lyricist Paul Williams, future chairman of ASCAP, who was blessedly oblivious to the fact that we barely made it off the ground alive.

David Crosby came out one day in his black Mercedes 450SEL to see "the madman in the desert." He braked to a stop in a cloud of dust and came walking out of the red fog like a Viking god with his handlebar mustache and hefty build, a gigantic smile on his face. I never had a passenger more ready or willing to put his life in my hands. He relished the ride even though conditions were difficult. I ended up taking a long tow, all the way up to ten thousand feet because that was the only way we were going to get a ride. I apologized all the way down and tried to explain why we weren't climbing up the side of the mountain. I needn't have bothered. He was happy as hell. A longtime sailboat skipper, he understood what it meant to be becalmed. We would be friends and shipmates through thick and thin.

I would often fly out over Death Valley, always peering anxiously ahead for the first sign of big cumuli. On one such trip, at about four thousand feet I stumbled onto a sprawling monster of a thermal in a little declivity between two spurs and climbed on an elevator to heaven. Suddenly a shape materialized under me and my first thought was: *midair collision.* Out of the corner of my eye behind my left wing something came up even with the glider and hovered off my left wingtip. I risked taking my eyes off the instruments and was taken aback by the presence of a large golden eagle pacing me around the thermal. This huge bird was dark brown and had at least a six-foot wingspan. Unaccountably, she was looking at me. Calm and regal she moved her body along the upper surface of my left wing, soaring all the while and yet exhibiting the most singular curiosity about the cockpit. I had to concentrate fiercely to stay in the thermal.

She came close enough to the cockpit that I could have reached out and touched her with a pool cue. I could see the fine reddish feathers shining around her ruff and shoulders. Her huge golden brown eye transfixed me.

She climbed past me. Now she was above my head and displaying her mastery of the air around us. She soared with the assurance of a virtuoso, wingtip feathers flared upward. She flicked her tail and adjusted her circle radius once or twice as she climbed until I had to crane my neck upward to follow her. She went up and away from me like a banshee. No machine could or would ever touch her.

I snapped my attention back to my instruments where my grasp on the thermal had started to slip. I was at about eight thousand feet. If I was going to Las Vegas, it was time to get moving.

Jimmy Webb and Glen Campbell meet for the first time, at the Grammy Awards.
(Courtesy of William Eastabrook)

CHAPTER TWELVE

And I have dined in palaces, drank wine
with kings and queens
But darlin' sweet darlin', you're the best thing
I've ever seen . . .
—Lowell George, *Roll Um Easy,* 1973

1967

I began work on a new concept album for the 5th Dimension called *The Magic Garden.* Bones Howe—who produced and engineered the first album—and I were to coproduce this record and Johnny gave us carte blanche.

I was bitter about my limited situation as a contract writer for Soul City. "I can't believe it Harv," I said one day as he was counseling me. "I've had two big records this year and the only way I can see it is I'm in bondage for the next seven years." There was a long pause in the conversation and then with a sigh Harvey Linnman rolled his big eyes heavenward, and placing the tips of his fingers together, said with an exaggerated vowel: "Not necessaaaaaaaaarily."

I stared at him, fascinated by his malevolent grin and the unwavering contact in his eyes that suggested a plot of some sort.

"All right, tell me about it, Harvey."

He smiled at the use of his full name.

"Weeell," he said, affecting a lazy Southern drawl, "it's lak this. Mr. Rivers has to fulfill the option on your contract once a year. In fact, by the end of the month." He licked his lips. "If he doesn't . . . there's noooo contract anymore."

Just like that? No contract? There were a lot of questions floating around in my head. What were the liabilities involved in screwing around with a contract when you were in a fiduciary sense the guardian of that contract? Our conversation thus far was probably already a conspiracy.

"What makes you think he'll forget about it?" I questioned.

"Oh, he'll forget about it, don't you worry." I wasn't randy to bed down with Harv but seven years in show business is a lifetime. I had never done anything remotely unethical in the world of business. My conscience kicked in. I should simply try to negotiate my way out of this deal, I thought. Nah.

The Devil stopped by my house in Laurel Canyon one afternoon with some marijuana, riding a brand-new Harley Sportster. We sat in the shade on the front steps and admired the paint job on the bike while we smoked. I told him I thought some changes might be coming down. I didn't know exactly where I was headed but I wondered if he would be interested in bringing his radio expertise into an enterprise of some sort, a label perhaps or maybe even a film company? Satan was most interested.

As the end of the month came closer I prepared for what I was sure would be a Sicilian storm of outrage when the ploy was discovered. To avoid confrontation with any unexpected visitors I moved into a hotel. I told the Devil what I was doing and he came by and kept me company while the betrayal unfolded.

Harvey prepared a letter disavowing any contracts, implied or otherwise, between Jimmy Webb and Johnny Rivers Music based on the fact there had been no renewal of the option. It hadn't been renewed precisely because Harv neglected to do so. I felt like shit.

Johnny, for all his imagined faults, had been good to me. He had given me the star stuff. I had lived under his roof. He had given me a studio and an orchestra. He had promoted my music to other artists, which is something that publishers swear they'll do but they rarely, if ever, deliver.

In the days that followed my discomfort faded a little when I became acquainted with the torrent of possibilities that suddenly poured through an unobstructed door. I could now have my own publishing company and own my own copyrights. Harv immediately staked a claim on a rightful share of any proceeds from this new publishing firm. We spent hours in his office pouring over the range of options and he began drawing up his own contract with me. I can't help smiling at the thought.

I came up with an idea for the name of my new company. It was from the bridge of "Up, Up and Away": "suspended under the twilight canopy." That's the way I felt. Suspended and uncertain of the future. But the "canopy" was an overarching protection for a variety of business pursuits. I would call the company Canopy.

One afternoon, after we had been in meetings for days, Harv and I pulled out of 9255 Sunset Boulevard and onto Doheny in the new Maserati he had bought off The Monkees, and we stopped at the light at the intersection of Doheny and Sunset.

Johnny Rivers pulled up next to us in his red Ferrari, adjacent to me on the passenger side, and glared at me with a look that was emasculating. His face was pale and frozen in a grimace. I felt a dagger of ice in my belly. The light changed, monolithic gears turned in the galaxies hanging over our heads, and he drove on.

Harv looked at me and must have read my utter despair.

"You've got to pay your dues, kid." He smiled.

My factory coating of innocence was peeling off at an alarming rate.

In a subdued frame of mind I packed my bags for a trip to Oklahoma. I hadn't seen my father or my brothers and sisters in over a year. Dad had married the wife of a former church member named Ken Sadler, who had died three years ago, within weeks of my mother, in the twisted metal of his truck. He left behind his wife, Lily, and two sons, Garth and Randy. When Dad moved back to Oklahoma he had begun to see Lily socially. After a suitable interval they had joined their fortunes together. Now, in the same house, was my brother Tommy, who was a high school basketball superstar, the two "little boys" Randy and Garth, my sisters Susan and Sylvia, and Dad and Lily. I showed up with presents for all. The crown jewel was a miniature Ferrari from FAO Schwarz, with a real gas engine, perfectly scaled for ten-year-old arms and legs.

Over supper, I told my father I was starting a new company and I wanted him to come out to California. I needed some perspective on people that were beginning to surround me.

He told me he would have to think about it and talk to Lily. He said his heart had not really been sincere in delivering the gospel for a while.

"My beliefs have changed," he said. "I don't believe half the stuff that comes out of my mouth. I'm at the end of my rope in the pulpit."

"It'd be reassuring to know you were there to help me, Dad," I said.

My brother Tommy had been on the All-State basketball team two years in a row and was fully six and a half feet tall. He carried the family banner in the athletic world, and his team was on their way to the state tournament for the third time. I told Tommy quietly if he won the state championship I would throw in a new Corvette. Was I right to be meddling in my father's affairs in such an overt manner? I had spoiled their simplicity already. This was Jimmy's magical mystery tour and I wanted to bring everybody with me, no man or woman left behind.

Back in Los Angeles, during the last days of 1967, Lou Adler and Bobby Roberts sold Dunhill Records to a cigar-chewing record mogul of the old school named Jay Lasker. Harv set about planning a creative deal for Canopy Productions at Dunhill.

The first day I walked into his office, Jay was bubbling over with enthusiasm for his new acquisition. Behind his desk was a sign that read in large letters: "You hear a lot about Vincent, but what about Theo?" This veiled rebuke to the artistic temperament referred to spendthrift and layabout Vincent Van Gogh and his organized, businesslike brother Theo who worked at a real job and got little or no credit for supporting the family. I picked up on it right away: "Artists, be on your best behavior."

In exchange for producing a number of albums for Dunhill Records exclusively, Jay Lasker gave Canopy a great deal of money and the promise to promote and market those releases at the full extent. Jay put me in Lou Adler's old office and furnished it with a genuine Louis XV desk. The wall behind my desk was decorated with an old French painting of balloonists making a massed ascent from a park. Looking on was an admiring crowd of ladies and gentlemen dressed in the parachute-like skirts and top hats of the Victorian era.

When in his best form, Jay could talk on three telephones at the same time and smoke a cigar while playing a remixed demo for a reluctant jock in Duluth. If his mark remained unconvinced he would heave his ample bulk out of the chair and bring his hand down on top of his desk with the force of a sperm whale's fluke. Then, his face, as red as a cardinal, would gradually give way to a possum-eatin' grin. Another station on the record. He was of that old school who roused themselves at four in the morning and by five were "on the phones" speaking with every Top 40 program director in America.

In 1966 I hadn't made enough to be required to file a tax return. In 1967 Harv predicted I would probably make well over $60,000.

While producer Bones Howe worked on the 5th Dimension's *The Magic Garden* with me, he was also producing another project across town. Bones called up one night in a very serious mood, which was unusual, as we clowned around for the most part. I hoped all was well with the 5th Dimension and no feelings had been hurt, which was a constant concern.

"No, nothing like that," Bones replied. "I'm nearing the end of production on an album with the Association. I'm imagining a kind of climactic tour de force for the end of the album. I've always thought you would be the guy to ask about this. Can you imagine a classical piece for Top 40 radio with different movements and tempos? I would like to use a full symphony orchestra. I'm talking about something probably no more than ten minutes long, with singing parts for the band, solos, the whole shamazola. What do you think?"

The Association, known for hits such as "Along Comes Mary," "Cherish," and "Wendy," was fresh off the Monterey Pop Festival and had been my favorite band when I was in high school. I knew I was going to say yes. He probably knew that just as well as I did, but I gave him the courtesy of thinking about it for a full twenty seconds.

"I could do it. You came to the right place."

"It comes with the usual caveat," he said. "I need it yesterday."

"Then you will have it yesterday!" I declared theatrically. Then we both calmed down a little. This was seriously a hell of a lot of work. It would take time to just imagine what shape it might take.

"This is a single, right?" I asked. He laughed. "Let me think about it, Bones," I urged. "I could let you know in a couple of days if I'm making any headway. Meanwhile, shop it around." He was still laughing.

"See you at the studio," he said. *Click.*

I sat down at the piano and idly tinkered with the right hand. This could be my magnum opus for Susan Horton. It could be symbolic of the meltdown of our love affair, the sad last night at MacArthur Park. I couldn't deny I was still missing her and the relationship that had never really happened.

My right hand found a D minor chord. I began thinking of images from the park, cozy symbols of innocence, like Susan feeding the birds and enticing them into her hands. She was gentle enough to do that. The lunches on the grass, a birthday with a small store-bought cake that had green icing. I started playing. A downpour with the two of us footracing through the rain and up the steps in front of her office building. I began to keep a notebook on one side of the keyboard and filled it with vignettes from "Mac Park." Events and conversations, all real. I wasn't creating a sucker punch for unwary listeners. I was pouring out my soul on a surreal canvas.

Three days later I surfaced. I looked around, stunned by the storm of dirty Kleenex and rancid beer cans, the dozens of busy, unkempt pages half stuck together by Scotch tape so they looped over the grand and touched the floor on both sides. I hadn't eaten. I had fallen asleep a couple of times at the keyboard and awakened with my face playing a G13 with a demented fourth. At those intervals I had crawled under the piano and buried myself in pillows for a couple of hours. As soon as I had been able to, I roused myself and continued. I was deep into the score, writing French horn parts and strings, woodwinds, and percussion. During the entire process I took no drugs of any kind. I was getting ahead of myself. I needed to call Bones.

He answered on the fourth ring.

"Bones?"

"I'll hafta call sum bak," he answered. I looked at my clock. "Oh, my God, it was three in the morning!"

"Bones, I'm sorry, but I needed to let you know. I've written it."

"What?" He was suddenly wide-awake. "Can I hear it?"

"I'm going to sleep for a while. I can play it for you tomorrow."

Before long I was nervously waiting outside of United Western Recorders, walking back and forth beside my car and holding a folded manuscript that felt very, very heavy. Around 10 P.M. Bones came out into the parking lot and said, "Here, I'll take you right into the studio."

A huge slab of the building slid back to reveal a spaceship-like bright interior. The Association, all nine of them, stood around their amplifiers surrounded by empty pizza boxes, Chinese food cartons, and pyramids of stale cigarette butts. I slipped through and the crew closed the loading door behind me. The group gave me a warm welcome and I shook each hand as I was introduced.

Eventually I sat down on the piano bench in front of the grand. As I lowered my behind down onto that little landing pad, with Bones sitting down alongside me to turn the pages, my cheap jeans gave way in the seat. With a sound like Errol Flynn unzipping a tautly trimmed sail and riding his dagger blade all the way to the bottom, I arrived at a seated position. To their credit the band tried not to laugh. But eventually, as I swelled up luridly around the face, there were gasps and then giggles and then guffaws. I had split my striped pair of pants.

"C'mon, guys, let's cut him a break here, this is business," Bones said as he tried valiantly to restore some sense of decorum.

I pushed my mortification as far back into my gut as I could, and then played "MacArthur Park," singing in my tremulous tenor as Bones studiously turned the pages. The band listened courteously to all seven and a half minutes. It felt long to me, but that's what the doctor ordered and I could feel their interest heighten with the up-tempo section, tailored especially for them. Then came the Wagnerian chorus reiterating the opening theme and the crashing finale, where I rolled the low notes on the piano to communicate a massive prospect of symphonic splendor.

There was silence. Nobody said a word at first. Then came a round of hearty congratulations on a job well done and more handshakes and suddenly I was back in the parking lot.

Bones called me up the next day.

"The dumb sons of bitches are not going to do it. I told them the day 'Mac Park' goes to number one with another artist will be the day they need to start looking for another producer," he grumbled.

"You don't mean that," I said.

"I fucking mean it," Bones insisted.

Various stories have been floated about these embarrassing yet simple events from time to time over the years. The Association were not discourteous and did not mistreat me in any way. Artists have the right—nay, the duty—to select what they deem to be the best material for their projects. I've never cried over a turndown.

Ninety percent of all songs ever submitted were turned down at least once. Bones was pissed. I just went out and bought new jeans.

Not long after, a telegram arrived for me from London. DEAR JIMMYWEBB (STOP) COME TO LONDON (STOP) WILL MAKE GREAT RECORD (STOP) LOVE RICHARD

1968

Harv and I went to England to talk to Richard Harris in January. This was my first flight outside the United States. There simply was no place on earth, nor has there ever been, like London at the end of the sixties. Anyone who traveled or lived there at the time will be happy to vouch for it. From the first rattle of the Cockney cab-driver's accent to the streets droning with strangely shaped vehicles and red double-decker buses, I was an instant Anglophile.

As Harv sat rigidly in the center of the cab trying to look dignified, I bounced from one side to the other shouting, "Oh, look at that!" as an interesting building came into view, or, "How old is that one?" at the driver, pointing at the rococo exterior of a Victorian house.

"Very old," he replied drily. "It's all bloody old, Guv."

All the structures looked like palaces to me, even the British Museum. He took us to Belgravia, extraordinary because virtually every house was painted white and had white pillars flanking the front porch and doorway. It was London's most fashionable and affluent neighborhood. At 37 Chesham Place, we pulled to the curb and took egress from the pudgie black London taxi.

The number 37 was engraved in a delicate flowing script on a brass plaque, clean and shiny as glass. We rang the bell and a scrappy young fellow with thinning red hair and wiry frame bound out into the street, saying, "Welcome, welcome, I'm Dermot!" He flashed a diabolical grin and, snatching up as much luggage as he could carry, led the way inside.

"I'm Richard's brother, by the way, the real brains behind this outfit!"

I was swept up once again in the stout arms of King Arthur, or if you prefer, Dicky Harris. He picked me up and twirled me around the room like a pathetic rag doll until his excitement and affection were temporarily satiated. He plopped me down in a stuffed chair by the fire and introduced me to Dermot for the second time, and again to the young Kathe Green, who had a fine blush to her cheek.

We settled into the cushy sofa and had our first real English tea. There were little pots of very strong, hot tea and some other pots that contained piping hot water and milk. There was also a silver platter covered with tiny triangular sandwiches made with odd ingredients—cucumber for instance—and sweet biscuits. Richard quoted Seán O'Casey and Kathe played her acoustic guitar. The wind whined coldly outside but was mostly unnoticed.

I had brought a portfolio of songs with me and soon we moved to the proper grand piano in the corner. As I played. Richard became more and more animated.

"Good God!" he would mutter. "Bloody fantastic!"

I was close to the bottom of the pile when I ran up on the bulky manuscript to "MacArthur Park," one I had very nearly left behind as impossible. With a sigh I began the opening motif in the right hand of the piano and then the crashing ascending cadence in ⅜ time. I began to sing.

> "*Spring was never waiting for us girl*
> *It ran one step ahead as we followed in the dance . . .*"

"Fucking tremendous!" Richard shouted. He was on his feet, walking and singing along as I played and sang. He cried. He orated.

"I'll have that!" He slapped the top of the piano with the flat of his hand like a gunshot. "Now, Jimmywebb, that's a song fit for a bloody king!"

Well, it was long enough, tall enough, and wide enough; also, in the zeitgeist of the era, it was obscure enough to confound even the most inquiring intelligence.

He made me play it forty times if he made me play it once. I was shredding my nails. He insisted I tape it instrumentally and then *he* sang it forty times. Harv and I finally got sick of it and checked into the Carlton Hotel, only a brisk walking distance away.

I slept well in England that night. Some long exiled version of me, locked in my genes and chromosomes, or perhaps my spirit, or even a likeness in another dimension, was glad to be home again. Home after all those years.

We returned to the United States with eleven solid song choices. My plan was to cut all the tracks in L.A. with the storied Wrecking Crew and then cross the Atlantic with the unmixed tapes to overdub Richard's voice. I would update him with tracks as they were finished and he would practice singing them in my absence.

On February 29, the Devil and I, Harv, Jay Lasker, the 5th Dimension, Glen Campbell, and countless other stars went to the Century Plaza Hotel for the Tenth Annual Grammy Awards. There were perhaps four or five hundred people in attendance and a couple of local news teams outside as we went in. The Grammys were then an "inside" industry ceremony, not a show that would fill a 25,000-seat sports arena and be seen around the world.

I had two songs nominated in the Song of the Year category: "Up, Up and Away" and "By the Time I Get to Phoenix." The 5th Dimension was nominated for Record of the Year and Best Group Vocal Performance, as well as Best New Artist for "Up, Up and Away." Glen Campbell had been nominated for Best Male Vocal Performance for "By the Time I Get to Phoenix." Even the kid who did the artwork on the 5th Dimension album cover, Wayne Kimball, was nominated for Best Album Cover. The two albums gleaned other nominations as well. I began looking forward to the ceremony, but I was convinced any chance I might have had to win the Song of the Year Award had been sabotaged by the fact I had two songs nominated in the category. My supporters wouldn't know which song to vote for. How could I possibly win?

We sat at a round table, front row center. I was very nervous in spite of the fact I didn't fancy my chances of winning. Jay chewed on his cigar and leered at me with his good eye and a lopsided grin.

"Don't worry, kid," he said with a high school smirk at Harv and Lucifer. "It's in da bag." He looked over both shoulders and hunched down into the white collar of his tux.

I was aghast. *In the bag?* Surely John Hartford would take home the gold for "Gentle on My Mind," a song I would gladly call my own. Then there was "Ode to Billy Joe," a hauntingly offbeat mystery novel in three verses by Bobby Gentry that could win for sheer originality. I watched the proceedings innocently without any real thought as to who would be taking home the little Edison phonographs. Eventually I heard the presenter say, ". . . and for Song of the Year," there was a pause, "Jimmy Webb for 'Up, Up and Away'!" A wild cheer swelled behind me. I stumbled up to the podium through a storm of "Attaboys!" and strangers clapping me on the back and beautiful women grasping at my clothes.

I had not prepared a speech and I don't know what I said except that I thanked Hal Blaine. Like a shot he was there, too, both arms wound completely around me. In that moment I could hear him whispering to me in Bob Ross's little clapboard studio, "Stay with it kid . . . you could be real good at this." Jay Lasker was there to give me a hug and a conspiratorial wink. Did he have foreknowledge? Had he done any fixing? I wouldn't begin to suggest such a thing. The tumult and euphoria continued as I stumbled backstage in a happy delirium for photos and on-the-spot interviews. Outside I heard the 5th Dimension receive the award for Best Vocal Performance and Best Contemporary Performance. Glen was represented as well for Best Pop Album of the Year and Best Male Vocal Performance.

Glen called me a few days later to ask for a "follow-up" to "Phoenix" and asked me specifically if I had "something about a town." I told him I appreciated his interest but I had just about exhausted the Rand McNally phase of my career. "Well, could you make it something geographical?" he almost pleaded. I told him I would spend the rest of the day on it and get back to him.

By about four o'clock I had come up with a song I did not believe was completely finished, but I called Glen and Al at United Western Recorders and told them about "Wichita Lineman." They wanted it right away. I agreed, with the caveat that it might possibly need a last verse. I met Glen in person a few days later, on the set of a commercial for General Motors, a business deal that would leave me with new Corvettes every year for the next three years.

As we were wrapping up the commercial I invited him over to the house to hear some of my back catalog and the roughs on "Wichita Lineman."

He walked into the music room carrying his Ovation in a sculpted case and sat down on the crappy couch. He whipped out acetates of "Wichita Lineman" and I said to him, "You know this song isn't really finished."

"It is now!" Glen crowed.

I listened to the beautiful intro with an especially catchy bass lick from Carol Kaye, the minimal strings gracing the upper registers, and then Glen's vocal, a match for the melody that must have been made in heaven. Verse three rolled around and I found out what they had done about the missing verse. Glen had detuned a guitar down to a "slack key," Duane Eddy style, and simply played the melody note for note, an extreme compliment. A lightbulb went off in my head.

"Hey, I've got something over here, Glen, it might be nothing but . . ." I turned to an old Gulbransen electric organ sitting on the opposite wall. I kept it around because it had a lot of electronic presets on it, bells, strings, harps, and other effects. We didn't have samplers or synthesizers in those ancient days. I selected a preset that was one of my favorites. I played open fourths and fifths up and down the keyboard with only two fingers using an F chord. The organ emitted a sound like a satellite or some other high-powered electronic device; the open fourths and fifths shivering up and down in a fascinating tintinnabulation loaded with reverb.

"That's fantastic!" Glen marveled. "How did you do that?"

"I'm not doing anything." I laughed. "That's the Gulbransen."

We played the rough of "Wichita" and the organ at the same time. It was a perfect fit.

"We have to record that!" Glen exulted.

"It sounds good," I cautioned, "but the organ weighs a ton."

He got on the phone to S.I.R.

"Hey! Shorty, I need you to come over to Jimmy Webb's house and pick up a great big organ and take it down to Western. 'Kay?"

Later that night we overdubbed the Gulbransen on the fade of "Wichita Lineman." You can hear it there to this day, sounding a little like the Northern Lights, like vibrating signals from outer space moving upward and downward in fourths and fifths.

When we had recorded all eleven tracks for Richard Harris's album, including large brass and string sections, as well as "interludes" that we intended to insert between tracks, Harv and I boarded a transatlantic jet and returned to London for the vocal overdubbing with Mr. Harris. The task was a challenge, namely to capture the vocal essence of a hard-drinking, heavy-smoking Irish thespian who was widely known for his mercurial temperament.

We had reserved a small studio on the outskirts of London called Lansdowne. Richard would not undertake a trip to the studio without a giant, chilled pitcher of Pimm's No. 1 Cup, a traditional British concoction that tasted no more threatening than a strong cup of lemonade but packed the wallop of a bad-tempered Oklahoma jackass. Richard was a novice and yet performed admirably with this one caveat. The fact is, recording him strained the existing technical envelope and taxed his physio-mental endurance. Between his enthusiastic efforts and a careful utilization of multitrack recorders we were able to isolate favored lines and passages and retain them for editing. At times inexplicably we would find ourselves working on one word. We tried at great length, for instance, to coax Dick into singing the words "MacArthur Park." It always came out "MacArthur's Park" as though a fellow named MacArthur owned the park. Our editing was not advanced enough to nip the "s" off of MacArthur's. We had to be extra sensitive to our inexperienced artist in order not to break his spirit. We finally let it slide. It would be "MacArthur's Park" forever.

Richard would sit in the studio on a high stool, his pitcher of Pimm's snug on a nearby table. Between attempts on the material he would regale us in the booth with detailed anecdotes about various famous anatomies he had known along with sound effects. He might, as the evening progressed, launch into Shakespearean so-liloquies and versions of his own poetry, both of which were damn good. He was never visibly drunk or incoherent on the job. He seemed to have a workable détente with the Pimm's and it was, in fact, a reliable clue as to the length of the session. When the Pimm's was exhausted, the session was over. In the early hours of the morning we would board his Phantom V and drive the Lansdowne Road back to his flat.

One night we were sitting around the fire at Richard's with Barbara Parkins and Lindsay Anderson and a famous ex-fighter, along with Clement Freud and many other members of Richard's usual eclectic mix.

The drinking and the discussion came around to The Beatles, an unavoidable topic in London company. A theoretical question arose from Lindsay.

"Who among the four is really most responsible for their great success?"

"Obviously Paul," I blurted without my social filter engaged.

"Bollocks!" Richard exploded. "I hate people who say that! Every cunt in the world thinks he has some insight into The Beatles."

"It's only an opinion," I dared to say in my youthful timbre.

"Well, take your bloody fucking opinion and piss off!" He caught me by surprise. I hadn't seen the angry Richard before. He had always handled me with kid gloves. The fact that historical research and certain autobiographers, most prominently Geoff Emerick in *Here, There and Everywhere*, have verified McCartney's single-minded obsession with perfection, that Paul at that time was re-recording Harrison's guitar parts, overdubbing drums in addition to playing bass and piano, buttress my original opinion. Over the years, however, I have come to respect with something akin to reverence the influence George Martin as producer had over the musicianship of The Beatles, not to mention the fact that he and Geoff were the great enablers of experiments like "A Day in the Life" and "Strawberry Fields." George was the mastermind who made "Yesterday" and "Eleanor Rigby" into realities. I'm confident every member made a valuable contribution and I'm sure that's what Harris wanted to say.

I walked out of the apartment, not used to being yelled at, and walked back to the Carlton Hotel in a slight drizzle. Miraculously this rift was mended in the sober light of day with a great round of hugging and kissing. There was, I'm sure, the sudden realization on both sides that we had crossed that fabled Roman stream mounted on the same horse and we needed each other to get to the other side.

We almost lost control of it again when we started bringing rough vocals home from the studio for Richard to audit and rehearse. His voice was too loud, he complained, even though improving the vocal was the whole point. He was insistent on meddling with the process. Later, when he had begun to feel cocky about his vocals and was admiring some of the finished composites, he complained just as bitterly that the *orchestra* was the culprit and we should turn it down a little for God's sake! He continued to complain about the orchestra and demanded a remix as the record was being mastered later in the year. This was circumvented.

Vocals finished, Harv headed back to California to work on the Dunhill and Universal deals. I moved in with Richard and settled into a small but comfortable room. It featured a gigantic Victorian bathtub with feet and a sunny curtained window looking out on the roofs of Belgravia. We were good mates again for a while. Parties were frequent; Richard never tired of showing off his luxurious flat. One night it was a human circus as usual: Michael Caine was there; Doug Hayward, the tailor to the stars; the former British Middleweight World champion, scarcely understandable after several severe injuries to the cranium; Sammy Davis, Jr.; Samantha Eggar; Oliver Reed; and so on. I remember on this particular night he had invited his freshly divorced wife Elizabeth and her new beau Rex Harrison. He had done this to show his universal tolerance for all living things but secretly despised the slightly fusty, aging actor.

I had seized an empty chair on the edge of the crowd. Looking across the densely populated room I caught a glimpse of a fantastic-looking chick sitting in a similar chair on the opposite side. It became a game of peek-a-boo, her venturing a smile, and me waiting for her to be revealed for a second in which to wave slyly. The first

thing I thought was that her eyes were impossibly large, not plaintive like the ones in the ubiquitous Keane paintings of the time, but
entrancing. She had high, almost primitive cheekbones and a thin
proud nose. Her hair was pulled back so I could see her tiny and
perfectly formed ears, as her petulant and generous mouth smiled
at me in frank curiosity. I couldn't take my eyes off her. I stood up
and went straight to her like a puppy dog.

I don't remember exactly what we said to each other. I do remember asking her if she was alone; she said that she was, for the
moment. Haltingly I tried to explain who I was and what I was doing
there. She listened, seemingly fascinated. "I am very familiar with
your accomplishments," she said and told me about her husband,
Leslie Bricusse. I was impressed. The Bricusse/Newley collabora-
tions for *Stop the World—I Want to Get Off* were familiar to me. The
songs were of an extremely high quality and I studied good things.
At one point when she and a girlfriend decided to leave I remember
her saying, "And what mischief are you going off to, Mr. Webb?"
She was flirting a little. I walked her to her car, a Mercedes 300, a
very imposing purpose-built limousine, sitting halfway up the street
with a driver lounging inside. He leaped out to open the car door.

I took her hand, as though to help her into the rear of the car,
and blurted out, "I want to go with you," with all the subtlety of a
moonstruck calf.

"Don't be silly." She laughed, but hesitated, and my picture of
the world trembled a little at the edges of the frame.

"Call me tomorrow, Richard has my number. I'm Evie." The ostentatious Mercedes made a great whooshing noise and she was
gone with just a suggestion of her French perfume still floating in
the air. English girls were new to me. There was nothing in the
world as wonderful as the sound of her voice. It was like wind on
the water.

Jimmy Webb, Thelma Houston, and Marc Gordon. *(Courtesy of Thelma Houston)*

CHAPTER THIRTEEN

And all this science I don't understand,
It's just my job five days a week
A Rocket Man, I'm a Rocket Man
Burnin' out my fuse out here alone
And I think it's gonna be a long, long, time . . .
—Bernie Taupin, "Rocket Man," 1972

1968, London

I invited Evie to dinner and she in turn invited me to a show. We ate at a trendy restaurant called Papillon, where the surrounding tables whispered and focused so much energy in our direction that Evie got to her feet and addressed the crowd.

"I have perfect teeth"—she displayed these—"and ears"—she

lifted her raven hair to display her ears like tiny seashells—"and I'm *his bird!*" She laughed hysterically right in their faces and as I stood she kissed me. I asked her to lose Leslie and marry me numerous times, but she was slow to react.

We were brazen enough to attend Sammy Davis, Jr.'s, show at the Palladium, where he put on his whole classic vaudeville act, including rope tricks and quick-draw displays with loud gunshots. He danced the old soft-shoe as he covered "Mr. Bojangles" and sang the hell out of Tony and Leslie's "What Kind of Fool Am I?" The table was crowded with friends of the Bricusses. After his show Sammy came out and joined us. He and I had a most spirited conversation about civil rights, which ended with his demanding, "Why doesn't someone write a song called 'When Can Brown Begin?'" I wrote the title on the back of a linen napkin and carried it away with me.

Sammy was close with Evie and her husband, but he tried to take me in stride. He recorded some of my songs, "Do What You Gotta Do," "Wichita Lineman," "Up, Up and Away," and some of her husband's songs, "What Kind of Fool Am I?" "The Candy Man," (both *w.* Bricusse and Newley), and I can only squirm at the emotional gyrations Sammy was probably experiencing, seeing me with her. But he was the prototypical mensch, quick to smile and physically demonstrative. He would have been remarkable if only for the inexhaustible energy he stored in such a small and seemingly fragile vessel. I have scarcely seen another grown man with such a childlike, almost emaciated frame. However, on stage, as one of the most riveting of performers, he achieved titanic dimensions. Evie adored him.

My home base in London was the penthouse at the Playboy Club. Some might sneer, but they were among the most spacious and private rooms on Park Lane. My suite sprawled across the whole top floor of the building; the casino and club were tucked in a couple of floors below. An outdoor patio and balcony separated from the living space by glass doors hung precariously on the outside of the building like a breathtaking amusement park ride. From this perch, an immense slice of London's daily life was on display in the streets below.

I invited Richard Harris, Kathe Green, Lady Pelham-Clinton-Hope, and some other guests over for a Champagne brunch on the deck outside. I arranged for a Rolls-Royce Phantom V to stand by at the Playboy Club for a trip to the venerated Connaught in Grosvenor Square, where I planned to collect Evie in a covert getaway, so she could join the party. I greeted my guests, one an executive from EMI, who brought me their entire collection of classical albums in a huge crate. We stood outside in the fine spring weather, sipping Champagne from flutes and chatting, oblivious to the fact that thousands of activists and demonstrators were forming a march at Trafalgar Square to protest the war in Vietnam, led most prominently by Vanessa Redgrave. They were headed in our direction.

The phone rang insistently inside the suite and I went to one of the old-fashioned London telephones in its heavy cradle. I picked it up half expecting Evie's voice, but quickly had to reorient myself as I recognized the caller.

"Hello, is this Jimmy?"

"Ye . . . uh," I replied in a moment's panic.

"Hi, Jim, this is Paul McCartney."

I searched for the right response. Not too fatuous but not unfriendly. I wanted to sound like a cool guy.

"Hi, Paul," I said. "How are you?"

"Oh, fantastic. Listen, Jim, I'm doing a record with Mary Hopkin and I'm getting the best writers to do her songs. I've spoken to Brian Wilson."

"Oh, great, fantastic!" I blubbered.

"I was wondering if you might want to write a song for Mary."

"Oh yes, that sounds fine." What was the matter with my brain, my tongue? I sounded like some phony prick who was staying at the Playboy Club.

"What do you need for her, Paul?" I retreated to my bedside manner.

"Oh, anything, just anything really. Brian's writing a song about puppies."

"Uh-huh, well, thanks for the honor. I'll try my best."

"Okay, Jim, thanks then. We'll be in touch. Cheers."

That was it. I was humbled and excited. Lopsided really. It was one of those bends in the river that could lead to something stupendous. Why didn't I bear down? *Right then.* Of all the industry people in the world I wanted to know, Paul McCartney was the most admired.

There was a hubbub out on the balcony. I dropped the heavy receiver back into its cradle and the watch work of pinioned wheels and levers that changed the scenery of life whirred and another set came wheeling in on hydraulic pistons, one backdrop ascending into the proscenium with this universe while another came whining down on steel cables stretched taut.

I went to the patio, where everyone was staring off toward Trafalgar. Vanessa Redgrave with her rippling mane of reddish gold hair was easily recognizable in the vanguard as she passed our overlook. What a noble, splendid sight she was. The leading edge of a throng of twenty thousand people came into view on the roundabout where Victory reigned in her rampaging four-horse chariot and lifted a laurel crown in her outstretched right arm, high above the Victory Arch. There was a color guard of red banners rippling in the breeze on the front ranks: some were flags of the British Communist Party, others of the Soviet Union, the Union Jack, and other smaller fry but the unifying theme was the color red. I gaped. The Communist Party wouldn't dare go on parade in Times Square, yet here was the hammer and sickle, bold as brass.

It seemed decadent to be standing on a penthouse balcony while the battle raged in Vietnam, watching courageous people of different political dispositions gathered in such numbers for a common cause. We watched, fascinated during a few moments of silence and our Champagne flutes were set aside as the marching mass came up even with our balcony, chanting, waving signs and banners. It was an ocean of humanity that quickly paralyzed traffic on Park Lane and suddenly I had a concern for Evie at the Connaught Hotel. The march was headed in her direction. I grabbed my coat and called downstairs to alert Terry Naylor that we were getting ready to leave.

There was a chorus of *ooh*s and *ah*s from the walkway and I stuck my head out to see what happened. Unaccountably the entire column of activists and demonstrators had come to a screeching halt, bunched up in the middle of Park Lane a couple of blocks north of us. The throng was staring upward at one of the prominent balconies on the Park Lane side of the Dorchester. I focused on a pontifical apparition that had suddenly appeared on the balcony in question.

"Bloody hell," I said, already adopting the expressions of the Richard Harris crowd. "Do you see that?"

"It's fucking Tiny Tim," Richard cackled, unable to restrain his glee. And by God it was. The androgynous, soprano-voiced, ukulele-playing recording artist, famous for his revival of a twenties number called "Tiptoe through the Tulips" (*w*. Al Dubin), had appeared in his trademark waist-length hair on a balcony far above the crowd. His arms were elevated and spread wide in imitation of a papal blessing.

Such is the power of momentary celebrity that Tiny Tim almost derailed the massive march of protest. Seriously, a number of hardened activists actually dropped to their knees. However, a more single-minded contingent of dissenters moved on purposefully toward the general area of the Connaught. On high Tim continued to wave and yoo-hoo delightedly.

"They're headed for the American embassy!" said Lady Pelham-Clinton-Hope. I bolted for the elevator. Six floors below, Terry Naylor was waiting in his gray uniform, white shirt, and black tie, complete with military-style bonnet and braid.

"Terry, we have to make all haste to the Connaught Hotel."

"Yes, sir." He smiled, revealing the conflicted array of large teeth in his uppers.

I dashed across the street and got into the back of the waiting Phantom. Terry opened the driver side door just after.

"There is a lady waiting, Terry, must hurry," I spoke as he slammed his door and settled behind the wheel. He started the beast and accelerated away from the curb. I was momentarily pushed back into the coachwork.

"This crowd is a bit out of order, sir," he commented as we made a hasty right turn on Audley Street, proceeding northwest and parallel to the line of march on Park Lane.

We managed the next four blocks, but at South Street the crowd poured across the intersection in a rowdy river that seemed to slowly carry us along toward Grosvenor Square, the site of the U.S. Embassy. We crept impatiently, at times almost nudging the demonstrators, who repeatedly slapped our high metal fenders hard and yelled "Tory!" or "Fuck the U.S.!" We were being mistaken for diplomats.

I agreed with our antagonists on principle but persisted in my attempt to extricate a lady from a situation that seemed balanced on the thin edge of riot. As we approached Mount Street the crowd pressed closer to the car and we were now caught up in its inertia, creeping toward the corner, a block west of the Connaught, which reigned supreme on the corner of Carlos Street.

Police vehicles were audible in ever-closer proximity with their seesawing electronic sirens playing the theme of the constabulary: two pitches repeating a tritone interval. The crowd roared in response as though to say "Bring them on!" Ahead we could see blue-clad vehicles and blinking yellow lights but the movement of the protest was increasingly random and unpredictable. It swirled. We pressed on.

Once we negotiated the corner, we were within sight of the Connaught, a Victorian ice cream cake of a building, bountifully decorated with quaint early-twentieth-century rococo. When we came up even with it I toggled Terry again.

"Sit tight, Ter, I'm going after Evie."

"Would you like me to fetch her, sir?"

"I'll get her. Take care of the car."

"You're the guvnor." He tipped his hat and I made my exit.

I pushed my way around the corner and found myself in front of the quaint entrance to the hotel. I saw Evie crowded into the little anteroom behind the glass doors, a bleak look on her face that struck me in the heart like an arrow.

"Baby!" I yelled through the door. "Let's go!" She smiled readily.

With me pulling and her pushing we got her through the door and, dodging the most physical displays of civil disobedience, we made it around the corner to find Terry under siege. Protesters were pounding on the car with protest signs and bare fists, apparently oblivious to the fact that there was only an innocent working-class driver inside. Evie and I pushed and shoved our way to the car through a barrage of verbal abuse. I opened the big door against the crowd and ushered her safely inside. With a sigh of relief I slammed the heavy door closed and at that moment one of the most dramatic spectacles of my life transpired.

Over a hundred mounted officers had made a charge to clear Grosvenor Square. Some of the grittier combatants had made a stand and physically engaged the police. Most of the throng, however, had made a sudden retreat directly south on Carlos Place. As Evie and I settled in the car this wave of protestors surged past the Connaught and into Mount Street. It was chaos. The bulk of the demonstration piled up around us, clinging to our door handles and each other, suddenly taking refuge behind and around the big car, faces pressed against the windows, cheeks and noses squashed against the glass. Behind this press of fleeing demonstrators appeared the flak jackets and riot helmets of cops; bobbies toting batons and tear-gas launchers. Many in the crowd turned, ready now to fight. A pitched battle erupted with the Rolls suddenly thrust into the role of a barricade. A cop on foot was rushed by three spoilers and bent backward over the gleaming bonnet of the big machine. Through the glass we saw him disarmed and given a severe beating, his helmet rolling off and into the street. He left behind a faint, theatrical spray of blood and saliva on the windscreen. Terry was pale but determined. Hanging his big arm up on the divider he began tenaciously and carefully to back us up Mount Street.

It took a half hour to extricate ourselves from the aftermath of the so-called Battle of Grosvenor Square, eventually landing us back on Curzon via Berkeley Square. We drove past the White Elephant, eatery of the stars, finally laughing with relief, and drew up to the Playboy.

I stood with Terry for a moment as he helped us out of the back.

"Very cool under fire," I complimented.

"Glad to be of service, sir," he acknowledged, a bull of a man.

Evie and I went up the elevator even as escapees from the confrontation scattered through the neighborhood toward Kensington and other tube stations. Upstairs, we gladly joined our friends who greeted us like long-lost comrades. We stepped out on the balcony with champers and watched a peace warrior, limping from the fray, as he carried a red flag bearing the hammer and sickle proudly into the lengthening shadows of Hyde Park.

1968, *New York*

The Devil and I went to visit Frank Sinatra at the Waldorf Astoria. It was a goodwill mission; we didn't mention Jimmy Webb's television special for Universal, but we blatantly intended to influence him favorably. Mr. Sinatra maintained a residence at the Waldorf. We rode the elaborately decorated elevators to one of the upper floors and were immediately admitted to the apartment by Sarge Weiss, president of Sinatra's publishing interests and keeper of the calendar. The soles of our shoes disappeared in the lush straw-colored wool carpeting of the living room. The colors were muted, the overall impression one of spaciousness and well-chosen antique furniture punctuated with tasteful works of art, all lighted by the full-length plate glass windows facing the Hudson River.

The demigod of American pop music arose from a chair and walked toward us, his blue eyes alight with energy. He extended his hand and the irresistible flash of white teeth against a Palm Springs tan and his ready smile completely disarmed me. Why, there was no doubt we were going to be compadres and make a television show together! He wore a one-piece beige leisure suit. He was in excellent shape and looked lithe even in such a revealing garment zipped up the front. He, thankfully, did not ask me when I was going to get a haircut. He said: "It's a pleasure to meet someone who is actually writing *music!*" And for a moment his face was more serious. What does one say to someone when, more than anything, one wants to make a favorable impression? His career was soaring after a hit record with daughter Nancy called "Something Stupid" and another solo effort, "Strangers in the Night."

"It's an honor to meet you, sir" was the best I could muster. The

Devil shook hands with him as well and we were ushered to a plush couch facing a couple of armchairs where the four of us were seated. There was something not completely direct about him, I decided. Not egocentric but perhaps he was just unwilling to involve himself in any unnecessary intimacy. He was not brusque; he was brisk. We chatted for a while about songwriting, a subject obviously close to home with him. "You know, kiddo, you write a great saloon song!" he complimented me. "'By the Time I Get to Phoenix' is the greatest saloon song ever written." He asked me if I would like a drink and I declined. He ordered a Jack Daniel's: two fingers straight up, and lit a cigarette from a silver box on the coffee table.

He began to mention me in the same company with Hoagy Carmichael, Jimmy Van Heusen, and Harry Warren. I felt my collar getting tighter. However unfashionable it may be or implausible it might sound, I am a somewhat modest person. These names were from a golden age and I didn't feel as though I belonged in such rarified company. I was more comfortable when the conversation edged toward more contemporary writers, Lennon and McCartney and Paul Simon, whom Sinatra also admired. As Sarge attended to a nonalcoholic drink for the Devil, Mr. Sinatra walked me over to the plate glass windows facing the west side of Manhattan, and beyond that, New Jersey.

"Jimmy, over there is Hoboken. I was born over there." He stood in silent contemplation for a moment.

"Let me tell you, it takes a lot longer to get from Hoboken to the Waldorf than it takes to get from the Waldorf to Hoboken."

"Yeah, I guess that's the theory of relativity, right?" I proffered helpfully.

"Well, not exactly." He looked at me slightly annoyed. I repented deeply for a comment that I suddenly realized made me sound like a smart-ass.

"You know, I recorded your song 'Didn't We?'" he said as we turned back to our armchairs. We sat and fresh drinks and cigarettes appeared as though by magic.

"There was a broad"—he paused thoughtfully—"probably a little bit before your time, but I had a thing. I thought it was going to kill me . . . or maybe both of us."

He looked at me, amused, and his blue eyes glinted.

"Some chicks, they get under your skin and they stay there."

I nodded.

"But I know you know what I mean." He smiled, but I didn't. I had endured a bumpy ride or two but at that time I had never been knocked down by an eighteen-wheeler. Not yet.

"Ava," he said finally.

I recognized the cautionary note in his words for a young flash in the pan like myself. We talked briefly about doing a whole album together before a certain change of tempo in Mr. Sinatra's speech was, to my alert ear, a precursor to the end of the meeting. A week or so later I called him from my cabana at Universal and asked him flat out if he would do my television show with me. His reply was an enthusiastic, undiluted yes. Diablo and I jumped up on top of my desk and did a Mexican hat dance.

1968, Los Angeles

Marc Gordon called again, always a good omen. He told me he had made a wonderful discovery in the person of one Thelma Houston, a young singer who was unsigned, and he wanted me to hear her before he took any other steps. We agreed to meet the next afternoon and she showed up with a list of songs she was prepared to audition. She was a fountain of joy and happiness, her smile an endless source of pleasure. I fumbled about for a couple of minutes setting her key and found out she could sing strongly across a broad spectrum, possessing a remarkable tessitura.

She sang and when she put her shoulders back and opened up, the penthouse windows rattled in their frames. When she finished her third song I turned to Marc and said, "Okay, fine, when do we do the record?" Thelma and I began rehearsing on almost a daily basis.

In the performance of music, particularly between an accompanist and a singer, there occurs a deep mixing of souls. We were of different races and backgrounds yet music creates a powerful confluence based on the interpretation of each precious note, a telepathy conveyed through the eyes and ears that addresses the unspeakable. It draws the participants together with an irresistible magnetism. I discovered there was little to nothing I could demand of her musically that she could not deliver tenfold. She was of the ilk of an Aretha Franklin or Mahalia Jackson. I resolved to craft the best arrangements of my career. We would push the envelope for Thelma. We would eclipse what we had done for Richard Harris. In her I had found the perfect instrument. I was at the height of my powers, I had the songs and a technical team that would bring this project to perfect realization. I had the Crew, all to myself. The budget was expansive. Any strength I found wanting was erased by one of Thelma's twinkling smiles. It was a dream project.

One night, working on one of the tracks, I went on for sixty-eight passes (takes). There were tape boxes piled all over the control room. After take sixty-eight Armin, the chief engineer, flatly refused to continue. I probably blew off a little steam over it. If I had it to do over right now I would fire his ass and find another studio.

The next day I was summoned to Jay Lasker's office. I wasn't used to being summoned. I was even more taken aback when I walked into Jay's office and saw Armin sitting there. Both of them ganged up on me with the bedside manner of a couple of psychiatrists addressing a difficult child. I wasn't to waste money in the studio anymore. They had been around the business long enough to know when a producer's behavior was becoming obsessive and compulsive. I could have laughed out loud. Armin had been up to take eighty and ninety with Johnny Rivers and Lou Adler, and who knows how many with John Phillips or Brian Wilson, whom he coddled? I tried to explain that any investment was worthwhile if we were successful in achieving *perfection*. What would Aretha Franklin's first album be worth? They seemed unimpressed by this line of reasoning.

I looked around me in disbelief. What was my engineer doing

in this office? Were these guys communicating behind my back? Yes. Of course. Talking about cocaine and grass and such. Armin had set himself up as ex-officio executive producer of my pet project. Eventually I obliged their meddling paternalism by shedding a brace of tears out of sheer frustration.

I went away from the meeting with deep resentment for Jay and a feeling that bordered on hatred for Armin. Armin had been one of *us*. Bad form indeed for him to run tattling to the record company about some supposed laxity of mine, if that's indeed what he'd done. I went back into the studio no less determined to create a flawless product. I didn't change my mode of production. I used as much audiotape as I wanted. I scarcely spoke to Armin. Gone was the once-warm camaraderie we had shared. He had gone over to *them*. What an ass-kissing move that was.

Rock 'n' roll was coming of age and the men at the top were determined to turn it into a rigidly controlled, corporate *business*. Modern-day fans can judge the efficacy of such stewardship.

It was during the Thelma Houston tracking dates that the Crew and I first noticed a startling metamorphosis in volume control expert Mike Deasy. When Deasy walked down the street people were apt to ogle his buckskin-fringed jacket adorned with wampum beads, matching pants, and Robin Hood–peaked cap with a pheasant plume. With his mountain man beard, he looked like a cross between Daniel Boone and Davy Crockett, his midriff belted with a hand-braided thong and hung with a powder horn and hunting knife. Deasy's favorite guitar was an aging Strat carved with Native American symbols.

One day, Mike walked into the studio for the date and everybody stopped short and just stared. Deasy was wearing a dark blue suit, wingtips shining, completely clean shaven. He looked like a freaking advertising executive. He played well, if not particularly inspired but drug-free, and when the session ended he walked out.

In dribs and drabs the story behind this unprecedented transformation became a part of Hollywood studio mythos.

Deasy and a friend had outfitted an old van with an eight-track professional recorder and old studio parts, effectively jury-rigging a mobile recording unit. On the weekends they would pull the old panel truck into an alley behind a club or concert venue and record whatever was going on. They went to Griffith Park one Sunday afternoon and recorded the Korean congregations worshipping outside.

The two musical gypsies were told about a group of free spirits who lived out on the desert, played some "far out" music, and were generous with various and sundry high-quality drugs. The latent frontiersman in Deasy must have leaped at the chance to go out under the night sky and sit among the sage and mesquite with a group of outlaws similarly inclined toward the philosophy of the pioneer throwback.

He went out to record the group a couple of times. One night, however, he was told the evening's ritual would be a feast in his honor. The leader of the band, Charles Manson, let Mike know he was to be inducted into membership in the desert rats club and receive the privileges and assume the obligations thereto. He was to become head music teacher and guitar instructor for the clan. For how long? Well, Manson told him, forever or 'til he died, whichever came first. Mike felt the first pang of fear. He was more or less coerced into taking a dose of LSD by some pretty girls and persuaded to join in a ritual. All the participants stood around a fire with their hands linked and chanted Charlie's poem for the occasion, said to be a blood oath.

Mike Deasy was missing for two days. He finally appeared at home, weeping hysterically and raving to his wife. "They tried to take my soul." He went out and got a new haircut and a blue suit. A few months after completing Thelma's album, he and his family moved to Oregon where Mike eventually became an evangelist.

Thelma Houston's album escaped from ABC Dunhill. It seemed as though the label blackballed it deliberately. *Sunshower* has been praised for forty years as a seminal debut by one the greatest of America's ingénue singers. Paul Shaffer told me once it was the best arranging and producing of my life. However, I watched in dismay as our dream project floundered at the bottom of the charts. One of the songs—"Everybody Gets to Go to the Moon"—made it into

William Friedkin's blockbuster drug flick *The French Connection*. A serviceable copy of Thelma's record was included in a nightclub scene by a good group called the Three Degrees.

When artist relations go south at a label it often happens in a hurry yet invisibly. It's like sitting and looking at a glass of milk on the porch and trying to guess the exact moment when it's no longer fit to drink. I had missed it at Dunhill. I had no idea I was in trouble there until the day I saw Armin Steiner sitting in Jay's office. No heads-up from Harv or the Devil or Howard Golden? We had grown complacent. I had salaried employees at Canopy Music pulling down $80,000 a year and not getting a single song covered in a film. I closed the expensive Canopy Productions office on Sunset Boulevard to keep it from bleeding to death. My father went to Curb Records. At about the same time Harvey Lippman succumbed to cancer and was interred with little pomp or ceremony.

Recalling the circumstances of my departure from Johnny Rivers Music, it is no less than astonishing that Harv had summoned Johnny to his bedside to ask for some sort of absolution. Johnny obliged him. One day I will owe Johnny such a phone call as well. My suddenly unstable continuum was seemingly turning sideways and unreeling on its edge. Like a toy gyroscope wavering on the edge of a glass, I was trying to walk it like an acrobat, striving not to fall into a worse mess.

1968, Las Vegas

I was invited up to Sodom and Gomorrah on another occasion by Mr. Sinatra to see his show at Caesars Palace. He made specific mention that I should bring my father as his special guest. This was a big deal for Dad, but I should add I was treated as nothing less than a visiting potentate. As we checked into Caesars Palace, pulling to a stop adjacent to the fountain, a half block long, we were swarmed by valets and bellmen. A uniformed hotel employee greeted me on behalf of Mr. S and informed me we were checked in and our money was no good in the hotel. There was even a marker waiting at the cashier's cage for a thousand dollars, and he gave me the code. We took our keys up to a typically overstated Vegas suite on the penthouse floor that was flagrant in its abuse of columns, mirrors, carpet, and square footage.

In the afternoon I met with Mr. Sinatra in a conference room fitted out with a piano and, in a routine that would repeat itself many times, he sat comfortably in an overstuffed armchair and sipped at a highball glass containing Jack Daniel's straight up while I played the piano and went through a dozen or so songs. On that occasion I remember specifically playing a song called "Winter Clothes" that he went for but was holding something back.

"It's not done yet, is it?" I asked him with a smile.

"It's such a great idea, kid. If we could rework the lyrics for me it would make a big difference," he retorted with a wry smile. He took a couple of puffs on a cigarette, one of perhaps two or three he would smoke during a session. I knew the song was missing something and kicked myself for showing it too early. There is extremely delicate timing involved in exposing material to an artist. I had probably lost a cover by overplaying my hand but I was so damned anxious to please him.

That evening Dad and I had our own table snugged right up to the stage in the middle of the house. As our candle flickered and the density in the room increased ten-fold, I watched the spotlit curtain and listened to the band jostling the stage as they took their places. With a great blast of sound, the band hit the warm-up music, a very brief overture that accompanied the raising of a gilt lamé curtain that must have weighed hundred thousand pounds. Nelson Riddle stood in the center of the stage holding a baton, his assets arrayed around him. Stage right sat the ranks of a string section numbering at least twenty violins, violas, celli, and a couple of concert basses. Immediately behind him at his custom-made drum set was Hal Blaine taking some time off from the grind of Hollywood studio work. With him was a lineup of rhythm players, two percussionists with their glittering array of chimes, glock, wind chime, and other toys. Two guitarists sat huddled over their music stands bearing the

"Nelson Riddle" logo, one electric and one acoustic. An electric bass player stood nearby and to his right a seven-foot Steinway with an elegant but graying stick of a man at the keys. This was Bill Miller, Mr. Sinatra's lifelong accompanist. Stage left was a who's who of jazz greats on six trumpets, five trombones including a bass, two French horns, six or seven reeds including a specialist on oboe and flute, two baris, a quartet of tenors, and at least a couple of alto saxes. This was a far cry from Monterey and my single chime.

The music paused. There was a tympani roll and a voiceover.

"Ladies and gentlemen, Caesars Palace Hotel and Casino presents a man and his music, Frank Sinatra!" There was a moment of implosion when it seemed all the air had been sucked out of the room. The familiar middle-aged man with a good tan and twinkling blue eyes walked on singing "I've Got You Under My Skin." (w. Cole Porter) A woman toward the back of the room passed out with a moan and the crowded sea of glitterati erupted in a volcanic shout of approval. This is what they had come to see, not the legend, not a disembodied voice on a tiny speaker, but the living, breathing animal. It was the fantasy we had seen in the movies: the posh nightclub, the full orchestra, and the timeless songs that had seen them through dates and proms, weddings and wars. I looked over at Dad. There was a glint of moisture in those deep blue eyes.

Somewhere in the cheap seats they were placing the unconscious woman on a gurney and wheeling her out for a hot toddy. The show barreled on hit after gargantuan hit. "Last Night When We Were Young," (w. Yip Harburg) "The Lady Is a Tramp (w. Lorenz Hart)" and then in an interlude Sinatra said, "Ladies and gentlemen, I'd like to do a brand-new song by one of today's most talented songwriters, a young fella who writes like a giant, Mr. Jimmy Webb."

A hulking searchlight like a relic from a World War II battleship swung in my direction and lit me up in white like a specimen under the microscope. My first instinct was to duck under the table.

"Stand up, son, the man is talking about you," my father chided, and I slowly got to my feet and received one of the rare moments of acclaim that guys in my racket enjoy. Mr. Sinatra was a lover of songwriters and never stinting in praise of the creators. Songwriters were credited throughout most of his shows and I learned a great deal about the history of my craft just by listening.

I resumed my seat and he sang "Didn't We?," a song engraved in history because of his and Barbra Streisand's and a couple of other fine recordings. The rest is a blur. The surreal effect created by someone of such international and historic acclaim addressing a little song I wrote when I was a teenager was dizzying. Once the music ended, escorts materialized and we went backstage to talk to the great entertainer. In this case it really was "backstage" as Mr. Sinatra had a full-size house trailer sitting deep upstage behind the curtain that backed the orchestra. Dad and I walked up to the Airstream with our guard and knocked on the door as though we were visiting friends in the heart of a wilderness. Mr. Sinatra took my dad out front to teach him to play a little chemin de fer. At hundred dollars a bet, Pop didn't last long.

We stuck around for a couple of days. One night Mr. S took my father and me to the Jockey Club for an early dinner and the two of them chatted away like old army buddies. They talked about the Andrews Sisters and Tex Beneke and the Big One. After a while they forgot I was there. The encounter changed my dad. He had a little more spring in his step after that. He started wearing a big diamond ring on the fourth finger of his right hand. He was a made guy.

1968, Los Angeles

When I got out of the elevator I could hear the phone ringing in my apartment. I sprinted to the door and skinned my knuckles keying the lock to get in and pick up the phone. There was much in the wind. I was loath to miss a phone call in those days.

"Jimmy?" It was Evie's mellifluous alto on the other end.

"Hello, little mouse."

"I can't stay here. I need to get out." She was sobbing. There was a hullaballoo in the background. Someone yelling.

"Can you come get me?"

"Watch for the car. I'll pull up right in front."

I drove as quickly as I could without drawing any heat. I pushed down busy Sunset Boulevard toward the heart of Beverly Hills, made a right on Benedict Canyon, and then another at trendy Tower Road.

A barefoot figure clad in flowing white came rushing down the steps of a big rancher. She ran out into the street clutching an overnight bag and a pair of shoes. Evie.

I braked quickly and leaned over and opened the passenger door from the inside. She slipped into the bucket seat, tear-stained and smelling of the same perfume she wore the night I met her.

"Oh, my God, he's gone crazy!" She sobbed. I kissed her.

"We will get you away," I reassured her with a hug and putting my hands back on the wheel revved the engine and almost took off. But just as the car began to roll another figure—this one bespectacled and wearing pants and a long-sleeved shirt unbuttoned at the sleeves, Leslie—threw himself in front of the car and splayed out over the hood, one of his hands right in front of my face on the other side of the glass.

I opened the door and got out. I figured we were going to have a jolly old duel of fisticuffs over the damsel. Maybe he really did love her.

"So, you've come into the light," he heaved. "Why don't you leave my fucking wife alone?"

"I'm here," I said, looking at his hands.

"If you had any balls you would come into the house like a gentleman," Leslie challenged.

"I'd be happy to."

I went around and helped Evie out of the car and the three of us walked back up the steps and into the living room. I am sure the room was very opulent and calculated to impress but in the insanity of the moment my eyes fixed upon an item that I instantly recognized: a chord organ.

We had come to that moment when it was time for something

to happen. An undignified scuffle probably would have occurred if David Hemmings hadn't stumbled in from the hallway wearing a bathrobe and scratching his shock of blondish hair.

"What in the diabolical blazes is going on around here?" he complained, seating himself beside Evie and placing a protective arm around her shoulders.

"Oh, my God!" he suddenly exclaimed. "You must be Jimmy!" He jumped to his feet.

"What a pleasure to meet you, old boy! I'm a tremendous fan, you know, and a friend of Richard's." He pumped my hand enthusiastically.

Leslie was mortified. Here he was looking for an ally to join in on the vilification, and houseguest Hemmings had turned out to be a Jimmy Webb fan. He turned on Evie.

"So make up your mind. This jacked-up country oaf or me, what is it to be?"

She whimpered.

"Stop yelling at her, for Christ's sake," I said.

"Leslie, good fellow." Hemmings shifted smoothly into the role of peacemaker. "Perhaps there's a way we could just all sit down and discuss this like adults."

Leslie ventured that since I wasn't an adult he couldn't see how that would be feasible.

"Evie, I'm going to go," I said, my voice shaking a little. I strove to keep it strong and even. "If you want to go with me there is nothing that's going to stop me from taking you out of here."

I looked Leslie straight in the eye, but David got between us.

"Listen, James—Jimmy, is it? I would love to get together and have a dinner sometime when you're in London perhaps," David interjected, maintaining the social ambience. I recognized him as a perfect rogue, fundamentally untrustworthy and likeable to the core. I turned for the doorway after giving Evie a kiss on the cheek and pumping David's hand enthusiastically. I walked out the front door, and halfway down the walkway Evie caught me.

"I'm going with you," she said. She had her little bag with her and we regained the cozy cockpit of the 'Vette. I fired up the ignition and flipped on the heater as we both shivered from the stress of confrontation in the chilly December weather.

My offers of marriage and hers of divorce hung in midair uneasily and I let it ride. After the weekend, she went back to her husband.

I, in turn, leased out the former Philippine Consulate.

Four blocks from Grauman's Chinese Theater, it was a faithful copy of a grand Spanish hacienda on a street called Camino Palmero. I asked Harv to move in with me. "We need a house big enough for you and me and the Devil and lots of groupies and any stray hippie who needs a meal or a place to crash."

Harv's eyes got very big. "Really?"

He couldn't get over the image of flower-clad free-love chicks draped all over the furniture. Harv took one suite of the house, I took the other. The Devil got his own room. A hipster mama cook, her handsome bartender boyfriend, actress daughter Patricia Highland and three-year-old granddaughter all moved in as well. The toddler's name was Petrie, and she was screeching hell on roller skates. Who morphed into a fine young woman over time.

I signed two writers and sleeping arrangements were made for them as well. They would also theoretically back me in the band I was intent on putting together. My philosophy was, if there's enough money, the more the merrier. And it looked like there would be enough money.

Word of our "co-op" travelled through the street scene rather quickly. A regular parade of uninvited guests began to show up for nourishment or shelter. The Devil and I made a rule for the entire household: do not invite strangers over for drugs.

My popularity was soaring. My picture and long articles had appeared in *Time* and *Life*. Fan pulps went wild with the story that I was dating Sally Field: FLYING NUN GOES UP, UP, AND AWAY. She was a wonderful girl and for a while my brother Tommy double-dated her sister Princess. The word "wunderkind" was bandied about. I had to ask someone to look up what that meant.

1968, London

I was invited to a Beatles session through the auspices of Harv and Ron Cass. I hopped on the next Pan Am flight back to London.

Unbeknownst to me, The Beatles were very antsy about visitors in the studio though I would have found that attitude perfectly understandable. In his book *Here, There and Everywhere* Geoff Emerick described their prickly demeanor when confronted with looky loos and front office types while at work. As Harv and I navigated the narrow alley called Queen Anne's Court, searching for the nondescript entrance to Trident Studios in Wardour Street, I could scarcely believe our good luck.

We hit the buzzer and a figure appeared in a window overhead. "Ooh is it then?" he yelled. Harv made the introductions. A strapping young man in jeans and a rumpled T-shirt admitted us with no further security measures. Besides some upbeat music faintly audible through a door in front of us there was no sign of life in the foyer. No groupies, no guards or receptionist, just an expressionless young fellow escorting us along a corridor decorated with award discs. It seemed a long walk toward the tinny timbre of the music, echoing, it seemed, from another era.

Honey Pie, my condition is tragic
Come and show me the magic
Of your Hollywood song

We opened a door into the control room and I dropped onto a black leatherette couch, as far away from the action as possible. After shuffling uncertainly for a moment Harv did the same. The name of the game when visiting a film set or recording session or backstage is to make yourself as small as possible. Nothing grates on my nerves like an unsolicited opinion or even unintentional noise from a visitor. Therefore, I kept quiet and tried to observe and remember as much as possible for the day when I might want to write it down.

Directly in front of me the wide window, found in most studios, revealed that the studio itself was one floor below the control desk. I had no view of the goings-on down on the studio floor, though I could hear the familiar Liverpudlian chatter of some of the most famous voices in the world. The take had broken down and The Beatles were talking.

They were consulting with a silver-haired gentleman seated behind the board, the word *gentleman* not being chosen lightly because starting with his appearance he could have been nothing else. He stood, speaking softly yet firmly, radiating confidence and trustworthiness. He was tall, almost gangly, and yet his stance was erect and noble. He was an astounding-looking man. So this was George Martin. I had half-expected a tubby, balding, uncouth, sweating record producer. This individual looked as though he had descended from the cast of Korda's *The Shape of Things to Come*.

As the session progressed, with no one having taken the slightest notice of my presence, I emboldened myself to stand up. Now I could see clearly into the mysterious lower chamber of the studio. On the left side, McCartney sat at a grand piano wearing jeans, a T-shirt, and a sweater tied loosely around his neck. He seemed to be making the lyrics up as he went along and was stopping the takes frequently. Linda Eastman sat behind him on the piano bench, motorcycle style, her arms tightly around his neck, chin resting on his shoulder. I was amazed that he could play or sing at all with this considerable handicap but he seemed to be inordinately cheerful, chortling and wisecracking constantly. The deliberately banal lyrics continued:

> *Honey pie, you are driving me crazy*
> *I'm in love but I'm lazy*
> *So won't you please come home*

On the right side of the studio was another tableau. John Lennon, long-bearded and adorned by a thick fall of dark brown hair, sat on an intricate rug of Indian design, legs folded in the manner of a yogi. He sat calmly and for the most part silently, cradling an acoustic guitar on his lap, which appeared to be a Martin D-18. He strummed along with Paul sometimes and sometimes not. Close by sat Yoko Ono in support, occasionally kissing or trifling with his hair, sometimes resting her right arm around his shoulder. Candles and incense burned around them in a semicircle creating the impression of an improvised altar.

Standing between the two collaborators and their respective girl-friends, George Harrison diffidently plucked at an electric bass on a strap, spaghetti thin and seemingly at a remove from the other two.

And what of the fourth? There was no sign of any drums and yet I could hear them snapping along on the two-beat rhythm, high hat and bass drum. Ringo's voice was clearly audible on the studio monitors.

"How long am I going to have to stay in here?" he asked at least once.

"Hello?" he would inquire plaintively.

"Is anybody listening?"

The truth is no one appeared to paying much attention to him. He was in a drum booth directly beneath the control room, a sort of windowless cell, where he whiled away the hours sequestered from human contact.

The arrangement of the personnel was somewhat strange to my eye. No American band would play without eye contact from the drummer, who was—in spite of much demeaning banter to the contrary—often considered to be the most valuable of members.

There was much symbolism to be read into the physical arrange-ment of the onetime "mop tops."

After a few runs at the track, which seemed focused primarily on Paul's piano, Martin and McCartney decided it was time for a listen and the band broke. John was invited in for the playback but declined.

"I'll just stay here with me drums," Ringo also responded, mo-rosely.

After a short delay, Linda and Paul burst through the door laugh-ing, and Harrison followed. The second engineer fiddled with some tapes and suddenly it seemed a whole other track, featuring a lot of electric guitar, was on the overheads.

"Hey everybody, I want you to meet Tom Dowd from Atlantic Records!" Paul announced to the room and I looked at the control room door, expecting to see the engineering/producing legend from Atlantic Records. There were no new arrivals. George Martin extended his hand in welcome to me. Confusedly I got up off the couch.

"I'm Jimmy," I said to George Martin who smiled at me with sympathy and a bit of pity.

"So Tom," McCartney said, too loud and right in my face, "fantastic, you're such a legend and all! Want to hear a track?"

"I'm Jimmy," I said extending my hand. Paul ignored it.

"Take a listen to this, Tom," he barreled ahead nodding at the second engineer. A button was pushed and a guitar solo blared at his extraordinary level, which I would learn was standard for the group. George Martin eventually lost an hearing in both ears. I stood nervously beside him and yet being trained to listen analytically, I automatically evaluated the playing. For originality and powerful rendition, it was superb.

"So Tom, what do you think of that take?"

"Very good," I said, "but I'm not . . ."

"Good, then I have another take . . ." He nodded at the second engineer and a different guitar solo thundered in the tiny room. Once again I automatically concentrated on the performance. He would get no hackneyed answer from me.

"That one was very good as well," I said honestly. "Amazing."

"Which one would you choose, Tom?" Everyone else in the room, Harrison, Harv, Martin, and balance engineer Barry Sheffield stood simply watching. I was bewildered. Did Paul McCartney actually think he was speaking to Tom Dowd? If so he was pretty high on some very good shit. If he knew he was talking to me, he was having me off royally.

"I wouldn't make a decision like that for you, Paul," I said. I was getting pissed.

"Well"—he laughed, a demented court jester—"I guess we'd better get back to work."

They stood and listened to "Honey Pie" a couple of times. Any additional opinion of mine was not solicited. They all trooped back downstairs and only George Harrison paused as he passed me to say, "Fantastic arrangement on 'MacArthur Park,' Jim." He smiled and shook my hand warmly.

As they left the control room so did I. Harv trailed me into the alley.

"What the hell was that all about?" Harv seemed genuinely confused.

"Paul called me last year and asked me to write a song for Mary Hopkin's album," I clarified.

"So?" he asked me.

"I guess I should have tried a little harder," I said with resignation. It was the only reason I could think of for such bizarre theatre. Henceforth, Paul and I were never what you could call friends.

Jimmy Webb and Art Garfunkel rehearsing. *(Courtesy of the author)*

CHAPTER FOURTEEN

Driftwood in its voyage steered by stars
Blown by wind to landfall close ashore
Through the spray, swept away
To the coastline tossed and torn
Thrown high and falls to rest like people
Baby like you and I
—JLW, "Driftwood," 1978

1972

San Francisco's morning was a symphony of white clouds and wind-scoured blue sky. The Golden Gate Bridge and Sausalito, Pacific Heights, and Coit Tower loomed. The Bay was dotted by a hundred white gouache sails in a quickening breeze, all vibrating to the frequency of blinding sunlight.

I was there to meet Art Garfunkel and his gifted engineer/ producer, Roy Halee. Art and Paul Simon had broken up two years earlier to splashy headlines. Since Paul wrote all the songs, Art needed material and was actively screening top writers such as James Taylor and Stephen Bishop. I was honored to be invited to audition.

On Russian Hill I walked into a cavelike environment—down a hallway and into a control room where it could have been midnight. In the holy of holies there was always a sacred mantra of peaceful, climate-controlled tranquility, emphasized by the soft acoustic shapes that covered virtually every surface. Amid a star map of colored lights and glowing VU meters I found Artie, relaxed and leaning against the console. He was tall and lithe. His bearing was aristocratic. Roy Halee—an imposing figure in his own right with the round face of a burgher—sat in the captain's chair and puffed on a slightly curved briar pipe. They greeted me warmly.

We traded the essential social trivialities for barely a minute and then Art walked with me out into the studio where the subdued lighting revealed a seven-foot Steinway and the studio's interior, resembling a cubist painting with its baffles, angles, and geometric blind corners. It was a fitting surround for a man of intellect who had studied architecture at Columbia University and earned a degree in art history.

Art coolly sized me up as I took a seat at the grand and ripped through a few chords to get the feel of the instrument. I had come unarmed. I had no lyrics or lead sheets, only the repertoire in my head. I played songs for him, uncorked a couple of good ones, and he nodded but gently coaxed me onward. He had not heard what he wanted to hear.

I had a new song I'd written in London for Rosemarie. I regarded it with suspicion as Rosemarie had dismissed it as "silly," but I took a chance and launched into "All I Know." Art stood seemingly spellbound while I played the simple intro and then gradually increased the volume and intensity until the climactic last line.

There was a moment of uncertainty and then a smile broke out on his face.

"That's very good, Jim, *very good.*"

He peered through the control room window and Roy nodded

and emitted a puff of cherry-scented smoke from the pipe clenched between his teeth. They had been recording.

Art invited me back inside where the three of us listened to the rough performance of "All I Know" on the studio monitors. "I think we could make a hit out of that, don't you, Roy?" Art said. I was exploding internally with joy at my good fortune. It was a historic moment. "All I Know" would be Art's first hit single after the Simon and Garfunkel breakup.

I found a house I liked, called Campo de Encino, and Evie agreed to come give her mark of approval. As we drove downt the hill she looked at Van Nuys and laughed hysterically.

"Jimmy? The Valley? Really?"

When I showed her around the property she was duly impressed, though not everything was perfect. She didn't care for the bathroom upstairs.

"You need to put a tub right there," she said, pointing to the corner, "with a Jacuzzi and a bigger window." I called Jerry Rubenstein and told him to go ahead with escrow.

Rosemarie and I seemed helpless to do anything about our situation. We continued to meet in the aching, dramatic, and physically overwhelming atmosphere that permeates adultery like a bittersweet poison. Whenever she could see me she would.

We drove to Solvang, an ersatz Dutch village north of Santa Barbara, and browsed through the tourist shops, buying shell necklaces and faceted glass pieces from discarded chandeliers. We spent the night in a kitschy mid-California landmark called the Madonna Inn, drinking Champagne. At dawn we were out in the almost empty parking lot turning doughnuts in the Cobra and listening to *Son of Schmilsson*, singing along and laughing hysterically until security guards stopped us. We ran back to our room, where the nightstand phone was ringing.

It was Art Garfunkel. I looked into Rosemarie's eyes and felt the blood draining from my face. Artie was at a recording studio in Hollywood. He was perplexed because the string arrangements I was supposed to write for an 8 A.M. session didn't seem to be on hand, nor was there any sign of my copyist and it was almost time for the session to start. I could hear an orchestra tuning up in the background.

So potent was my preoccupation with Rosemarie (it was veering into mental illness), I had forgotten this recording session completely. There would be no arrangements for the musicians that morning and haltingly I began an apology that would last the rest of my life. What I had done was unpardonable. There isn't much a producer can do with a string orchestra that has no arrangements. In the dollars of the day that session was going to cost Artie around ten or fifteen grand at least. Lamely I offered to pay for the date. He ended the call abruptly and I couldn't blame him. How could I *forget* a string date? If such a story were circulated in town, it would hurt me.

Rosemarie and I jumped into the Cobra, drove south on the PCH, and parked in a turnout high over the immensity of the Pacific far below. Here the noise of swells colliding with burly boulders was muted and modulated by the onshore breeze.

"I love you, Rosemarie," I said.

"I love you, too, Jimmy."

As we stood, me with my foot up on a rock, Rosemarie with her arm around my shoulders, lost in the music of wind and wave, something extraordinary happened.

It started with a few birds circling unevenly a hundred yards out toward the sea and slightly south of us. Behind them the afternoon sun was partially obscured by a sudden massive cloud that sent shafts of golden light to the ground. More birds joined until there were perhaps a hundred individual birds circling a half mile out, their wings catching the irregular ministrations of direct sunlight and flashing an indecipherable code. I could feel it and knew Rosemarie felt it, too. Something was going to happen; exactly what I could not tell, but the gaggle of birds moved closer to shore and their increasingly excited cries became a suspenseful soundtrack. A hundred birds became a thousand. They broadened their circle into a sizeable noisy cloud. For reasons unfathomable, more arrived on the scene of what seemed a deliberate congregation. Their number had subtly grown to proportions Alfred Hitchcock would appreciate. There must have been ten thousand by then. It was a wide gyre of beating wings, quite close and circling like a typhoon, their shrill cries discouraging normal speech. We took an involuntary step back and almost into the path of another car that had pulled into the turnout to get a closer look at the huge massing of birds. Eerily, their numbers continued to multiply.

"Good Lord," I prayed.

"I've never seen anything like it," Rosemarie said, her voice small and thoughtful.

The living pillar had tripled and individual birds became hard to distinguish, as the swirling column seemed to be slowly revolving about a mile out to sea from wave top to cloud base. This might well have been all the birds on the coast all the way to San Francisco gathered together. Of course we assumed, as lovers will, that the whole thing had been laid on for our benefit by the angels. Eventually the mega-gaggle began to thin and birds fled in droves over our heads and away. It was the end of a most solemn convocation.

"Why don't we just break it clean?" she said to my sad surprise. "Entanglements make people unhappy and ruin so many happy memories. We have a chance to keep this clean and free of anything bad."

"Of course, you're right. We should do the adult thing." I bluffed bravely.

"You'll always be my Cloudman," she said, and kissed me sweetly.

1972

David Geffen called and asked if I would like to produce the Supremes. I thought Motown was a small receding speck in my rearview mirror and suddenly here they were with a dream project. The one little hang-up: Diana Ross was leaving the group to pursue a solo career. Well, of course! That's what successful groups do. It is so hard to come up with that elusive chemistry, that prime number that can't be divided by anything except itself, and when you have it—a virtual money machine—well, of course you break it.

Jean Terrell was a powerful singer, more from the Aretha Franklin mold of gospel influence than the "little voice" sound of Diana Ross who she was set to replace. Her brother was World Heavyweight Champion Ernie Terrell. Replacing Cindy Birdsong was Lynda Laurence. I heard a number of sides and demos by her and, satisfied that Mary Wilson was still on board I thought, why not? Perhaps we could rework the franchise and cut something that would take advantage of the singer-songwriter wave currently inundating the nation.

The girls didn't blink an eye when I walked in the first night with "All I Want" by Joni Mitchell. They were ready for changes to their traditional repertoire. I also had the hopeful "When Can Brown Begin?" The label wasn't looking over my shoulder so I ran with it. I worked the group hard. So hard in fact, that one night Jeanie came in with a note from her doctor. It was brief:

"Dear Mr. Webb, could you please refrain from requiring Miss Terrell to sing any notes above a high C? I believe she is damaging her vocal cords. Yours truly, Dr. So and So."

I laughed and looked at Jean and said, "You're puttin' me on, right?"

"If you think so," she said. "Next time I'll have my brother come over and 'splain it to ya."

Okay. I still wasn't getting the sound I needed. I called Darlene Love and she brought in Fanita James and Jean King and *now* the sound was fat. The Supremes backgrounds had never sounded so good. We finished it up and turned it over to the label. They promptly brought in Shirley Matthews and Deke Richards to produce a "single." This turned out to be Stephen Schwartz's lovely song "I Guess I'll Miss the Man." They turned it over to the art department.

The cover was a close-up of a dandelion puffball backlit by a setting sun. Now, if I wanted to call attention to a new album by a bunch of new Supremes I would put their goddamn pictures on the front of it and call it "The New Supremes." This product, almost impossible to recognize as a Supremes album, was called *The Supremes (Produced by Jimmy Webb)*. When I saw the cover, I knew it was a goner. The whole genetically engineered mess hit the floor like a chunk of lard. It achieved the lowest chart position in Supremes history: 129. So much for "When Can Brown Begin?" Even though the album scored a respectable twenty-seven on the Billboard R&B chart, none of my productions for this album were ever released as a single. Revisionists laud this album and say it was among the best of the Supremes but I'm sure that is not correct. There was only one real problem with it: it wasn't the Supremes.

1972

In September, *Letters,* my third album, was released. I had a new look on the sepia-toned *Letters* cover: a long beard, shoulder-length hair, and ungroomed mustache. This was not your father's Jimmy Webb. I had written a comical homage to Harry Nilsson called "Campo de Encino" (which he eventually recorded). I covered Glen Campbell's "Galveston" as an elegiac opening featuring a masterful, acoustic guitar intro by Fred Tackett. I covered a forgotten Everly Brothers album cut called "Love Hurts," written by the incomparable Boudleaux Bryant. (It would be recorded at least forty-seven more times by a wide range of artists.) "Simile" was a song I had written about the letter I sent to Joni Mitchell. "Once in the Morning" was a cocaine song, a satire on Freud's Rx to patients suffering "from the ennui"; he prescribed a dollop of coke "once in the morning and once at night." Freddy had written some punchy Stax/Volt horns for the track. In "Catharsis" I imagined I'd castigated an old friend who had betrayed me. I was the first artist in history to put the word "fuck" on record in a little ditty called "Song Seller," which took the piss out of the record industry:

> *I'll cut you a track that's truly truckin'*
> *If you want me to I'll sing about fuckin'*
> *Sing about it fast or sing about it slow*
> *I want to hear it on the radio though.*

Is it possible I was trying to do too much on a simple phonograph record? If true then I paid the price for it. There was a rumor Mr. Sinatra wasn't happy about the four-letter word I had put on "his" label. I was adamant about including the word "fuckin'" on the pressing in spite of real pushback from Warner. I needn't have worried. The future of foul language in pop music was in safe hands.

It probably doomed the album, in spite of positive reviews. The record did not "break out." Not one DJ dared play the unexpurgated version of "Song Seller," insider rock masterpiece or not. We went about the required tour, but came off the road tired and disillusioned.

When I got back home I told Susan Horton as nicely as I could that it was time for us to go our separate ways. I would take care of her finances for the time being and she shouldn't worry. My life was overburdened and careening out of control. My recordings, most of which Susan had sung background on with my sister, also named Susan, were critical successes but not hits. It didn't seem to be very important. I had another obsession. Just a short drive over Benedict Canyon was Sunset Boulevard, where Rosemarie lived.

Stained glass window at Campo de Encino. *(Courtesy of Janice Linnens)*

CHAPTER FIFTEEN

If I could do it over, there'd be some changes made
I'd paint with brighter colors, I'd stay out of the shade
I'd make everybody happy with the lessons
I have learned
I might not find the joy in life but I'd leave
no stone unturned
I'd leave no stone unturned
—JLW, "Sandy Cove," 1993

1969

I tried to buy the Camino Palmero house but it was not for sale, at any price. The whole street, a synoptic garden of silent film's golden hours, would fall under the wrecking ball. In their place would rise chockablock apartment buildings in the ticky-tacky style.

This tight commune, the interwoven braids of my hippie life-style, began to untangle. I bid farewell to the crew as each one shipped off.

I had never lived alone. I was ready for a clean house and, no matter how hard it was to endure, unblemished solitude. I found it two blocks away at the corner of Sunset and LaBrea, at the Hollywood Versailles, a Tom Brady Hail Mary from Grauman's Chinese Theatre. The Versailles was a gleaming new tower with panoramic floor-to-ceiling views of Franklin Ave. and the Hollywood Hills. I settled into the penthouse with a hospital-clean, stainless steel kitchen. The movers had to dismantle my windows and hoist the nine-foot Yamaha skyward with a giant crane. A crowd of onlookers gathered, perhaps in hope of a catastrophic musical sforzando. I held my breath as my only piece of furniture came floating into the living room nine floors above the beating heart of Hollywood.

When the nominations came out again for the Grammys it was a mixed blessing. Happily I was nominated for Best Orchestration Accompanying a Vocalist for "MacArthur Park." Glen Campbell was nominated for Album of the Year for *Wichita Lineman*. The committee in their wisdom—or for other reasons—had seen fit to omit either "Wichita" or "Mac Park" from the Song of the Year category. The songs that were chosen were "Little Green Apples" (Bobby Russell), "Harper Valley PTA" (Tom T. Hall), "Hey Jude" (Lennon and McCartney), "Honey" (Bobby Russell), and "Mrs. Robinson" (Paul Simon). In my opinion, Simon was the guy to watch. It was interesting that grizzled veteran Bobby Russell was facing the same quandary as I had the year before: He had two horses in the race. When I was a kid he had written "I Saw Mommy Kissing Santa Claus."

"MacArthur Park" had been an extraordinary record. Every time it was played on the radio I was paid for three song performances. Never before and not since would a "song" change the face of commercial radio in such a dramatic way. We had given The Beatles a sudden jolt. They rushed into the studio with George Martin and lengthened the fade on "Hey Jude" in order to make it over seven minutes (7:11). It was not a coincidence, George Martin told me. He said group members stood by the control desk at Abbey Road watching the VU meter and carefully dialed down the repetitious fade in "Hey Jude" in order to close the margin on the 7:21 of "Mac Park." The fade in "Hey Jude" had been lengthened by creating a tape loop.

I loved "Hey Jude." I remember dancing to it at Tramp with Evie draped around my neck. I think we first truly fell in love during that long fade.

1973

Rosemarie was involved in a traffic accident on Sunset Boulevard barely a half block from her house. A few reliable sources told me her husband and his friend, a doctor, had taken her to Hawaii for rest and recuperation. I was told she had received an injection to tranquilize her for the trip. This detail, for some reason, drove me right up the wall. I imagined she had been taken against her will, or in some serious condition. I became paralyzed. I rarely left the house and the immediate vicinity of my telephone on the off chance she might call me.

I went over every detail of every conversation she and I ever had with forensic concentration. I wrestled with the possibility that she might be gone for good, that it was all just a ruse to put me behind her. I drifted onto the downslope of insanity without even trying. One time I put the Vaughan Williams Symphony No. 6 on my turntable and turned up my Altec 604s as high as I could stand. I rang her and when the answering machine responded with a cheery greeting I left a recording of the warlike music in the first movement.

I stopped eating. I stared at the telephone. I talked to the damn thing. Weeks slipped by in a haze of marijuana smoke and doses of strong cocaine. I was losing weight. I could not move forward nor could I retreat. David Geffen called about the new record and I presume my response was incoherent. Soon afterward Sandy Gallin called good-naturedly wanting to know if I had lost my mind.

"Yes, I believe I have," I responded.

One night I opened a drawer in my bathroom hesitantly. Inside were two videos: *I'll Take Sweden* starring Bob Hope, and *A Hard Day's Night*. I watched the Bob Hope movie and recognized Rosemarie. She was a few years younger and seemed strangely immature. She cavorted in a bikini and laughed at Bob's painfully dumb jokes during a leering, innuendo-packed scenario that seemed hopelessly out of sync with current tastes. I watched it again. I didn't feel her there somehow. I watched *A Hard Day's Night* and eventually The Beatles arrived at the Ed Sullivan Theater for their big debut and there were some chorus girls about. Lovely, tall girls dressed in feathered headdresses and sequined costumes revealing perfectly tapered legs. I saw her on a backstage circular stairway in her avian costume and the ache was unbearable. I forwarded and reversed the videotape over and over. Up and down the stairway she went endlessly until I realized there was no way I could pull her out of the screen and hold her in a fluorescent embrace.

Then one day she called. She was as matter-of-fact as though she had just stepped out for a smoke on the patio. Yes, she was back and feeling much better. She was sorry she hadn't called but she had been watched. She had been held prisoner.

Prisoner? Yes, her husband had gone insane. That made two of us. I didn't care. She was alive and speaking, laughing, chirruping on the line. The color began to bleed back into the landscape. I looked around me. The surrounding area appeared to be the nesting place of a large raccoon. She offered to drive over but I put her off for a day in order to clean the place. It was inhuman the way she just dropped back into my life, apparently with no intimation or concern for the tailspin she had induced. Never mind. We were still on.

I got on the phone to David Geffen, who offered me a berth. I had already had my three bites at the solo album apple but it was no act of philanthropy on David's part. He thought I could do it. I asked him if he would be comfortable with Robin Cable, the affable and tireless first engineer on *Nilsson Schmilsson,* at the head of our new project. Robin would know the best English studios and musicians. David gave me the go-ahead. I became more animated as the electricity began to flow and the amperage increased. I began to consider dates and pencil in travel arrangements.

When Rosemarie got out to the house it was as though we had never parted. I could not let on how shattered I had been. We lounged by the pool, her favorite spot, and I tried to keep the conversation chipper and casual. Sometimes it was difficult.

"There must be hundreds of beautiful girls out there who would fall all over you," she opined while we sipped on mimosas. "Why don't you find someone a little less complicated?" This mix of sophistication and placidity in regard to a sensation that burned in my breast like a white-hot poker almost unhinged me.

"Hmm." I pondered calmly. "Maybe I'll just do that. I could find someone younger as well."

She turned the pitcher of mimosas over my head. I jumped into the pool to escape and it became a water fight and then a laugh fest and eventually lovemaking. I asked her what she wanted for dinner and she said, as though setting me an impossible task, "I want a three-pound lobster from the Palm!"

It was twenty miles away and at least an hour through the predinner rush. This was complicated by the fact that the Palm absolutely and without exception refused to prepare food to go. I called up Don Gee at Starlight Limousine.

"Don!"

I could all but see his heels clicking together as he saluted. He had mastered the art of smiling on the telephone, realizing one can actually hear a smile over the line.

"Yes, sir. What can I do for you this evening?"

"Don, I want you to go over to the Palm and sit down in a booth. I want you to order dinner on me. Order *two* three-and-a-half-pound lobsters steamed and then broiled. Order creamed spinach and chop/chop salad. Eat one of the lobsters. Have them put the rest in a pooch bag and bring it over to the ranch."

"Yes, sir," he replied briskly. "Immediately, sir." Click.

The story got around. People would come up to me at a party somewhere and ask, "Did you really . . . ?" Uh-huh.

1969

The release of "Galveston" was a great housewarming gift in Encino and another hit for Glen Campbell, who was by then becoming a small industry. It went to number four on the top ten. The record also prompted a letter from the mayor of Galveston, Texas. It was an invitation to serve as Grand Marshal at the Shrimp Festival and Parade on the small island just off the Gulf Coast of southeast Texas. It was an area haunted by the ghosts of Jean and Pierre Lafitte, who had held illegal slave auctions on the island in the early 1800s. Generations of storytellers had greatly inflated the Lafittes' reputations as brave fighters and "swashbucklers." The island was also famous for surviving Isaac's Storm, a horrific hurricane and tidal wave that had demolished the prosperous, bustling city in September of 1900, killing at least eight thousand people, most of whom drowned.

I don't know why I said yes. It was a nonpaying gig and there was no concert to justify the time it would consume out of my schedule. I suppose I was infected with the first symptoms of hubris; the idea of being cheered by a crowd of thousands became irresistible. In my single-mindedness I selected from my wardrobe a Pierre Cardin spacesuit, a tartan in gray, green, and red featuring a long coat and his odd circular zippered collar.

I flew down to Galveston unescorted, and was greeted at the airport by a committee of local dignitaries whose collective jaws dropped at the sight of me in my round shoulder collar, festooned with nickel-plated zippers and pull rings. They couldn't take their eyes off my hair, no doubt the longest they had ever seen in the real. Once a couple of them had replaced their false uppers and got over the initial shock, we began to discuss the master plan for the day's activities. The working shrimpers of Galveston, in that day quite numerous, would parade their festive decked-out workboats past a reviewing stand where I would be observing. Good. No problem. I would be presented with the keys to the city and photos would be taken. A simple task. Then I would move to the rear seat of a Cadillac convertible joined by Miss Shrimp Boat Festival, a lush coed to whom I was elaborately introduced. Being a proper Southern belle she disguised any surprise she may have felt for my spaced-out costume. We would be together for a few precious moments, waving to the crowd that would line the parade route. I would be on my way back to Los Angeles by nightfall.

The day was partly cloudy and mostly fair so I reacted with sheer delight when they told me I would be riding to the reviewing stand on my own speedboat. The good ol' boys and I went east to a pier a few miles down the shore of Galveston Bay. Tied up there was a hellacious-looking drag boat with a fully chromed Dodge Hemi engine exposed behind the two bucket seats perched precariously on the prow. On the stern was proudly emblazoned in red flaming letters: *Hellstar.*

The guys were surprised to see me clamber eagerly aboard and secure myself with no assistance. The mayor introduced me to my driver, Tiny, an affable giant who seemed to downscale everyone and everything he touched. The aluminum steering wheel on the drag boat shrunk to the diameter of a coffee saucer in his hands as big as hams. With a sudden eruption of white smoke and a sound like an ill-synchronized firing squad, the massive power plant ripped into action with the loping gait of a full race cam. Tiny fed her spurts of gas to keep her running as the fellows on shore gave a gigantic shove and we drifted away from the dock on waters that were as placid as a goldfish pond. The boat turned into a trace of a breeze and started west along the coast, Tiny slowly but surely edging up the throttle.

It is a unique experience to be strapped to the front of a waterborne missile straining to leave the wet surface. My long hair blew back past my ears and began to tie itself into interesting knots. We ran out from behind a protective promontory and into a chop, which—at our speed—caused my teeth to chatter uncontrollably.

"Well, Jimmy, should we stop pokin' along here?" Tiny asked with an innocent grin.

"Hell yes," I said in my gruff voice, putting on my Southern accent. "Let's stop pokin' around." He shoved the throttle up to about eighty-five percent and *Hellstar* lunged forward into warp drive, taking short flights above the water and free-falling back with bone-rattling jolts and spouts of spume and foam. "Soaked to the skin" is more than a cliché. It is a precise physical moment when clothing reaches its maximum moisture absorption level and the body loses its ability to maintain a normal, life-sustaining temperature. Tiny looked at me with his disingenuous grin and asked, "Yokay?"

"Ungggg," I said through clenched teeth, nodding. He delivered me to the waters off downtown Galveston looking like a thrice-drowned rodent, long hair plastered to my skull, clothing steaming slightly as a hot sun broke from behind a cloud. I submitted to being helped ashore by the mayor as Galvestonians gazed upon their poet laureate. For the most part they were impassive. There was a palpable atmosphere of disappointment. This was it? This was the guy who wrote the song? Their kids turned away, bored.

I sat on the reviewing stand with Miss Shrimp Boat Festival, watching the fleet pass in review and attempting to rehabilitate myself with a sheaf of paper towels Tiny shoved helpfully into my hand. Galveston was largely a blue-collar environment. They looked at me with an unmistakable challenge in their gaze. It was the unspeakable "who are you to profit by us?" I looked just like the kind of fool who had never done a lick of work in my life. Too late to change into jeans and a Pendleton shirt, however. I began to think seriously about how far I had drifted from the agrarian authenticity of my youth. At the same time I was defensive. I had worked hard for every goddamn thing I had achieved. I was the captain of my own vessel. I fished for a different animal, but it was certainly no easier to haul aboard. Thus, mentally reconstructed, I accepted the keys to the city to a smattering of applause and entered the Cadillac with Miss Shrimp Boat and big Tiny driving. We joined a cordon of fire trucks, marching bands, and policemen on motorcycles to drive slowly down Galveston's main street.

At first I thought I was hearing things. I thought my survivor's guilt had finally wrested away control of my innermost helm.

"Hippie asshole." I felt something rattle against the paper cup of water I held in my hand.

"Go back where you came from, sissy." Something hit me right on top of the head and then bounced into Miss Shrimp Boat's coif where it was clearly visible. The mutterings of mutiny were all too real. It was a shrimp. Suddenly it became the thing to do. Pelt the songwriter with prawns, everyone! Shrimp began to arc over the crowd and fall into the backseat of the Cadillac.

"Welcome to Galveston!" A whole cup of boiled shrimp landed in my lap. I became concerned for the welfare of my escort who had committed no crime except to sit in the same car with me. I leaned forward and talked mean to Tiny.

"Get us out of here before someone gets hurt."

"Yokay." Tiny grinned.

Miss Shrimp Boat Festival was on the verge of tears.

At the end of the parade route I gallantly kissed my queen on the cheek, disengaged myself from my hosts politely, and quickly as possible escaped from the greater Galveston area. I never wore a Pierre Cardin suit or scarf again. Ever.

1973

Rosemarie decided one day out of the blue that everything would be fine and she could see a future for us but only if we lived at the beach. If she thought this would discourage my ardency she miscalculated. I drove her down to Malibu and checked into a nice hotel on Carbon Beach and spent the afternoon on the phone setting up real estate appointments.

The next day we saw five houses. Rosemarie went over these different offerings with concentrated precision. I offered no resistance. I even managed to show a little enthusiasm for these overpriced gilded cages. I remember looking at one particularly elaborate mansion that was tagged at an outrageous $400,000. It was the one Rosemarie wanted. Today that four hundred grand would probably not pay the property taxes.

"Let's get it, doll!" I exulted, taking her into my arms. "If it makes you happy!" I called Jerry Rubinstein and told him I was putting Campo on the market and buying a beach house. He was stunned but he didn't argue with me. He started putting together an offer and a loan.

That night we were watching television in bed as the ocean chanted through the open balcony doors at the hotel. A caressing breeze toyed with the curtains and then subsided. Rosemarie arose from the bed slowly and calmly. She picked up the telephone and ordered a cab. I could only watch. She took her street clothes out of the closet, cast her sleeping gown into her bag, and got dressed.

"You're leaving again."

She said nothing, just closed her overnight case and checked her Louis Vuitton tote bag to make sure she had everything. She walked over to my side of the bed and sat down on the mattress. She gave me a sad smile and kissed me sweetly on the cheek. She walked out and closed the door softly, leaving me miles from my own bed on that lonely beach. There was finality to her silent good-bye. I lay there for a while and then stoically put my shit together and checked out. When I got back to Campo I called Jerry Rubinstein.

"Jer. You know that beach house thing?"

"I'm working on it."

"Don't," I said, and hung up.

I didn't hate her. I loathed myself for being such a schoolboy. Nobody makes a fool of anybody, country music notwithstanding. Fools are volunteers and when the dust settles they have no one to blame, no lawyer, no sympathy, and no recourse.

I hired a yacht out of Marina del Rey: a symbolic voyage to celebrate the ending of such a brutal affair. Gary Kellgren, who owned the Record Plant, had been talking about the possibility of taking a recording studio to sea as a business venture. I frequently chartered a small ship called *Magnifico*, a World War II hospital ship, the sister ship of John Wayne's famous *Wild Goose*. Kellgren decided we would put a studio on board and take her on a trial voyage. In my unfettered state I jumped at the project and made further preparations for my album with David Geffen. Enough howling at the moon. I became a proponent of Ava Gardner's famous theorem: "Love is nothing."

It had taken two full days to install the studio aboard ship and waterproof everything. The handsome, unflappable Gary Kellgren (with his briar pipe clenched in his teeth) joined Harry Nilsson, Micky Dolenz, Garth Sadler Webb, Jesse Ed Davis, and other legendary sidemen. My father and his new lovely girlfriend were there. The boat's owner, an ex-con named Rick Compton, was at the helm and backing him was his faithful first mate and cabin valet Sid. A dozen berths were filled with nameless souls who are lost to this feeble memory, but many of them were exceedingly beautiful girls.

Spirits were high when we shipped out for Avalon on Catalina one sunny afternoon. We were somehow convinced we were making history. Margaritas were traditional on the *Magnifico* and virtually the entire crew had one as we exited the tight network of slips and pilings and headed west through the outer harbor, huge man-made jetties a half mile apart on either side. Kellgren's playback system cranked into life at plane crash volume, rendering Eric Clapton's forbidding version of "Cocaine." A cheer went up on the boat. All scientific considerations aside, this was going to be one hell of a party.

Under ideal conditions we found recording at sea was not so hard. We recorded in the gentle swell, a test track whose basis was a publishing discovery by Kellgren called "Mothertrucker." There were some conflicts between the noise of auxiliary generators and soundproofing but nothing that could not be solved in a prototype. Both the vessel and the players rocked gently.

That evening the entire crew went ashore using various forms of transportation, including a monstrous Boston Whaler, as Kellgren and I chartered a small restaurant on the waterfront. Compton had left the ship—all sixty-two tons of her—securely anchored and, to discourage intruders, with the television in the main salon on and turned up loud. Lights burned everywhere there was a lightbulb. It seemed to my rudimentary maritime judgment that someone should have been left on watch, but I wasn't the skipper.

We tucked into the catch of the day and ordered bottles of wine for twenty people. I am sure we made a serious dent in their cellar. Kellgren also brought along his famous Igloo cooler, a tiny thing that held a bottle of iced Champagne and a quart of fresh orange juice, baking soda, and cocaine at all times. There was a particular ritual associated with these items but not one that would be demonstrated in a public place.

Ribald stories were told, laughter in ripples dominated the conversation of our intrepid adventurers. It was easy to get lost in overlapping accounts of studio lore featuring all the big players: Lennon, Jagger, Clapton, and other members of Kellgren's glittering clientele.

Suddenly Compton roared, "*Shit!*" The veins on his big bull neck were about to explode. "The friggin' boat is loose!"

A glance out the picture window revealed the lights of the *Magnifico* just disappearing over the horizon. All the guys piled out the front door in a mob leaving the ladies to settle the astronomical bill. Half of us jumped into the swift Boston Whaler with its 70 hp Mercury engine and took off chasing our home, our belongings, and a quarter-million-dollars' worth of recording gear. The Whaler was a rubber inflatable that tended to bounce over the water. With each bounce most of us caught a mouth full of the old briny. We closed with the *Magnifico* quickly.

"We have to be careful here," Compton warned in a hoarse yell. "If there are people aboard they could be armed. This could be a drug deal."

He cut the throttle and we came up gingerly on the big flat stern with its proud name.

"The boarding ladder's still down," I contributed, thinking of all the exotic weapons I had in my cupboard in Encino. That's the problem with lethal arms. You can never find one when you need one.

"She's not making way. She's in the tide," asserted Compton. The currents in the Catalina channel are notorious for their strength and unpredictability. We crept up by the boarding ladder, engine idling, and Compton hopped on board. We waited uneasily, half anticipating a ruckus until Compton's hulking silhouette appeared at the top of the ladder.

"Sid! Come aboard and get down to the engine room. Let's get power on this bastard before we hit something! You guys come on up. This is just a case of incompetency." He shot the long-suffering Sid a look that would shrivel bacon as he passed him at the top of the ladder and the rest of us trooped aboard. A subdued captain guided us back into the Harbor where we retied ourselves to the mooring with several newly minted experts looking on. With everyone back aboard it was grass and booze and a little coke and then, quite late in the morning, there was bed. My father was aboard but shunned the drug use and stayed in his cabin. We brought our languorous Hollywood schedule with us.

LIVING WELL IS THE BEST REVENGE, Lou Adler had printed on his business cards. I thought of Rosemarie as I drifted off and re-solved that I would savor my share of that revenge.

I was awakened by the smell of scrambled eggs and bacon. There were a dozen people lounging on the stern and eating breakfast. Down below someone was playing "Mothertrucker" on the console and seemed to be doing a rough mix. I heard the soloing of indi-vidual instruments and the repetition of certain sections, part of the ordinary studio routine but nevertheless remarkable on a spar-kling blue ocean.

After a few minutes the engines rumbled and the keel shivered for a moment as the big Cats came on line. I walked up to the bridge and saw Compton hunched over the chart table, my favorite part of the ship. We would head north out of the San Pedro Channel and, just skirting Santa Monica Bay on our starboard beam, make for the Anacapa Islands, three big rocks—one with a lighthouse—about seventy miles north by northwest of our position. These rocks were the gateway to the Santa Cruz Islands: Cruz, Rosa, and Miguel, each one an uninhabited ecological treasure. It was a playground to those who knew its secrets.

I went to the portside rail and looked over to see my father steer-ing a little boat up to the boarding ladder. In the early morning he and his pretty date had gone fishing. Their skiff was filled with enough fish to feed everybody aboard. At least three yellowtail tuna in the fifteen- to twenty-pound range and a half-dozen cod, some of them distended by the difference in pressure when they were hauled up from two hundred feet or deeper.

Once aboard, Pop stripped off his shirt, borrowed a butcher knife out of the kitchen, and began the task of turning the fish into seafood on the swim step. He had a stomach of iron and he carved his way through the shocking disembowelment with a smile on his face as a crowd formed among the passengers, many who had never seen a spectacle of such forensic interest. Harry was paler than I've ever seen him.

"Jimmy, I mean no offense, but your father is a fucking barbar-ian." He spit on his way to the head where he spent quite a long time.

Later, I was at the helm with the skipper when Gary came flying through the door.

"There's something back here, man. You have to come check this out!" His voice was high and excited. Virtually everybody on board was focused on something in our wake. It was not something in the sea they were pointing at, but something above water. A disc-shaped object was about a thousand yards off our stern, floating a thousand feet above the water. The upper surface of the disc had a domelike swelling that blended gently into its smooth round shape. Most of the people on that deck were half in the bag already. We were as unreliable and unqualified a band of dopers and alcoholics as one could have amassed on the whole West Coast and in no sense do I expect this story to meet with even polite skepticism; and yet it was there, calm as cheese, and we were there, crazy and giddy, but seeing it.

I took it to be about forty or fifty feet in diameter at least, with a possible one hundred. That it was following us was undeniable. Compton stood there, and Kellgren and Harry and I just grinned at one another. Sure. Why not?

Champagne was opened and guests began to drink toasts to the "spacemen" and to talk to them as though they were alongside. This took a disturbing turn.

"Why don't you just come over here and kiss my ass?" one of the second engineers shouted out.

"Yeah, fuck you guys from outer space. Chomp on this!" somebody else said, and it quickly became a vulgar display of human manners culminating in the dropping of pants and the mooning of fellow voyagers in violation of the most ancient rules of maritime courtesy.

It seemed as though in a huff, the effortlessly agile craft disappeared in a straight line over the scruffy ridge of Santa Catalina. The party doubled down on this departure. Comments meant to be amusing were launched such as: "That'll show the little green bastards." Or, "C'mon down and have a snort, shorty, join the party?" Finally there was a shout twice as loud as all the rest: "Fuck you, interstellar assholes with your little gray dicks! Invade us already!"

The disc cruised back slowly, only nearer. The merrymaking ceased. I ran toward the bridge where Sid was tending our course.

"Is the radar on?" I asked even as I saw it was. There was a sizeable blip four hundred yards off our stern and trailing us. There was abject silence on the stern, only the sound of wind, waves, and the grumbling diesels. Our vaunted white yacht was not even a toy compared to this thing, whatever it was.

The brief interval of involuntary communion ended suddenly. My ears popped and the miracle was gone. It darted away in classic UFO fashion, disappearing over the island in a starting display of technical superiority. Ours was a tough audience indeed but even my irrepressible shipmates were subdued by these events. The crew drifted into small groups and conversed quietly, glancing at the sky occasionally.

By sunset we could see Anacapa light and no wonder. All aboard crowded to the bow, undaunted by spray and wind to see the three short flashes of white light separated by almost forty seconds of darkness until the three dashes were repeated again. We passed by the Anacapa Islands and moved toward Santa Cruz, a gigantic undecipherable shadow. The lighthouse faded behind in a corona of Joseph Conrad's "opaline mist" suffusing its probing beam, and then we passed beyond as though entering another world, reering west toward the big island of Santa Cruz. It was getting late, at least ten o'clock, and still we powered into the night looking for Devil's Cove, a spectacular landscape of beach and cavernous rocks on the south shore.

I started out of a nap on the big bench seat at the back of the wheelhouse. "There it is," said Compton, examining the radar intently. He held a big fat thumb up against the fiery image that illuminated once every thirty seconds as the radar signal made its sweep.

With a lot of shouting, a little cursing, and much backing off of the anchor to ensure it was firmly buried, we came to rest. The insistent vibration of the engines ceased. Placidity descended over the craft as we watched the surf glowing with phosphorescence some distance away. An acoustic guitar materialized above decks and Jesse Ed Davis played "Blackbird" and variations. Steaks hit the grill in the galley and a pipe was passed around, rich with aromatic, honey-flavored hash. Smoke drifted. It was chilly above decks and sweaters proliferated among those who hadn't already collapsed in sleep.

The skipper had found a calm spot in the lee of one of the island's outthrust haunches. As the ship's systems were powered down and only essential lighting remained, the evening softened further into the flicker of lighters and glow of candles and cigarettes and joints. Voices ceased their cacophonous silliness and became a murmur that rose and fell with the swells, disturbed only by the odd wiseass remark and disembodied laughter from somewhere far forward.

I found Kellgren sitting in a chair on the poop with his little Igloo cooler. In these surroundings its workings could be revealed. Gary took a pinch of baking soda and placed it under his front lip like a chaw of tobacco. To this was added a healthy line of top-quality cocaine. There was an immediate chemical reaction between the two accelerated by a shot of Champagne held in the mouth and then purged by orange juice. This process, as far as I know his exclusive invention, would supercharge the alkaloid directly through the membranes of one's mouth into the bloodstream. I indulged in the experiment with mixed emotions. Cocaine was already becoming a problem for me. Making it more potent was something I shied away from. I was doing my best to "manage" a problem that was overtaking me anyway.

I went to sleep in my private stateroom. I had a tiny sink and two bunk beds but I didn't invite anybody inside. I still thought about Rosemarie at the most inopportune moments. She had a way of invading my thoughts whenever I saw a very pretty girl.

The sun was high when I awoke to a clamor of seagulls at the stern. One by one the beguiled travelers came awake in a wonderland from the dust jacket of a Jules Verne novel. The vampire kings and queens of Hollywood's night life stood on deck with mugs of wickedly strong black coffee and gaped at the opening shot of some gothic horror tale or better yet, the lair of King Kong.

The *Magnifico* was precariously close to the island. The scarred, cracked face of the cliff was only perhaps fifty yards away. When I stepped up on the deck I was in the middle of a silent crowd lining the railings. They all stared intently at something high above us on the face of the cliff.

"Jesus," I heard someone whisper under their breath. I pulled my glasses out of my pocket and suddenly the world was clearer. My father was on the island near the top of the cliff. He was free-handing his way down the flat rock wall just beneath the crest. He had no tether rope or even proper clothing. He was in a pair of shorts and a T-shirt. He was splayed out like a spider feeling for his next toehold.

"What in fucking hell is he doing?" I asked Harry, who was watching beside me.

"Shhhh!" Harry silenced me. "He's going after the baby goat, get it?"

I looked farther down the cliff perhaps fifteen or twenty feet and discerned a white ball of fluff, which might have been a house cat, huddled in a niche between two rocks. The animal was wedged in with no way up and a nasty fall in the other direction.

As I watched, my dad's foot slipped and his bare sole frantically searched for substance on the crumbly wall. Pebbles rained down in a miniature rockslide.

"Oooh!" the Greek chorus chanted in unison.

Dad found a foothold.

"Ahhh!" the spectators reacted with approval.

"Baaaah!" the kid bleated. It was very young and apparently help-less. Other goats were looking down from above. One in particular bleated constantly. The mother, I presumed.

My mouth was open to say, "Be careful, Dad!" but nothing came out. I watched him crab his way down the rock face wondering just what the hell he was going to do when he got down there. He would end up being trapped on a cliff. He worked his way slowly down from the summit at least twenty feet and finally secured himself in a kind of crouch right next to the tiny animal.

The kid made no attempt to escape capture. Dad reached out and scooped him up. Now he would have to climb up the sheer cliff with one arm. Nobody on the deck moved or spoke. I gripped the railing hard.

Dad set out. On the way up he would have to be doubly con-cerned with his points of purchase as losing his footing would almost certainly result in a fall. If that were to happen I presumed he intended to kick out and try to land in the ocean.

There was something epic in my father's climb up the rugged cliff with a baby goat in one arm. It was biblical somehow and reminded me of the old Baptist hymn "The Ninety and Nine." I prayed fervently that he would come to no harm. Notch by notch he groped his way upward using his free hand and feeling for support on the rock face. He shifted the little goat slightly one time but otherwise held it firmly in the crutch of his arm. At last, clinging to the top of the cliff, Dad passed the kid up to its mother. It walked away unsteadily but very much alive.

A great cheer went up on the yacht. I looked at Dad clambering up to safety. His reaction to the applause, if any, was invisible. I was not surprised by what he did. I was surprised that he was physically able to do it. It reminded me again that we do not know each other. None of us know any of us. Art Garfunkel said to me once, in a philosophical mood, "Jim, we are either completely like other human beings to the extent that there is no difference in the way we perceive life, the taste of wine, experience love, et cetera, or we are so essentially different from any other human being as to make a comparison impossible."

I only know this: To this day I do not know my father and would not claim to. I love him and respect him but I can in no way account for his behavior. All my life he would surprise me, sometimes for better and sometimes for worse. Never was a son more like a father in appearance and temperament. And yet we do not know each other.

Rev. Webb was brought aboard to hugs and kisses from all the pretty girls. After a day, we upped anchor and Compton backed us away from the rocky, threatening shore. The engines came to life and we made our way south. And so at about ten o'clock that night he steered the great white yacht *Magnifico* slowly down the channel at Marina del Rey like a ghost ship in the pearlescent ground fog that had suddenly materialized. One of our voyages had come to an end.

Ringo Starr and Jimmy Webb, London. *(Courtesy of Garth Sadler)*

CHAPTER SIXTEEN

For while it's true that the unexamined life
is not worth living,
it's also the case that the unlived life
is not worth examining.
—Robert McKee, 1997

1969

On March 15 I appeared on *Playboy After Dark,* chatted with
Hugh Hefner, and played a couple of songs. We got along well and
I found myself invited to "the mansion" in Beverly Hills on several
occasions. I usually went with high hopes of coming away with a
bunny or two but it quickly became obvious that the bunnies were
private stock and they weren't going anywhere, nor were they about
to invite some songwriter for a romp in the high-security area
upstairs or the darkened grotto, a popular feature of the pool. It

was never intimate. The mansion was always crowded with a few significant stars and a plurality of fringies crowded together like sardines in a can. A federal probe was in progress into alleged drug use at the mansion. We were told politely not to bring any. Often a current movie would be shown and we were actually expected to sit there and watch the damn thing. One night after a screening Hef asked me if I would be interested in scoring a picture and I assured him it was a subject never very far from my mind.

At the beginning of April one of the most influential records of the era was released by Simon and Garfunkel. The epic song "The Boxer" was a new kind of record that to my ear went beyond Spector's Wall of Sound. It was just as big but cleaner. The lyric hints at more than it reveals. To hear it is to walk into a movie and sit down somewhere in the middle of the show and then try to piece the plot together. I wanted to make records like that.

Against my better judgment I consented to appear on *The Dating Game*. Three bachelors sat on one side of a screen and a young girl sat on the other. The young girl proffered inane questions and each of "us guys" gave even sillier responses in hopes of winning the maid's favor and a free date, usually to Disneyland or Sea-World. I was the "secret" guest star. I didn't expect to win nor did I try very hard. Imagine my shock when she picked me. Imagine my distress when the "date" turned out to be a trip to Rome for a week. I swallowed hard and agreed to fly to Rome in the middle of a busy recording and writing routine. The young lady was pleasant to look at and had an outgoing personality. Once in Rome I found that far beyond a mere television promotion she looked on the trip as a kind of honeymoon. I had to be on the lookout for her in the long nights. Her chaperone was useless.

I found to my immense dismay that *Dating Game* had planned every second of our sojourn. We were on camera each day, visiting the Spanish Steps, Saint Peter's, the Trevi Fountain, and Alfredo alla Scrofa's golden spoon. After a couple of days I threw a star fit and started scheduling my own activities. It was a long and awkward week. Since I last saw her at the airport, I have neither seen nor heard from my date.

1973

By midyear if I wasn't snorting coke I was looking for some. Garth did most of the driving because I was wound up too tight. Far from the sophisticated party scene it was an ongoing cycle of binging on the stuff at night, drinking hard to blot out reality, and finally falling into bed with no real memory of going to sleep. To begin to function the next morning it was necessary to snort a line, and the cycle would begin again.

One morning I decided I wanted to drive. I went out to the garage where the Cobra waited patiently in its customized gold metal flake and light blue. I popped into the cockpit and turned the small key. The mill cranked over energetically at first but didn't catch. By the third attempt at starting, the battery was dead. I went up to the guesthouse and awakened Garth. He came down half asleep and helped me roll the machine out of the garage and point it down the steep driveway. I got in and he gave me a shove. It rolled off slowly, but by the time I got to the curve at the bottom of the driveway we were doing about thirty. Just before we hit the turn I popped the clutch in first gear and it farted a couple of times and died again.

I was in a rage. Cocaine is renowned for making users feel with an intensity that transcends the ordinary bounds of human emotion. The unbridled anger that comes with it has gotten a lot of people beaten senseless or killed. It could be said I wasn't in my right mind when I told Garth to bring his Camaro down the driveway to give me a pushing start. When he got there he took a hard look at the rear end of the Cobra and the front end of the Camaro.

"These bumpers are not a match. No way."

"Push this motherfucker until it fires up!"

He shrugged and slowly walked back and got into the Camaro. As gently as he could, he began pushing the Cobra along Encino Avenue. The Cobra fussed and backfired trying to start but more than likely the plugs were fouled or the timing was off or both.

We got to the corner and I waved at him and sat in the car seething. He parked and walked up to me.

"Uh, dude, you better have a look at what's going on back here." The bumper tubing was bent like a pretzel. There were spiderweb cracks in the gloss coat.

"God-fucking-damn it!" I looked up to heaven and challenged the lightning bolts. I could barely breathe; I was choked with fury.

"We'll try it once more," I said through clenched teeth, walking in tight circles, looking for something to attack.

I took my place in the car I loved so much, completely out of control.

"Faster, this time!" I yelled, without turning my head.

With a sickening grinding noise Garth eased into the Cobra again and I turned the corner.

"Faster, goddamn it!" I yelled, and with an occasional unavoidable bump he pushed me up to near fifty miles an hour on the long straight. The Cobra, as though in shock, had given up on trying to start, the proud motor just going through the motions. I coasted to a stop and pulled over to a grassy shoulder and parked her well off the street under some trees. I walked back to Garth's car without even looking at the obscene point of contact. I was no less incensed, but my fury had frozen into an icy wall.

He drove us home and I went to the stairs. I closed the heavy soundproof door at the bottom and went up to my room. I lay down on the bed and wept. The Cobra went back to Mike Fennel's.

Soon after, Garth and I shipped out for England and the new album. We moved into a mews house with a gated courtyard in Mayfair called Three Kings Yard. The flat was expansive for London with a living room and a roomy kitchen downstairs, a full bath and two bedrooms upstairs. I wouldn't have minded living there for the rest of my life.

Aside from California oranges and some albums, almost everything we brought remained in our suitcases. Within a few hours we had the telephone number of a lady nicknamed Chalita, who lived in Soho. Jesse Ed Davis and Harry Nilsson had agreed that this was the best connection in London. With the help of Chalita, my self-abuse continued unabated.

I met with Robin Cable for curry at a local Indian restaurant to talk about logistics. He mentioned almost straight off the bat that after *Son of Schmilsson* he had been involved in a very serious motorcycle accident. He still looked a little spaced out; he was forgetful and clumsy with his cutlery. He confessed his hearing had been affected for a little while but that he was now "back in fine fettle" and raring to get in the studio. I went back to the mews house seriously concerned.

We started cutting tracks with some of Elton John's favorite players: Nigel Olsson, drummer; Davey Johnstone, guitar; Dee Murray on bass; and Brian "Badger" Hodges, acoustic. Most of the rhythm dates took place at Trident. It so happened that Harry and Ringo Starr came by the sessions on occasion and the idea was floated that maybe Ringo would play on a couple of songs. This sounded good but I didn't take it too seriously. One afternoon I walked into the Trident control room and a very famous drum kit was sitting front and center. On the bass drum was the famous logo: THE BEATLES.

Ringo had come by to play, after getting his kit down from the rafters of the garage, by his account. He sat down and Robin asked him to hit his snare. Usually a half-dozen solid smacks on the snare would be enough to satisfy the most persnickety engineer and a few adjustments would be made. In a rare case perhaps a piece of tape would be laid across the drum or sometimes an object (Hal Blaine used his wallet) to achieve a muting effect. Instead, Robin rushed out and relocated all the microphones on the snare. Ringo whacked on that snare for two hours. Every drum was subject to the same rigorous testing standards. It took hours to tune the bass drum and adjust the mikes. Ringo sat patiently, thumping away with his foot. Sometimes he would come into the booth and look at me forlornly. When Robin bustled out to adjust yet another microphone he would lodge a gentle protest.

"Jim, why am I just whackin' me drums?" he asked with a little smile.

"I'm embarrassed, man. I will see if I can hurry him along." I blushed deeply.

"You know he's had a mash-up on his motorcycle?" Ringo asked, tapping his temple.

"Yeah, I've heard."

At last we were able to finish a basic track on "Walk Your Feet in the Sunshine" with Ringo playing a brilliant part, but in the process we lost him. He walked out of the studio amiably but determined not to do any more drum whacking. I went home that night grinding my teeth. If we could have just gotten our foot out, there was a slim chance he would have done the whole record with me.

We struggled along, and tackled the title piece and most ambitious track on the album, "Asleep on the Wind." We booked the Music Centre in Wembley, known then as DeLean Ley, a room that could easily hold a hundred musicians. Robin and I envisioned the largest recording session of modern times. It would be a kind of Berlioz super-orchestra with three pianos, three drummers, eight guitars, forty strings, twenty brass and woodwinds just to start. I checked with David Geffen personally before setting off and he okayed it. He believed there was a reason for me to make that record. He expected a return.

I began laying the arrangement out in the living room at Three Kings Yard. The prelude to the song was as long as a main title for a major motion picture. Thirty full orchestra pages were spread out on the living room floor in order to create a rough plan. I wrote a classically influenced tone poem depicting a sinking ship in a tumultuous sea, sending out a last desperate S.O.S., and this was merely the intro. A couple of weeks and several grams of coke later, the pages started going off to the copyist.

The day of the super session finally dawned. The little bar in the lobby of the studio was overflowing with string players long before start time. The rhythm section had been called early and I was already rehearsing them as Robin frantically fiddled with the control desk attempting to create a cohesive rhythm sound out of a score of rockers. The booth at the Music Centre is suspended above the hangar-like studio and looks down on the entire orchestra. On this day the view was awe inspiring from above as a forest of double basses took their places, and were joined by fifty-odd violins and violas. A host of cello players were seated with a special dignity. The French horn players uncased their shiny instruments along with the other brass in a field of open bells. A copse of woodwinds grew near

the podium on my right. Directly beneath the booth were three concert grand pianos and expansive drum kits surrounded by a music
store full of amplifiers for the eight guitarists. I mounted the podium with a strange calm. I thought about Rosemarie and how she
would laugh if she could see me in this situation. How she would
tease me and ask, "Don't you think you're overdoing the maestro
bit?" I was not partial to batons and usually conducted with my
hands but with this great host in front of me I opted for a modest
baton. I raised it. I carved the first beat.

A "clam" is a composing or copying mistake that causes a discor-
dant blot in a music passage. There were few of these if any as we
embarked on the dramatic voyage of "Asleep on the Wind," the title
derived from a line of dialogue by Tennessee Williams. I was immaculately prepared and the orchestra treated me with a gratifying
courtesy. There were no snarky asides about fingering or voicing. I
had made no mistakes in transposition, so the much-feared unplay-
able note did not materialize. I didn't hear one virtuoso crossly mut-
tering under his breath about the dubious location of the downbeat.
It went so quickly and so well it was almost over before I knew it. I
stepped off the podium sweating and emptied out. All of the Rosemarie music was recorded. There were other exertions ahead, but
the great labors of orchestration and tracking were behind me.

I invited Joni over to sing on a track and remarkably she came
and brought her D-18 with her. She sat in the living room at King's
Yard and played songs that were works in progress. I watched her
hands, her eyes, her fingers, and listened with unrelenting absorption. She allowed me to glance at some of her notebooks where
lyrics were written and copied and recopied. Her method was, to put
it simply, extensive and concentrated rewriting. Version after version of the same lyric would be tried, verses sometimes crossed out
completely and then re-created. These songs were to became the
lovely *Court and Spark* album. As she played, I realized she was
trying the songs out on us, subtly watching our reactions as we were
completely entranced by her.

Joni, my sister Susan, and I went to Trident one afternoon to
lay down vocals on "Walk Your Feet in the Sunshine." Our parts

were simple at first but by the time we reached the repeated fade we were multitracking interlaced contrapuntal doo-wop parts and having a ball. That night the studio crew and the Kings Yard Kids stormed a Portuguese restaurant. Joni was staying at the Dorchester and joined us. After a few vodkas, a chant went up for Joni to sing. She smiled politely and declined, citing her lack of any form of stringed instrument. Hanging above her head on the wall was a cutaway Portuguese guitar. I took it down and to my immense surprise found it playable. I handed it to her. She gracefully submitted and began tuning the antique. Its voice was deep and melodious. She sang, "I remember that time you told me 'Love is touching souls.' Well surely you've touched mine, 'cause part of you pours out of me in these lines from time to time." Every fork in the joint froze in midair at the sound of her voice. When she finished, there was raucous applause. She examined the guitar and toyed with the bridge and the tuning pegs. I went to the maître d'hôtel and privately asked him if I could buy the instrument. After some tense negotiations (it seemed it was a family heirloom) he agreed to sell it to me for a couple hundred pounds. As we were exiting the tightly packed booth after dinner I said to Joni, "Don't forget your guitar." Her eyes widened. I put it in her hands.

Considering I sung about her virtually every day, I had done a reasonably good job of living without Rosemarie. Weeks passed and I had become resigned to the fact that she was back at home where she probably belonged.

I was sitting in a window seat at the front of Kings Yard when I saw her come to the guard's booth and pause to flirt for a moment with the old geezer before he got out of his chair and opened the gate for her. She came into the courtyard walking straight toward me: the hair stood up on the back of my neck. She was wearing a pair of faded jeans and a silk blouse, platform shoes so high it looked as though she might fall off of them. Before she got to the door, I had her in my arms. With a look of sweet surprise she surrendered to me for a moment as a few drops of rain spattered onto the cobblestones. I held her close for a while and then she pushed me away laughing.

"Let's have a look at you then!" She laughed and scanned my face for any signs of wear.

"Aw, puddin' face. You're not looking after yourself," she chided. Or as Ava had said to Sinatra "Frank, you look like shit." A scrap of music floated from the wireless in the guard's station and she took me around the waist and eased me into a little waltz. I turned with her, still intoxicated by the physical effect she had on me. The rain became a steady sprinkle as we danced to the radio.

"Come in," I invited.

"Can't. I've got my poor husband with me." She laughed again.

"What, here?"

"Well, in the hotel."

I stopped dancing.

"You can't do this. You can't just come out of the rain and stove me in and then go off to your husband. I won't have it."

"It could be so simple," she countered. She just wanted a willing, uncomplicated lover. There was nothing preventing us from seeing each other now and again, was there?

"You might not believe this," I replied gravely as the rain began to pour. "But I feel sorry for that poor bastard. Don't come around to tease me anymore."

I turned on my heel and walked away from Rosemarie. I looked for her through the window and saw the guard walking away from his post, holding an umbrella over her head.

Harry blew into town to help me beat back the evil spirits. He invited me to move into his flat on Curzon Street and Garth and I jumped at the chance. Robin Cable and I had moved the album project into a mixing room. It was night after night of endless mixing dates that seemed to go nowhere. Robin continued to complain of headaches and difficulty hearing. A certain odd expression would cross his face at times and I could tell he was hurting real bad.

I would take the rough mixes back to the flat and listen with extreme care. The mixes were making me queasy. I was drowning in echo. The singer/songwriter movement was scaling down and drying out while I was adrift in a monsoon of echo cocktails and megalithic effects. We were literally on the wrong track.

I called Richard Perry one night on the transatlantic cable. In his deep, reassuring bass he told me he would be happy to give an opinion. I put a half-dozen roughs and a couple of reels in the mail to California, while guiltily working in earnest with Robin.

A few days later Richard called.

"I think you should get your masters and uh . . . come back to California."

It was like a pail in the face. Not just the water, the whole pail.

"I think Robin came back to work a little too soon," he said uneasily. He thought a lot of Robin. It was a bad position to be in.

"Right. Thanks, Richard." The circuit hung open for a moment and we listened to each other's breathing before the line went dead.

I sat there for five minutes doing the math.

"Gar?" Garth was in the bathroom taking a shower.

"Hello?" he said through the door.

"We're leaving!" I shouted. The water abruptly turned off.

1969

At the end of April, Capitol released "Where's the Playground, Susie?" to follow "Galveston" from the eponymous album. It made a quick run to number 26 and then slowly fell off. Glen moved on like a juggernaut to other writers and interpreted songs by Larry Weiss ("Rhinestone Cowboy") and Allen Toussaint ("Southern Nights") brilliantly.

Nina Simone's cover of "Do What You Gotta Do," one of Johnny Rivers' copyrights, had inspired June's release of two surprising covers, one by the Four Tops and the other by groundbreaking songwriter and Vegas superstar Paul Anka.

By the beginning of July, Isaac Hayes would release his cover of "By the Time I Get to Phoenix," eighteen minutes and forty-two seconds of drama. The record incorporated a lengthy improvised preamble by Hayes as he sets the scene for the lyric itself. To be fully grasped his concept must be heard, but it became an instant classic.

Later in the same month Waylon Jennings, a seasoned country

artist and one-time bass player for Buddy Holly, would cover "Mac Park" for the first time. He would record it three times in all, a record that has never been challenged and is unlikely to be surpassed.

I was rattling around in the big house I had bought. I had not yet discovered soaring or Cobras or mysterious women. I tiptoed around the fact that one day I called the Devil and invited him over for a drink—though he didn't actually drink. At least not like your usual alcoholic. I asked him about Susan. How was she? His answer was strange. She was living up in the mountains "with some weird people." He was distancing himself. The remark worried me because I still cared about her. A few piña coladas and half a bottle of Commemorativo later we were talking about taking a trip to Hawaii.

1973

Back in the United States I moved *Land's End* into A&M Studios. After clearing it with Joni I put the mixing in the hands of her producer Henry Lewy and I felt very good about that. She recorded frequently and routinely just across the hall from our little mixing suite. Lewy was widely respected for his soft hands on Joni's records. He began methodically to sort out some of the excessive production on *Land's End* and we did more work on vocals. He was absolutely trustworthy when it came to notes. If you were under you were under. If you were sharp he could hear it and would sound the alarm.

I spent the month of December in relative quiet. In fact I was getting quietly drunk on Christmas Eve when I heard someone knocking on the front door of my house.

I wobbled on my way to the heavy door that faced out on the verdant front yard and the walkway to the swimming pool. I opened it, peering through the crack suspiciously to see what misfortune awaited. The lighthearted lyrics of "Joy to the World" and the trilling of carolers burst like a firework over my work-weary ears.

Joni Mitchell, Linda Ronstadt, J. D. Souther, James Taylor, and Peter Asher, among others, stood in the chilly evening and sang three carols in four-part harmony. I stood there more than a little rumpled and probably needing a shave. I was genuinely overjoyed to see those smiling faces. They stayed only a short time, having many stops to make that night, and drove off like the very embodiment of Christmas. It may have been the best present I ever got.

Land's End really was my best shot ever for a hit album. The songs were at the extreme reach of my ability and nothing if not authentic. And it was in tune. England's finest musicians backed on every track. Not a penny had been spared. The owner of the label was my rabbi and mentor. It was the second release on Asylum Records and all over the country critics, for many reasons, were sharpening their pencils in anticipation of this high-profile bid. Most of them were supporters of mine and had held my position through three unsuccessful ventures. These critics, whom I had vilified in my first concert at Dorothy Chandler Pavilion, were ironically among my most ardent fans. I was a repeat underdog.

I suppose in all fairness I should add there were others who just didn't give a shit, and didn't take me seriously anymore, if they ever had. Fair enough.

When I considered an album cover, my thoughts immediately went to sailplanes and the way the hot air balloon had been used to focus public attention on the 5th Dimension's "Up, Up and Away."

We all naturally wanted to use photographer Henry Diltz, who had done hit album covers for America, the Eagles, the Doors, and—with partner Gary Burden—literally hundreds of other artists. He was the master of the "big picture," that perfect shot that captures the essence of the music inside the cover.

"We could go out to the desert with a couple of Panavision 35's," Henry said when I came to him with the idea. "We could get up in your plane and do it in one day. Do you think we could have helicopters following us?"

He was off and running with it. This bond between music and flight and the title *Land's End* was like a seamless piece of perfect luck.

I made ten flights that day, starting about noon and lasting through the afternoon. It became a deceptively simple routine. Henry and I would go up to ten thousand feet and take a tow all the way over to the mountain. When we reached Blue Ridge, about fifteen miles from the airport, we would release. It was a day of surprisingly strong lift, largely generated by a vigorous wind out of the west as it passed over the mountain. The maxim, oft-repeated among glider pilots, is "Wherever there is strong lift there is somewhere nearby heavy sink." Though we battled turbulence from time to time in an effort to get a stable shot, the ridge lift was fairly consistent and we routinely exhausted Henry's supply of film before we had to return to base for fresh rolls, water, and to stretch our legs. As we finished the tenth flight of the day we were looking forward to the most exciting part of the shoot: Helicopters were set to arrive with stabilized mounts to shoot air to air, full shots of the glider against stunning backgrounds. They were late to arrive, and loath to waste a single precious second, but Henry suggested we do one more pass.

My heart was well and truly into this effort but I was experiencing a little fatigue. I brushed it off and clambered back into the Schweizer 2-32's roomy rear cockpit as Henry struggled into the smaller front cockpit with the awkward and heavy Panavision. We towed out to Blue Ridge and a couple of times got slammed up against the canopy by some very impertinent turbulence. No big deal. Just part of the game. A low cloud was forming just over the crest and I deliberately let the glider become partially engulfed. It was a stunning shot for the camera. I flew the ridge until Baden-Powell loomed over us to the left. I put her up on one wing and made a tight 180-degree turn to port.

"Whoa!" Henry said from the front, and we both laughed as I rolled the big wing straight and level.

"Let's do it again," he said. "Only this time let's go in and out of the cloud."

Yes, but I didn't want to lose visibility completely within a few feet of the top of the ridge. I flew south again, checking my variometer, and discovered we were maintaining altitude at about 200-plus feet per minute. Close to minimums, but I began planning another run.

In the blackness above us, beyond the atmosphere, planetary clocks rang in alarm as the Brobdingnagian machines of the gods began to adjust the future. A black hole in time swept nearer to us in the invisible world. I was trembling on the edge of a razor blade and didn't know it. I laid the stick to the right in a medium bank as the sailplane swung its nose around the compass.

"This time let's try to get into something really hairy!" Hank exhorted. As I stopped the turn on a northerly heading I stared in horror at my instruments.

"We're already into something really hairy," I said.

"What?"

I was looking at my variometer, a special instrument that tells the pilot which way he's headed: up or down and how fast. It was pegged in the negative position. The ship was losing altitude by at least 1,500 feet a minute. I had been sloppy in the turn. I should have snapped it around in a crisp 180. I had turned the wrong fucking way, *toward* the mountain. I deepened my angle of bank and then flew directly at the ridge, perhaps a mile away. It was going to be close. I fiddled with my MacCready speed ring to find the best speed to fly. In essence the solution was to go like hell. I put the nose down and ran for the ridge at near red line. Turbulence batted at the glider like a kitten stalking a feather on a piece of string.

Making contact with the ridge would be unacceptable and not survivable. I ran right up to it. I could see the pinecones in the trees on the flank of it. With a sick feeling in the pit of my stomach I realized I would miss clearing it by at least the length of one giant tree. I would pile into the top of the ridge at high speed and we would both be killed instantly. At the very last second I turned away to port looking for a low spot or dip in the natural barrier. There was Vincent's Gap two or three miles to the north. I checked my variometer again and turned west into the canyon.

"We're going down," I said to Henry.

"We're going back?"

"Down there," I said, pointing toward the ground.

"Oh, really?" He took it in stride.

I looked over the side and saw a thin, snaking riverbed in the depths of the gulch. There was nothing else in sight and coming down in the trees was probably going to kill us.

"I'm going to make an emergency approach on that riverbed."

"I'm going to keep shooting," said Henry.

"Okay, good idea." I didn't want to scare him with the hopelessness of our predicament.

While I still had altitude, I flew up and looked for the smoothest part of the riverbed. It seemed to me it was more flat and level about halfway through the canyon. It looked almost inviting until I realized that every pebble in that riverbed was the size of a Winnebago and there were more than enough boulders and flood debris scattered about as to make it virtually impassable.

A cold fist gripped at my gut as I realized this was probably the end. I could hear Henry asking for angels to be there with us.

I entered pattern altitude at a thousand feet and began to fly my downwind leg parallel to the trickle of water and stony obstacle course of the river. I could hear Fred Robinson's voice saying, "Always keep flying the glider, never give up or abandon the controls."

I turned my base leg. It became more of a sharp steep turn in the narrow confines of the gulch. I straightened out on final. I let the glider settle, keeping it straight and level.

The tops of the pines floated up to meet us. A sense of universal placidity came over me. I thought of love and how it had governed most of my decisions. I could rest with that. The colors became intense. I noticed suddenly that the forest wasn't just green. It was fifty shades of green, all in a blur beneath the glider. There was a barely perceptible wrench that segued to an inconceivable deceleration, a half second of darkness, and then oblivion.

In a gradual accumulation of sensation, punctuated by the liquid calls of birds against a primeval silence, I began to realize I was not dead.

I slowly opened my eyes; the left one was not operating properly. Through the fuzzy forward view that my vision provided I could just discern what remained of the cockpit and Henry hanging inert in his five-point harness. I could see blood. Lots of it, dripping from his head. My first thought was, *God, please don't let me be the only survivor.*

I experimented and found I could move my left leg. I lifted it slightly and was able to touch him gently on the shoulder with my foot. I pushed.

"Nnnnnnngh," Henry groaned. My heart leaped in my chest. He was bloodied but not bloody dead. My arms felt like a mannequin's, my fingers stiff and shaking. However, I was able to separate myself from the glider by unfastening the quick release on the harness. I made sure I was still hanging on to it though. After all, we were half-way up a tree. Gingerly I made my way to the ground some ten feet below.

"Hank, you okay? Can you hear me?"

He looked at me and managed a smile.

I half-lifted him out of the cockpit, not easy to do with his fractured leg, and we both sat down on a nearby rock. I took my bandana over to the stream and wetted it. I brought it back so he could clear his vision.

"Your eye," Henry said with concern.

"Ah, it's okay. I can still see you." I grinned. "We made it Henry. It's a miracle."

He reached inside his shirt pocket and took out a ready roll.

"Want a joint?" he asked with a wide smile beaming through a bloody mask. We fired up the splif and inhaled deeply, looking out on a nature study from a weekend artist's sale. A tranquil little stream gurgled down through the rock-strewn hillside. Firs and pines grew on either side; a red-tailed hawk's nest loomed in a rough sphere of dead leaves and sticks in the top of a nearby big pine. Far above was the snow-crowned summit of Baden-Powell, the sun plummeting toward the west, the long shadows reaching out for us.

Jimmy Webb and Harry Nilsson on the *Magnifico*. *(Courtesy of the author)*

CHAPTER SEVENTEEN

Hope I die before I get old.
—Peter Townshend, 1965

1973

I had temporarily lost track of Harry until it became big news. John Lennon was in L.A. and he and Harry were on the Endless Hang, more widely known as "Lennon's Lost Weekend." It was common knowledge that Yoko Ono and John had agreed to a temporary separation with no caveats on behavior. Putting Nilsson and Lennon together without a buffer was one of the great bad ideas of all time. For a while I heard nothing about Harry at all. I continued to work at A&M.

The top hanger in Hollywood called me early on the morning of March 13. Five in the morning to be precise.

"Who the fuck is *this*?" I growled. "Do you know what time it is?"

"Jim, I already know the time," Harry replied in a hoarse conspiratorial whisper.

"Funny stuff." I propped up on one elbow.

"Jim, I'm coming over with John."

"John who?"

"John Lennon."

"Right. Yank the other one." I hung up and burrowed deeply into my goose down pillows.

By and by, the gate phone awakened me again.

"Jim, it's Harry and John."

"No, I'm not going anywhere with you," I protested, but leaned over and hit the button to open the gate.

I was still lying there, and very near resuming my nap when I heard someone pounding energetically on the kitchen door. I wrapped myself in a bathrobe, unsteadily navigated the steep stairs, and managed to push the heavy sliding door to one side. The first photons of diffused early light filtered through the titans of rock 'n' roll in the stained glass windows, including Lennon in cross-legged meditative pose. I walked yawning to the back door and saw the hulking figure of Harry Nilsson in a raincoat peering through a window in the kitchen door.

"Jim, we've been in a bit of scrape," Harry said. He was agitated and looking nervously outside. There was a limo sitting in the driveway.

"We?"

"I've got John Lennon out here."

It was an incredibly interesting fact but I was not an autograph hound.

"Bring him in."

"He wants to stay in the car."

I laughed hysterically.

"You think I'm going to fall for that?" I knew suddenly, with no reasonable doubt, that there were two hookers in the back of the car. I rushed outside and swung the rear door open, sticking my head inside. In the far corner of the compartment, looking small and owlish in his round specs, his white soft hands folded in his lap, was John Lennon.

"Hello, John."

"Jim," he acknowledged with a nod.

"Jim, we have a favor to ask," Harry said from behind me.

I carefully closed the limo door. Harry and I walked back into the house and on the way upstairs he explained his dilemma. In the late evening the night before he and John had gotten swacked on brandy and cocaine and, popping amyl nitrates like party favors, had gone to Doug Weston's Troubadour to see the Smothers Brothers in concert. Apparently the show wasn't as funny as the pair had expected and they started to heckle the Smothers Brothers. Lifetime fans turned on the hecklers. Tom and Dick defended themselves and tried to regain control of the stage. In the confusion John, for some unknown reason, went to the ladies lavatory and purchased a sanitary napkin from a wall dispenser. He managed to attach this to his forehead.

He returned to the table and he and Harry continued to insult the talent in spite of being told to shut up by a waitress. Witnesses reported that Lennon in a rare witless moment had shouted at her, "Don't you know who the fuck I am?" to which she replied, "You're some asshole with a Kotex on his head."

At this point Harry, being the designated caregiver (a danger sign), recognized the need to flee the premises immediately. As Harry and John pushed their way through the narrow passageway leading to the alley a woman stepped up from John's left and raised a flash camera for a close-up. John, according to who you chance to ask: 1. Didn't do anything; 2. Inadvertently pushed her; 3. Punched her in the face and broke her camera.

"So?" I asked Harry.

"We need you to ride downtown with us to John's attorney's office before the newspapers come out and sit for a deposition. John needs you to swear that you saw the whole thing and that John *didn't hit anyone.* That's the key thing, Jim, he *didn't hit anyone.*" He paused and took in a breath or two.

"Fuck no," I said. "I wasn't there."

"Jim, if you don't help us out John's going to get sent back to Britain. The feds have a hard-on for him."

"Going back to Britain isn't like going to the electric chair, Harry. They have women there and daffodils and cozy little pubs."

He stood and fixed me with a reproachful gaze.

"Do it for Derek. Do it for peace. Do it for The Beatles," he said, but he could not keep a straight face.

"I'm a bigger idiot by half than both of you put together," I said, pulling on jeans and a fresh T-shirt while Harry laughed with glee. Slipping into well-worn sneakers and tying them snug while sitting on my bed, I insisted on combing my hair and brushing my teeth, especially if I was going to lie through them.

We drove downtown from Campo, which was a schlep by any standard. Early morning traffic was crowding onto the Hollywood Freeway on-ramps. John sat impassively, quite noticeably gray of complexion. He said little. He looked like a man in a lot of trouble.

"That cunt," he said suddenly to no one. "I didn't touch her fucking camera." That this wasn't exactly a clear-cut denial did not escape me.

I was still groggy when I walked into a suite of high-priced offices downtown where a coven of somber besuited men sat in intense conversation. I was deposed and asked if I had been to the Troubadour the night before. A court stenographer waited with her curious little keyboard.

"Yes," I said with a somber and sober demeanor.

"Did you, Mr. Webb, see Mr. Lennon exiting the Troubadour night club?"

"Absolutely."

"Yes or no, please, Mr. Webb," I was admonished.

"Sure. I was with him."

"Mr. Webb, did you see Mr. Lennon strike any person, or lay his hands on another person in any manner whatsoever?"

"No, I didn't see him strike anyone." Which was the absolute truth.

We rode the elevator down in silence and it occurred to me that John Lennon hadn't bothered to look at me since I set out on this mission to save his bacon. A thank-you or conspiratorial wink would have been nice.

They drove me home. In odd fits of conversation that seemed to be taking place internally, Lennon fumed about the government and the unfair treatment he had received. There was to be no meeting of minds. There would be no expressions of gratitude. There was a great deal missing in the simple exercise of common courtesy.

They let me out at the kitchen door and John nodded again like a pontiff. I had done no more than was expected in that rarified dimension where The Beatles lived by their own special rules.

"Thanks, Jim," said Harry, walking me to the door. He knew it was a minor indignity but he also knew I had to do it.

"Get the fuck out of here and take your asshole with you," I mocked gently. The poor limo driver, looking like he was at the end of a sixteen-hour shift, set his bleary eyes on the road and drove them away. What was it about The Beatles that commanded such perilous loyalty at any price, and without any noticeable gratitude?

The charges filed by a female photographer quietly disappeared after a couple of weeks when the D.A. dismissed any action for "lack of evidence." Larry Kane wrote in his biography: "John was lucky."

Their mutually destructive aerial ballet temporarily preserved, John and Harry went into the studio with the brilliant but dangerously unpredictable Phil Spector. In an argument with David Geffen at A&M, five-foot-five Spector had lifted Geffen off the floor by his throat and pinned him against the wall. Geffen had tried to prevent Spector from taking control of a Joni Mitchell session. Spector then threatened him with a loaded gun.

It would be hard to exaggerate the level of drug use during the Lennon/Nilsson/Spector project. Harry came into my house one of those nights and spit a handful of blood into my kitchen sink. I was shocked. Not like a little old lady would have been shocked, but shocked as in deeply concerned for his vocal cords. I asked him about his voice.

"I left it on the microphone," he said with a laugh. Nilsson's tenor was a special gift, a mellifluous instrument with an unfettered agility and multiple layers of emotional nuance. John, on the other hand, had less to lose.

In the days that followed, the world seemed to grow dark. I was deeply unhappy without Rosemarie. I unabashedly turned to increased doses of drink and drugs in an attempt to alleviate my depression. I was urged by friends and family to "get some help" but found it difficult to surrender to a head doctor. My father was the man who had cured a particularly nasty abscess in his molar by going out to the garage and resorting to a pair of pliers out of his toolbox. I was his son.

It didn't seem to matter that she showed up again. The Watergate hearings had started and Hollywood was glued to the screen. She said we could have mimosas and watch them together. I may have been less than enthusiastic about the idea. She came anyway and hinted she would like to have a television at the pool in homage to the increasingly fine weather. Garth managed to wire up a big screen at the pool specifically for Rosemarie to watch Watergate. When she complained she couldn't see the picture properly, he was charged with constructing a kind of hood over the set so direct sunlight could not impinge on the screen. I once had reveled in gratifying her extravagance but I no longer got the same charge. I knew she would be gone in a few days with little or no explanation. Rosemarie means "remembrance." It seems as though I thought of her constantly at the expense of recalling anything else clearly.

The phone rang in my darkened bedroom where I had fallen asleep after restless hours around two or three o'clock in the morning. I rolled over cursing, trying to locate the phone. I found it under the bed.

"Jim." It was Harry's hoarse voice.

"No," I snapped. "That is a preemptive unilateral *no*."

"We're down at a hotel on the beach in Venice."

"Don't care."

"John is having some problems. The photographers are chasing us around."

"I can't hear you." I made static noises at the back of my throat.

"Jim, I just need a little favor. You're still up, right?"

"The house is crowded with people, can't leave, you know."

He ignored me. "Do you happen to have any hundred-dollar bills?"

"I just want to check and make sure that you just asked me if I have any hundred-dollar bills at three o'clock in the morning . . . (static) . . . sorry, just thought I . . . (static)"

"Unfortunately we are also out of wampum and we can't just go out into the street."

"What, are you guys grafted together now?" I complained.

"So it boils down to this. We want you, Jimmy Webb, to bring hundred-dollar bills and some hee haw down to Venice. Please. Do it for peace."

"Fuck you."

"Please. It's urgent, we have no cash."

I was wide awake by then so it didn't seem to matter as much.

"I've taken the tiny liberty of sending my chauffeur over to your house. He should be there anytime," Harry wheedled. The gate phone extension lit up and started beeping.

"You can tell his nibs that you sons of bitches have steel bollocks to do this to me again. I'm a respected member of the community, not your pusher."

"Right. Thanks, Jim, I knew we could depend on you!"

In the background there was a hysterical burst of laughter that sounded distinctly feminine. I made no obeisance to hygiene save swirling a mouthful of Listerine for two circuits and spitting it into the sink. I opened the secret door in the lazaret behind the bar and dialed the combination into my safe. I had road money in there and I was able to find ten or twelve hundred-dollar bills and an eighth of an ounce of the best cocaine in a clear polyurethane envelope. I walked out into the driveway to find the chauffeur standing rigid as a bridegroom beside the rear door of Harry's personal limousine.

"Good morning, Mr. Webb." His unwavering smile and heels clicking together were just a bit more than I could stand. I groaned in response and collapsed on the rear seat as he firmly closed the door. The gate opened automatically for exiting traffic as I closed my eyes.

We pulled into a somewhat low-rent section of Venice Beach and went down a side street toward the ocean. As he pulled to a stop in front of a threshold beachfront hotel with a NO VACANCY sign blinking in an upper window, the surf broke in a single clap of thunder and roared. One room on the second floor was brightly lit and laughter echoed down the street. I looked behind us and saw no sign of a tail. No police. No cameras. If Nilsson and Lennon were in this place, I thought, they were well and truly submerged in the substrata of L.A. society. I knocked on the door.

Inside, someone shushed loudly and the room fell silent. Harry opened the door, red faced and sweating, fully dressed with a papier-mâché grin plastered on his face.

"Jimmy!" he exclaimed, as though in complete surprise.

It was a kitchenette apartment, on the trashy side. Behind him I saw a beautiful Asian girl sitting naked on a Formica kitchen table. Her legs were spread wide and elevated on two supporting chair backs to put her in a position not unlike the one a woman assumes on her visits to the obstetrician. She was not May Pang. As I stepped through the door I saw Lennon crouched between her legs on his haunches, fully clothed. He was rolling a hundred-dollar bill into a thin tube and fitting it with studied precision into the young lady's vagina. She was delighted with this procedure, laughing while exhorting him, "More! Please! More!" Lennon glanced up at me coolly as I stood in the doorway, and resumed the rolling process, scarcely pausing to nod. In front of him on the table was a dwindling stack of hundreds.

"We're going for the Guinness Book of World Records!" Harry enthused and went over to encourage John and have a look at his handiwork. I woodenly reached inside my motorcycle jacket and took out the contraband and the cash.

"Uh, here's your stuff, Harry," I said, my voice weak from amazement.

"Come over and have a look!" he invited, taking the hundreds and the cocaine offhandedly, as though the boys were building a model airplane.

"I gotta run. You guys go ahead with, uh, whatever . . . good luck with that." I turned on my heel and walked out into the fresh cold air of the beach.

'Thanks, Jim," Harry called after me while closing the door.

A few days went by. Somehow a merry, merry, non-birthday party coalesced around me. It was an all-male ritual featuring Harry, Garth, Bruce Grakal, and Hilary Jarrard, Ringo's handler. Ringo himself was noticeably absent. The party didn't start rolling till about ten at night and immediately became a true blowout featuring cocaine, amyl nitrates—which I really couldn't stand—and some other chemicals, it would turn out, that had not been vetted for content.

I remember with distinct clarity sitting on the big organ bench with my back to the keyboard. High on cocaine and tequila and overtaken by a depression that was like being in freefall. I wanted only to be with Rosemarie under that starry desert sky, bundled up and driving my Cobra to a new life somewhere, anywhere beyond all this crazy shit and noise that continued to escalate like the accordion catastrophes in a Buster Keaton one-reeler.

Harry came over and sat down, reading my mood instantly.

"Look, I've got some product here. It's supposed to be Merc, wanna try it?"

He took a bottle out of his pocket and laid a pile on the back of his hand, hoovering it in one go. He dumped another and held it out to me. I hesitated for just a second. It didn't look exactly as expected, but what the hell, I took it all in one blast.

We sat there for an hour or a second, I lost all track of time.

I recall Harry on all fours, crawling around on the living room floor, saying, "Zardoz, Zardoz," over and over. I knew exactly what *Zardoz* was. It was a cult film starring Sean Connery about a bleak dystopian future where old age is dispensed as a punishment. In the film, a giant stone human head flew around from place to place distributing free arms and ammunition to the barbarians.

I started feeling sick to my stomach. The interior of the house was claustrophobic and now it seemed inhabited by hundreds of people, even though I knew that was impossible. I said nothing about my sudden illness but left the organ bench and walked out the back door of the house where I knew I would feel better. Just get some oxygen, that's all, and things would come back into focus. My stomach would stop doing one-and-a-half gainers into a yawning empty abyss. I walked down the driveway alone, keying on the runway lights that I had bought from an airport equipment company. One on each side, staggered down the serpentine length of the road. I was counting them. One, two, I remember counting three, oblivion. Oblivion. *Oblivion.*

There were moments when it seemed I almost broke through the surface tension of consciousness. People were in a panic. Harry was insensible, lying in a pile on the living room floor. They wanted to call an ambulance.

No, they weren't going to call for an ambulance after all because it would be in all the papers. No way they were going to call an ambulance and have the police in this. I was vaguely aware that they had taken Harry away and then I was back under fighting for breath. It felt like some creature had me by the heels and was dragging me down through realms of diminishing perception and illumination to dark regions. Places darker than the familiar nights on planet Earth. A new darkness, below all this.

There were creatures with blue faces, deformed and sinister. "We have you where we want you," they said to me. They were so happy they'd taken me down. I was not a religious guy. I had overdosed on the dogma of the Southern Baptist Church; a jaded but secret agnostic by the age of twelve. However, these ghouls were a real threat to my soul and my mental state. I invoked God and they howled in disappointment.

I've got to get away, I thought. If I can tread water, the world will come back. Instead I sank lower. My thoughts slowed. I passed through the realm of demons and was on a bleak, dark plain under a starless sky.

There were two of me. One suffered the most outrageous fear

and insult while the other watched, calm and unsympathetic. I knew somehow that this was the final theater. It was as though all my senses save the olfactory faded and switched off one by one. Now I was robbed of even my hallucinations and there was only smell. The air I struggled to inhale was bereft of any bouquet. It was the smell of artificiality, of plastic and synthetic rubber and other noxious, nameless compounds; the concentrated exhaust of chemical factories. It would be my last sensation, this God-awful stench that eclipsed the organic putrefaction of even a decaying corpse.

Garth has said that had he known the extent of the damage I had suffered he would have taken me to the hospital. Perhaps we appeared "passed out" in the sense that drunkards "pass out" and are merely put to bed in order to sleep it off. As it was, Harry was carted away in an automobile to engineer his own recovery, a miracle that has never been recounted to me. I had my own extremely serious problems to deal with. In the full glare of daylight I remained silent and apparently sleeping on the bed.

The weeks that followed were nightmarish for my family. My senses had not come back unaffected. The mechanics of reason had suffered. Great swaths of data had been seemingly degaussed overnight. The supposed sniff of high-quality "Merc" cocaine had in reality been a super dose of crude street level PCP, enough to kill an elephant.

Once I was up and walking around I was certain every object in the house was made of rubber. I would run my hand over the walls, the floor, and the furniture and ask my sister Susan or her boyfriend, Paul, who had volunteered to be my wardens, "Why has everything turned to rubber?" They reacted with bewildered, panicked expressions. I went out in the driveway to examine an automobile. I ran my hand over the metal. It was rubber as well. The black asphalt of the driveway was rubber. The trees in the orchard, the flowers growing by the front porch, all was rubber.

My sister Susan asked me if I wanted to play the piano. She and Paul took me into the living room where the Yamaha C3 waited patiently. It had, of course, turned to rubber. I looked at it. For the life of me I could not remember what it was for. The shape was familiar but its purpose evaded me.

I would sit on the bench and parse the keyboard, five black keys and seven white ones in a repeated pattern. There was something there. Sometimes I would almost get it. I sat and stared at the keyboard all day. They couldn't get me away from it. At the end I was crying. Real tears, not rubber ones, streamed down my face as I pounded on the stubborn keys. I was unable to evoke a single tune or chord. I looked into the faces of Susan, Garth, and Paul and saw real fear.

A month after the overdose I approached the piano in a pensive mood and sat down at the keyboard. What had been a cryptic puzzle lay before me in benign simplicity. I had rediscovered the code lying where I had carelessly dropped it in a maze of tangled neurons. I put out my hand hesitantly and ever so gently played middle C. I let it sing without interference in the cavernous cabinet of the huge instrument. My right foot lingered on the sustain pedal and I listened to the note blossom, change, and then die away. Like everything on earth. A template of all living things, all empires, all eras and eons.

In that moment I looked at the keys and knew I could play anything. I could play the "Star-Spangled Banner" or "Penny Lane." I could play "Clair de Lune" or "Jesu, Joy of Man's Desiring," "My Funny Valentine," or "Jailhouse Rock." I could play any song I had ever heard or any song I ever would hear. The warm tears cascaded down my face and onto my chest. Paul and Susan stood next to me, their arms around my shoulders, crying softly as my fingers moved through the chords of "Amazing Grace."

Jimmy Webb. *(Courtesy of Henry Diltz)*

TOP 100 CHARTS - UNITED STATES*

June, 1967	Up, Up and Away - The 5th Dimension	#7
June, 1967	Up, Up and Away - Johnny Mann Singers	#91
October, 1967	By the Time I Get to Phoenix - Glen Campbell	#75
November, 1967	Paper Cup - The 5th Dimension	#23
December, 1967	Up, Up and Away - Hugh Masekela	#14
February, 1968	Carpet Man - The 5th Dimension	#29
May, 1968	MacArthur Park - Richard Harris	#2
August, 1968	Montage, Love Generation	#86
August, 1968	Do What You Gotta Do - Bobby Vee	#83
October, 1968	Do What You Gotta Do - Nina Simone	#83
October, 1968	The Yard Went On Forever - Richard Harris	#64
November, 1968	Wichita Lineman - Glen Campbell	#3
December, 1968	Worst That Could Happen - The Brooklyn Bridge	#3

* Lists on these pages are highlights and are not complete listings.

March, 1969	Galveston - Glen Campbell	#4
May, 1969	Where's the Playground, Susie? - Glen Campbell	#28
June, 1969	Didn't We? - Richard Harris	#63
June, 1969	Galveston - Roger Williams	#99
July, 1969	First Hymn from Grand Terrace - Mark Lindsay	#81
August, 1969	By the Time I Get to Phoenix - The Mad Lads	#84
August, 1969	By the Time I Get to Phoenix - Isaac Hayes	#37
September, 1969	MacArthur Park - Waylon Jennings	#93
November, 1969	Wichita Lineman - Sérgio Mendes	#95
January, 1970	Honey Come Back - Glen Campbell	#19
April, 1970	The Girls' Song - The 5th Dimension	#43
January, 1971	Mixed-Up Guy - Joey Scarbury	#73
September, 1971	MacArthur Park - Four Tops	#38
October, 1971	I Say a Little Prayer/By the Time I Get to Phoenix - Glenn Campbell & Anne Murray	#81
October, 1972	Song Seller - The Raiders	#96
December, 1972	Didn't We? - Barbra Streisand	#82
September, 1973	All I Know - Art Garfunkel	#9
January, 1975	It's a Sin When You Love Somebody - Joe Cocker	#5
September, 1978	MacArthur Park - Donna Summer	#1
April, 1983	Easy for You to Say - Linda Ronstadt	#54
April, 2016	Famous - Kanye West (Jimmy Webb, Cowriter)	#34

TOP 100 CHARTS - U.S. COUNTRY

October, 1967	By the Time I Get to Phoenix - Glen Campbell	#2
November, 1968	Wichita Lineman - Glen Campbell	#1
March, 1969	Galveston - Glen Campbell	#1
May, 1969	Where's the Playground, Susie? - Glen Campbell	#28

September, 1969	MacArthur Park - Waylon Jennings	#23
1970	If This Was the Last Song - Billy Mize	#71
January, 1970	Honey Come Back - Glen Campbell	#2
October, 1971	I Say a Little Prayer/By the Time I Get to Phoenix - Glen Campbell & Anne Murray	#40
January, 1975	It's a Sin When You Love Somebody - Glen Campbell	#16
August, 1985	Highwayman - The Highwaymen	#1
October, 1987	Still within the Sound of My Voice - Glen Campbell	#5
November, 1988	Light Years - Glen Campbell	#35
1989	More Than Enough - Glen Campbell	#47
1997	Wichita Lineman - Wade Hayes	#55

TOP 100 CHARTS - U.S. ADULT CONTEMPORARY

June, 1967	Up, Up and Away - The 5th Dimension	#9
June, 1967	Up, Up and Away - Johnny Mann Singers	#24
October, 1967	By the Time I Get to Phoenix - Glen Campbell	#12
1968	By the Time I Get to Phoenix - Floyd Cramer	#32
1968	By the Time I Get to Phoenix - Harry Belafonte	#38
April, 1968	We Can Fly/Up, Up and Away - Al Hirt	#23
May, 1968	MacArthur Park - Richard Harris	#10
August, 1968	Montage - Love Generation	#19
August, 1968	All My Love's Laughter - Ed Ames	#12
November, 1968	The Yard Went On Forever - Richard Harris	#23
November, 1968	Wichita Lineman - Glen Campbell	#1
1969	Didn't We? - Robert Goulet	#33
1969	MacArthur Park - Tony Bennett	#39
1969	Wichita Lineman - Larry Page Orchestra	#33
March, 1969	Galveston - Glen Campbell	#1
May, 1969	Where's the Playground, Susie? - Glen Campbell	#10
June, 1969	Didn't We? - Richard Harris	#11
June, 1969	Galveston - Roger Williams	#21
July, 1969	First Hymn from Grand Terrace - Mark Lindsay	#24
November, 1969	Wichita Lineman - Sérgio Mendes	#34
January, 1970	Honey Come Back - Glen Campbell	#4
April, 1970	The Girls' Song - The 5th Dimension	#6

October, 1971	I Say a Little Prayer/By the Time I Get to Phoenix	#13
	- Glen Campbell & Anne Murray	
August, 1972	MacArthur Park - Andy Williams	#26
December, 1972	Didn't We? - Barbra Streisand	#22
September, 1973	All I Know - Art Garfunkel	#1
January, 1975	It's a Sin When You Love Somebody - Glen Campbell	#39
1977	Crying in My Sleep - Art Garfunkel	#25
September, 1978	MacArthur Park - Donna Summer	#24
April, 1983	Easy for You to Say - Linda Ronstadt	#7
1990	Adios - Linda Ronstadt	#9

TOP 100 CHARTS - U.S. DANCE

| September, 1978 | MacArthur Park - Donna Summer | #1 |
| 2013 | MacArthur Park - Donna Summer | #1 |

TOP 100 CHARTS - U.S. R&B

December, 1967	Up, Up and Away - The 5th Dimension	#47
January, 1968	Do What You Gotta Do - Al Wilson	#39
October, 1968	Do What You Gotta Do - Nina Simone	#43
August, 1969	By the Time I Get to Phoenix - Mad Lads	#28
August, 1969	By the Time I Get to Phoenix - Isaac Hayes	#37
September, 1969	Honey Come Back - Chuck Jackson	#43
September, 1971	MacArthur Park - Four Tops	#27
1977	By the Time I Get to Phoenix - Isaac Hayes	#65
1977	By the Time I Get to Phoenix - Isaac Hayes	#65
	and Dionne Warwick	
July, 1978	This Is Your Life - Norman Connors	#31
September, 1978	MacArthur Park - Donna Summer	#8

TOP OF THE CHARTS - UK

October, 1967	Up, Up and Away	#6
October, 1967	By the Time I Get to Phoenix - Glen Campbell	#52
February, 1968	By the Time I Get to Phoenix - Marty Wilde	#56
May, 1968	MacArthur Park	#4
June, 1968	By the Time I Get to Phoenix - Georgic Fame	#51
October, 1968	Do What You Gotta Do - Nina Simone	#2
November, 1968	Wichita Lineman - Glen Campbell	#7
March, 1969	Galveston - Glen Campbell	#14
September, 1969	Do What You Gotta Do - Four Tops	#11
January, 1970	Honey Come Back - Glen Campbell	#4
July, 1972	MacArthur Park - Richard Harris	#38
September, 1973	All I Know - Art Garfunkel	#51
September, 1978	MacArthur Park - Donna Summer	#5
April, 2001	Since I Left You - The Avalanches	#16
July, 2001	Frontier Psychiatrist - The Avalanches	#18
October, 2001	Dreamy Days - Roots Manuva	#53

Glen Campbell, Jimmy Webb, and Harry Nilsson. *(Courtesy of Henry Diltz)*

HIGHLIGHTS: JIMMY WEBB AWARDS & HONORS

- 1967 - Grammy Award, Song of the Year "Up, Up and Away"
- 1967 - Grammy Award Nomination, Song of the Year "By the Time I Get to Phoenix"
- 1968 - Grammy Award, Best Arrangement Accompanying Vocalists for "MacArthur Park" & Richard Harris
- 1969 - Oklahoma Baptist University Phi Mu Alpha Sinfonia honorary membership, Pi Tau Chapter
- 1972 - FAI Gold Badge 746 from Soaring Society of America
- 1985 - Grammy Award, Best Country Song "Highwayman"
- 1985 - The Wrangler Award, Oklahoma City
- 1986 - Songwriters Hall of Fame inductee (youngest member ever inducted)
- 1989 - ASCAP Special Award "MacArthur Park" most played composition in the American ASCAP catalog
- 1990 - Nashville Songwriters Hall of Fame inductee
- 1990 - BMI 50th Anniversary List, The 50 Most Performed Songs of Our First Half Century, #3 "By the Time I Get to Phoenix," #27 "Up, Up and Away"

- 1992 - Doctor of Music, Honoree, Five Towns College, NY
- 1993 - ASCAP Lifetime Achievement Award
- 1999 - Oklahoma Hall of Fame inductee (youngest member ever inducted)
- 1999 - Elected ASCAP Board of Directors
- 1999 - Country Music Awards Honors the 10 Most Played Country Songs of All Time ("Wichita Lineman")
- 1999 - BMI Top 100 Songs of the Century, "Up, Up and Away"
- 1999 - Lifetime Achievement in Songwriting Award, American Cinema Awards Foundation
- 2000 - Songwriters Hall of Fame Board of Directors member
- 2000 - "Wichita Lineman" most played song on American country radio stations in the twentieth century
- 2000 - Grammy Hall of Fame, "Wichita Lineman"
- 2001 - Achievement in Music Award by Virtuosi Chamber Symphony
- 2003 - Songwriters Hall of Fame: Johnny Mercer Award
- 2004 - Grammy Hall of Fame, "By the Time I Get to Phoenix"
- 2005–2015 - ASCAP, Board of Directors, Vice Chairman
- 2006 - ASCAP Voice of Music Award
- 2006 - Influential Songwriter Award by the National Music Publishers' Association
- 2007 - Honorary Doctor of Music Degree, Oklahoma City University
- 2010–2014 - Chairman, Songwriters Hall of Fame
- 2010 - *Rolling Stone* Magazine 500 Greatest Songs of All Time, "Wichita Lineman," #195
- 2012 - Ivor Novello Special International Award
- 2013 - Oklahoma Music Hall of Fame, Inductee
- 2013 - Great American Songbook Hall of Fame, Inductee
- 2015 - *Rolling Stone's* 100 Greatest Songwriters of All Time, #44
- 2016 - Academy of Country Music Poet's Award

NOTE: The 1968 Grammy Awards were presented at the 10th Annual Grammy Award Show for the previous year, 1967. The 1969 Grammy Awards were presented at the 11th Grammy Award Show for the previous year, 1968.

HIGHLIGHTS OF AWARDS & RECOGNITIONS FOR JIMMY WEBB WORKS AND COMPOSITIONS

1967—Grammy Award, Record of the Year
The 5th Dimension, "Up, Up and Away"

1967—Grammy Award, Best Vocal Performance, Male
Glen Campbell for "By the Time I get to Phoenix"

1967—Grammy Award, Best Performance by a Vocal Group
The 5th Dimension, "Up, Up and Away"

1967—Grammy Award, Best Performance by a Chorus
Johnny Mann Singers, "Up, Up and Away"

1967—Grammy Award, Best Contemporary Single
The 5th Dimension, "Up, Up and Away"
Johnny Rivers and Marc Gordon, Producers

1967—Grammy Award, Best Contemporary Group Performance
(Vocal or Instrumental)
The 5th Dimension, "Up, Up and Away"

1967—Grammy Award, Best Contemporary Solo Vocal, Male
Glen Campbell, "By the Time I Get to Phoenix"

1967—Grammy Award, Contemporary Single
The 5th Dimension, "Up, Up and Away"

1967—Grammy Award Nomination, Contemporary Single
Glen Campbell, "By the Time I Get to Phoenix"

1967—Grammy Award, Contemporary Vocal Group
The 5th Dimension, "Up, Up and Away"

1967—Grammy Award, Male Vocal Performance
Glen Campbell, "By the Time I Get to Phoenix"

1967—Grammy Award, Record of the Year
The 5th Dimension, "Up, Up and Away"

1967—Grammy Award Nomination, Record of the Year
Glen Campbell, "By the Time I Get to Phoenix"

1967—Grammy Award Nomination, Contemporary Album,
The 5th Dimension, "Up, Up and Away"

1968—Grammy Award, Album of the Year
By the Time I Get to Phoenix, Glen Campbell
Al De Lory, Producer

1968—Grammy Award, Album of the Year
Glen Campbell, *By the Time I Get to Phoenix*

1968—Grammy Award Nominations, Contemporary Pop Male Vocalist
Glen Campbell, "Wichita Lineman"
Richard Harris, "MacArthur Park"

1968—Grammy Award Nomination, Best Contemporary Pop Performance
by a Chorus, Ray Charles Singers, "MacArthur Park," Command

1968—Grammy Award Nomination, Record of the Year
Glen Campbell, "Wichita Lineman"

1968—Grammy Award Best Engineered Recording, Non-Classical
Joe Polito, Hugh Davies, Engineers for "Wichita Lineman"

1968—Country Music Award Nomination, Single of the Year
"By the Time I Get to Phoenix," Glen Campbell

1968—Country Music Award Nomination, Album of the Year
Glen Campbell, *By the Time I Get to Phoenix*

1969—Grammy Award, Best Country Performance by a Duo or Group with
Vocal
The Kimberleys & Waylon Jennings, "MacArthur Park"

1969—Grammy Award Nomination, Best Contemporary Performance Chorus
Brooks Arthur Ensemble, "MacArthur Park"

1969—Country Music Award Nomination, Album of the Year
Glen Campbell, "Wichita Lineman"

1969—Country Music Award Nomination, Single of the Year
Glen Campbell, "Galveston"

1978—Grammy Award Nomination, Best Pop Vocal Performance, Female
Donna Summer, "MacArthur Park"

1985—Grammy Award Nomination, Best Country Performance by a Duo or Group with Vocal
Highwayman (Waylon Jennings, Kris Kristofferson, Johnny Cash, and Willie Nelson)

1985—Grammy Award Nomination, Best Album Package
Virginia Team, *Highwayman*

1985—Academy of Country Music Award, Single Record of the Year, Producer
Chips Moman, Producer, "Highwayman"

1985—Academy of Country Music Award, Single Record of the Year, Artist
Johnny Cash, Kris Kristofferson, Waylon Jennings, Willie Nelson, "Highwayman"

1985—Academy of Country Music Award, Album of the Year, Record Company
Columbia Records, *Highwayman*

1985—Academy of Country Music Award, Album of the Year, Artist
Johnny Cash, Kris Kristofferson, Waylon Jennings, Willie Nelson, *Highwayman*

1985—Academy of Country Music Award, Album of the Year, Producer
Willie Nelson, *Highwayman*

1985—Academy of Country Music Award, Country Video of the Year, Artist
Johnny Cash, Kris Kristofferson, Waylon Jennings, Willie Nelson, "Highwayman"

1985—Academy of Country Music Award, Country Video of the Year, Producer
Joe Small, "Highwayman"

1985—Academy of Country Music Award, Country Video of the Year, Director
Peter Israelson, "Highwayman"

1989—Grammy Award Nomination, Best Pop Vocal Performance, Female
Linda Ronstadt, "Cry Like a Rainstorm, Howl Like the Wind"
Jimmy Webb, Writer on album, Arranger, Player

1989—Grammy Award, Best Engineered Album, Non-Classical
"Cry Like a Rainstorm, Howl Like the Wind" performed by Linda Ronstadt
George Massenburg, Engineer

1994—Grammy Award Nomination, Best Music Video
"Jurassic Park" (MacArthur Park), Weird Al Yankovic
Scott Norlund, Mark Osborne, Directors
Scotti Bros./Imaginary Entertainment

1997—Grammy Award Nomination, Best Traditional Pop Vocal Album
Carly Simon, *Film Noir*

2009—Grammy Award Nomination, Best Male Pop Vocal Performance
James Taylor, "Wichita Lineman"

2017—Grammy Award Nomination, Best Rap/Sung Performance, "Famous,"
Kanye West featuring Rihanna
Jimmy Webb, Cowriter*

2017—Grammy Award Nomination, Best Rap Song, "Famous," Kanye West
featuring Rihanna
Jimmy Webb, Cowriter

ARTISTS WHO HAVE PERFORMED OR
RECORDED JIMMY WEBB SONGS
(Partial List)

4Troops
5th Dimension
A., Johnny
Acoustic Guitar Troubadours, The
Aldrich, Ronnie
Alexandria, Lorez
Allen, Rags
Allen, Roy
Allyson, Karrin
Allman, Gregg
Alman, Jon Philip
Alpha Sout
Amen Corner
America
Ammons, Gene
Anckorn & Dolovich
Andreas, Christine
Anthony, Richard
Arbouretum
Arioli, Susie
Armstrong, Adam
Arnold, Eddy
Aro, Eric Van
Arrival
Arundel, Jeff
Asgard
Ashford, Annaleigh
Ashton, Wyn
Aspelund, Monica
Assembled Multitude, The

Association, The
Atlantic Bridge
Auguscik, Grazyna
Avalanches, The

Baird, Meg
Bailey, Razzy
Baker, Brett
Baldry, Long John
Band Perry, The
Ball, Michael
Ball, Steve
Bama Winds
Band of Her Majesty's Royal
  Marines
Banks, Cary C.
Barber, Matt
Bards, The
Barker, Simon
Barnes, Jimmy
Barnstormer
Barron Knights, The
Barzee, Anastasia
Bassey, Shirley
Beer, Phil
B.E.F. featuring Glenn
  Gregory
Beggar's Opera, The
Belafonte, Harry
Bell, William

Beloved
Bennett, Brian
Bennett, Tony
Bentyne, Cheryl
Beveridge, Tim
Biddell, Kerrie
Bilk, Acker
Billingsley, Wayne
Billy, Bonnie "Prince"
Birdsall, Megan
Blackmore, George
Blueground Undergrass
Bobo Willie
Boston Pops
Boulevard Big Band, The
Bourne, Katy
Bowen, Paul
Brabec, Jiri & Count B
Brand, Violet
Breen, Ann
Brennan, Bridin
Brennan, Walter
Brooks, Nigel, Singers
Brothers Four, The
Brown, Dennis
Brown, James
Brown, Noel
Brühl, Heidi
Bruner, Linda
Budd, Julie
Bundeswehr, Die Big Band
  der
Burke, Donna & Bill Benfield
Burlington Banjo Band
Butcher, Shannon
Button Down Brass featuring the
  Funky Trumpet of Ray Davies, The
Butz, Norbert Leo
Buy As You View Cory
  Band
Bygdén, Lars

Byrd, Charlie
Bystanders

Café Lounge
Caiola, Al
Callaway, Ann Hampton
Callaway, Liz
Camacho, Thelma
Cameron, Ruth
Cam-Pact
Campbell, Glen
Cannon, Ace
Cantrell, Lana
Carlton, John
Carlton, Larry
Carpendale, Howard
Carpenter, Karen
Carpenter, Ross
Carr, Vicky
Carter, Clarence
Casapietra, Björn
Casey, Al
Cash, Johnny
Cave, Nick and The Bad Seeds
Celtic Thunder
Celtic Woman
Central Band of the Royal British
  Legion, The
Cerisano, Joe
Chacksfield, Frank and His Orchestra
Chapin, Thomas
Charles, Ray
Charles, Ray Singers
Cheeze
Cher
Cherry, Don & Willie Nelson
Cheryl
Chicago Metropolitan Jazz
  Orchestra
Chicken Little (Film) "All I Know"
Chiffons, The

Chris & Carla
Christen, Nadia
Christensen, Julie
Christie, Tony
Cinderella (TV)
Clark, Alice
Clay, Tom
Clayderman, Richard
Clean and Narrow (Film)
Clements, George
Clientele
Clooney, Rosemary
Clouds
Cocker, Joe
Collins, Judy
Collins, Laura
Collins, Peter
Collister, Christine
Colman, Kenny
Colvin, Shawn
Como, Perry
Cooper Clarke, John & Hugh
    Cornwell
Conniff, Ray and the Singers
Connors, Norman
Contessas, The
Cooper, Ray
Corless, Freddie
Coryell, Larry
Country Cousins
Cowsill, Susan
Cramer, Floyd
Crawford, Jimmy
Creator, The
Criss, Sonny
Crosby, Bing
Crosby, David
Cruz, Edgar
Cumming, Alan
Cummings, Burton
Cunimondo, Frank

Curtis, King
Coughlan, Mary

Daly-Wilson Big Band
Damone, Vic
Darleens
Darren, Jenny
Davenport, Jeremy
Davidson, Dianne
Davis, Larry
Davis, Rhett
Davis, Ruth
Davis Jr., Sammy
Davis, Spencer
Day, Danny
Day, Donk
Dayton, Jeff
Declan
Dee, Lenny
Dells, The
De Lory, Al
Deninzon, Joe Trio
Dennis
Denny, Martin
Denver, John
DePaiva, Kassie
DeShannon, Jackie
Dewar, Bruce
DiNizio, Pat
Disco Fox Girls
Disney Travel Songs
Distel, Sacha
D*Note
Dobson, Bonnie
Dodd, Dick
Dominique, Miss
Donahue, Jack
Doonican, Val
Dorsey, Jack Orchestra
Douglas, Craig
Douglas, Jerry

D'Owen, Lance
Duffy, Mark
Duke, Doris
Durbin, Allison
Dylan, Bob

Earle, Brenda
Easton, Sheena
Ebstein, Katja
Eckstine, Billy
Edelhagen, Kurt and His
  Orchestra
Edwards, J. Vincent
Elephant Micah
Eliran, Ron
Elliot, Cass
Ellis, Tinsley
EMI Music Pub
Emmons, Buddy
England, Buddy
Eriksen, Torun
Erskine, Peter
Eternity's Children
Ethereal Architect
Evanko, Ed
Evans, Dave
Everly Brothers, The
Executives, The

Faith, Percy and His Orchestra
  and Chorus
Fame, Georgie
Fargo (Film) "Up, Up and Away"
Fasano, Barbara
Fatback Band, The
Feeling, The
Feinstein, Michael
Felice, Dee
Feliciano, José
Fender, Freddy
Fender, Jack

Ferguson, Maynard
FernGully (Film)
Ferrante & Teicher
Fiedler, Arthur and The Boston
  Pops
Five for Fighting
Flack, Roberta
Fleming, Joy
Fleming, Renée
Fleming, Tommy
Flowers Pops, Mike
Ford, Dean
Ford, "Tennessee" Ernie
Forsyth, Bruce
Fortunes, The
Fountain, Pete
Fountainhead
Four Freshmen, The
Four Guys
Four Lads, The
Four Preps, The
Four Statesmen
Four Tops, The
Fox, Albert Choir
Franklin, Aretha
French Connection (Film)
  "Everybody Gets to the Moon"
Friends of Dean Martinez
Fusion

Gaebel, Tom
Gardiner, Boris
Garfunkel, Art
George, Cassietta
George, Lowell
Geraci, Sonny
Ghosts of an American Airman
Gil, Vince
Gilberto, Bebel
Girls from Petticoat Junction, The
Givers, Van

Glass, Gavin
Glover, Sheilah
Golden Ring
Gomez
Goober and the Peas
Goodees, The
Goodman, Benny
Goodrich, David
Gordon, Dexter
Gormé, Eydie
Grace, John
Grant, Amy
Grant, Peter
Grappelli, Stéphane
Greco, Buddy
Greene, Jack
Greenwood, Lee
Gregorianik
Gregory, Glenn
Grey, Eugene
Griffith, Nancy
Grimethorpe Colliery Band
Groban, Josh
Groove Coverage
Groovie Ghoulies
Grunt Futtock
Gunderson, Jack
Gustafsson, Rigmor
Gustafsson, Rune
Guthrie, Arlo
Guy and David

Haden, Charlie and Pat Metheny
Hadley, Jerry
Hadley, Tony
Haenning, Gitte
Hamilton, Judd
Hamilton, Scott & Friends
Hall, Jim
Harkin, Harry
Harkness, Gordon

Harland, Kelly
Harrington
Harris, Richard
Harrison, Joel
Harrison, Michael
Hartley, David
Hatch, Tony Orchestra
Hayes, Isaac
Hayes, Wade
Hayward, Justin
Haywood, Nick Quartet
Hazeltine, David
Healey, Mikael
HEC
Heller, André
Helms, Jimmy
Hendricks, Eddie
Herman, Woody
Hietanen, Pentti
Highwaymen, The
Hill, Mike
Hirt, Al
Hirte, Michael
Ho, Don
Høstrup, Fini Quartet
Hofmann, Peter
Holland, Amy and Michael
   McDonald
Hollenbeck, John
Holloway, Brenda
Holy, Onie J.
Hopfenmusig
Hore, John
Horse
Horseshoe Road
Houston, Thelma
Howell, Doug
Humphries, Les
Hunter, Nancy
Hurst, Mike Orchestra
Hussey-Regan

Hutch, Willie
Hutcherson, Bobby

I Nomadi
Ian, Janis
Iced Earth
In-Mood feat. Juliette
Incredible Shrinking Man, The
Infinity
Ingmann, Grethe
Innocence

Jackson, Wanda
Jacott, Ruth
Jankowski, Horst and His Studio
    Orchestra
Jazz at the Movies
Jean, Nikki
Jefferson
Jeff Duff Band
Jennett, Mark
Jennings, Waylon
Jess and the Bandits
JJB Sports Leyland Band
Johnny Maestro & the Brooklyn
    Bridge
Johnny Mann Singers
Johnston, Freedy
Joling, Gerard
Jolley, David
Jones, Anthony Armstrong
Jones, Dean
Jones, Janie
Jones, Jimmy
Jones, Tom
Jordan, Sheila
Julie & Carol
Jungr, Barb

Käfer & Søren Sebber
Kalkbrenner, Fritz

Kallmann, Günter Choir
Kalvik, Finn
Kawakami, Tsuyoshi and His Mood-
    makers
Keller, Mark
Kelly, Nancy
Kelsall, Phil
Kendricks, Eddie
Kennedys, The
Kenoly, Ron
Kent, Mary
Kenton, Stan
Kerr, Catherine
Keystone & Kimberleys
Kihn, Greg
King Harvest
King's Singers, The
Klein, Mimi
KLF
Københavns Politi Orkester
Köhncke, Justus
Kool & The Gang
Koorax, Ithamara
Körbert T.
Koyanagi, Yuki
Krahn, Jerry
Kramer, Wayne
Krgovich, Nicholas
Kunkel, Leah
Kush
Kwasniewska, Aleksandra
Kymm, Nevis

L. Sound & Arts O
La Femme Verte
Ladybug Transistor, The
LaFave, Jimmy
Lages, Eduardo
Lake, Alan
Landgren, Nils
lang, k.d.

Larry's Rebels
LaRue, Stoney
Lass, Martin
Last, James
Last Unicorn, The (Film)
Le Grand Orchestre de Paul Mauriat
Leander, Mike and His Orchestra
Lee, Albert
Lee, Albert and Hogan's Heroes
Lee, Byron & The Dragonaires
Lee, Johnny
Lee, Peggy
Lee, Shawn
Lefèvre, Ray
Lekman, Jens
Lemon Jelly
Lemonheads, The
Les Sirocco
Lessack, Lee
Lettermen, The
Levert, Gerald
Lewis, Ramsey
Liberace
Ligertwood, Alex
Light, Enoch & The Brass
    Menagerie
Linden, Marc van
Lindroth, Lloyd
Lindsay, Mark
Links, The
Lipton, Peggy
Löfgren, Anne-Lena
Logan, Johnny
London Philharmonic Orchestra
London Pops Orchestra
London Sound & Arts Orchestra
Longthorne, Joe
Longmire, Wilbert
Loring, Gloria
Los Blues
Lounge-O-Leers, The

Love, Darlene
Love Generation, The
Love Serenade
Lowry, Ron
Luca, Loes & Ruth Jacott
Lullaby Players
LuPone, Patti
Lynn, Vera
Lynne & Mike
Lynne, Shelby

MacNeil, Rita & Frank Mills
Madden, Dee
Magic
Magic Hands
Main Ingredient, The
Majestic Wind Ensemble
Mann, Aimee
Manousos, Paul
Mantooth, Frank Jazz
    Orchestra
Manuela
Maravella Orchestra
March, Peggy
Marcovicci, Andrea
Marsh, Natasha
Martin, Dean
Martin, Tony
Marvin, Hank
Masekela, Hugh
Mason & Dixon
Match, The
Mattea, Kathy
Mayhan, Judy
McCorkle, Susannah
McCoy, Freddie
McDermott, John
McDowell, Kristopher
McEntire, Reba
McGovern, Maureen
McGuffie, Bill

McKee, Maria
McKuen, Rod
McMillion Jazz Orchestra
McNair, Barbara
McNeely, Larry
McRae, Carmen
Meco
Medley, Bill
Menzel, Idina
Merenbooty Girls
Merrill, Buddy
Merritt, Max
Meters, The
M.I.A. Maya Arulpragasm
Michaels, Marilyn
Michell, Keith
Midler, Bette
Miller, Mrs.
Milo, Billy
Mingus, Charles
Minnelli, Liza
Mitchell, Ella
Modern Folk Quartet
Moon Loungers, The
Monopoly, Tony
Monro, Matt
Monroe, Gerry
Montenegro, Hugo
Montenegro, Neil
Moon, Keith
Moore, Misty
Moore, Pete Orchestra
Morgan, Lorrie
Morgon, Tim
Morse, Neil
Mottola, Tony
Munarheim
Munich Symphonic Sound
   Orchestra
Myles, Heather
Mystic Moods Orchestra, The

Na, Youn Sun
Nabors, Jim
Nail, David
NAS
Nascimento, Milton
Navarro, Ken
Neal Morse Band, The
Negro Problem, The
Neighborhood, The
Nelson, Jim
Nelson, Willie
Nergaard, Silje
Nero, Peter
New Apocalypse, The
Newman, Lee
Nicastro, Michelle
Nicoletta
Nilsson, Harry
Nocturnes, The
Noelia
Nolan, Mike
Norby, Cæcilie
Nova, Heather

O'Connor, Hazel
O'Day, Anita
Ohio State University Marching Band
Okkervil River
Old Friends
Oler, Newell
Olsen, Niels Noller
Olsson, Mats
Only Men Aloud
Optiganally Yours
Oranj Symphonette
Orchez, Tony
Oregon
Original Five
Originals
Oskar, Juan
Óskar, Páll og Casino

Ovenden, Julian Overstreet, Tommy

Page, Patti
Paige, Elaine
Pan-Pan Wen
Paris, Priscilla
Pastor, Guy and Company
Paul, Billy
Payne, Freda
Pearlfishers, The
Pelander, Bob
Pellow, Marti
Perfect View
Perjanik, Mike, Complex
Pia, Ulla
Picardy Singers, The
Pierce, Bobby
Piket, Roberta
Pipedreams
Pitre, Louise
Plastic Penny
Pop Zeus
Powell, Susan
Presley, Elvis (bootleg)
Presley, Reg
Price, Rick and Sheridan, Mike
Priscilla
Prodigy
Prysock, Arthur
Psychotica
Puthli, Asha

Queers, The
Queler, Liz and Farber, Seth

Radu, Dino & GSO
Rajput & The Sepoy Mutiny
Randolph, Boots
Randy
Rangel, Moses

Rankin, Kenny
Raye, Collin
Raymonde Singers Etcetera, The
Reed, Jerry & Chet Atkins
Reed, Les
Reese, Della
R.E.M.
Rene & Rene
Revelation
Revells, The
Reyburn, Julie
Rhoden, Pat
Rhodes, Red & The Detours
Ricciotti Ensemble
Rich, Lewis
Rihanna
Rivers, Johnny
Robbins, Rick
Roberts, Malcolm
Roberts, Sherri
Robinson, Smokey
Rockin' Berries, The
Ronnie Kole Trio
Rodriguez, Daniel
Rogers, Chet
Rogers, Julie
Rogers, Kenny
Romani, Graziano
Ronstadt, Linda
Ros, Edmundo and His Orchestra
Rose, Haroula
Rose, Kathryn
Rosmini, Dick
Ross, Andy Orchestra
Ross, Diana
Rossi, Juliano
Rowe, Bob
Rowles, John
Royal Philharmonic Orchestra
Roybal, Lenny
Ruffin, Jimmy

Rumer
Russell, Brenda and Howard Hewett
Russell, Gene
Ryan, Lloyd
Ryan, Saint John
Ryder, Freddie

Sam Houston State University Choir
Sammes, Mike Jazz Ensemble
   Singers
Sandoz Lime
Sarducci, Guido, Father
   (Don Novello)
Satton, Lon
Savalas, Telly
Sawyer, John
Scarbury, Joey
Scarlets, The
Schatz, Warren
Scheelings, Anita
Schofield, Pete and The Canadians
Scott, Parker
Scud Mountain Boys
Seeley, Jeannie
Serendipity
Serrie, John
Setrakian, Mary
Setti, Matteo
Sex In Public
Shank, Bud
Sharp, Brian
Shaw, Sandie
Shelley, Peter
Shepherd, James Versatile Brass
Sheri, Stephanie
Shiratori, Emiko
Shirley, Don
Shocked, Michelle
Shyette, Lowell
Simon, Carly
Simon, Joe

Simonal, Wilson
Simone, Nina
Simpson, R. D.
Sinatra, Frank
Sinatra, Nancy
Sinfonia '72
Singh, Judy
Sister Double Happiness
Sister Sister
Sitt, Sonny
Slater, Andrew
Slyke, Jim Van
Smith, Jason
Smith, Jimmy and The Trio
Smith, O. C.
Snarski, Rob
Snell, David
Soli Deo Gloria
Som Ambiente
Soulful Strings, The
Sounds Orchestral
Soupy Sales
South Notts Brass Band
Southern, Sheila
Southfield, Jim
Sparklehorse
Spartz, Doug
Speake, Jim
Spotnicks, The
Springfield, Dusty
Springfield Rifle
St. John, Barry
Stan & Doug
Stephenson, Tyler
Stevens, Connie
Stewart, Amii
Stitt, Sonny
Stone, Jonmark
Stone Temple Pilots with Glen
   Campbell
Straker, Peter

Strangers, The
Straw
Strawberry Children, The
Streisand, Barbra
Strollers, The
Stryker, Dave
Suite Steel
Summer, Donna
Youn Sun, Nah
Sunday's Child
Sunshine, Margot
Supremes, The
Surprise Package
Sweden
Swing Out Sister
Swing Wing
Syme, David

Tangent, The
Tapio, Kari
Tartaglia, John Andrews
Taylor, James
Tee, Willie
Templeton Twins, The
Temptations, The
These Animal Men
Thomas, B. J.
Three Degrees, The
Tinkerbells Fairydust
Toivonen, Jarkko
Tokyo's Coolest Combo
Toneff, Radka and Steve
  Dobrogosz
Tormé, Mel
Toto
Toussaint, Allen
Towers, Lee
Travellers, The
Trythall, Gil
Tucker, Tanya
Tura, Will

Turrentine, Stanley
Soli Deo Gloria
Tuxen, Nils
Tymes, The
Tyler, Bonnie

Uesugi, Akiko
Ukulele Orchestra of Great
  Britain
Ulvan, Therese
Underwood, Carrie
Unicorn
United States Air Force Band
Ünüvar, Atakan
UP (Film)
Upstarts, The
Urban, Keith
Urge Overkill

Vale, Jerry
Valentino, Sal
Valles, Norma
Van Dyke, Earl
Vanoni, Ornella
Vast Majority
Vaughn, Billy
Vee, Bobby
Velasquez, Regine
Ventures, The
Via Vegrandis
Villagers
Vocal Majority Chorus
Vogt, Susanne
Vogues, The
Vollmar
Vondráčková, Helena

Walden, Lois
Walkabouts, The
Walker, Scott
Waller, Gordon

Wanderley, Walter
Waples, Al and the Incredibles
Ward, Clifford T.
Ware, Terry
Warnes, Jennifer
Warren, Jennifer
Warwick, Dee Dee
Warwick, Dionne
Watts, Anne
Watts, Ernie Quartet
Wayland, Sean
Webb Brothers, The
Welsman, Carol
West, Paula
Westerberg, Paul
Weston, Kim
Weston, Glenn
White Buffalo, The
White, Bob
White Jr., Josh
White, Louisa Jane
White, Tony Joe
Whitman, Jerry
Whyton, Wally
Wienerschnitzel
Wilde, Marty
William & Michael

Williams, Andy
Williamson, Nicol
Wilmot, Gary
Wilson, Al
Wilson, Brian
Wilson, Cassandra
Wilson, Jim
Wilson, Nancy
Wilson, Rita
Windermere, John
Winter People (Film)
Wisner, Jimmy
Wisur, Vigdis
Wooden Wand
Woofers on Tour
Wopat, Tom
Wrecking Crew, The
Wressnig, Raphael
Wunderlich, Klaus
Wu-Tang Clan

Yankovic, Weird Al
Yoakam, Dwight
Young-Holt Unlimited
Yorkshire Imperial Metals

Zumpano

ARTISTS WHO HAVE RECORDED
"MACARTHUR PARK"
(Partial List)

Adams, Mark, 1977
Aki, Erkan, 2007
Allen, Rags, 2000
Amen, Corner, 1969
Anderson, Jim, 2007
Anthony, Richard, 1969
Ashton, Wyn,
Atlantic Bridge, 1970, 1999
Band of Her Majesty's Royal
    Marines, 2001
Banks, Cary C., 2009
Barron, Knights, 2010
Bassey, Shirley, 2014
Beatles, The, 2000
Bennett, Tony, 1970
Beveridge, Tim, 2002
Billingsley, Wayne, 1986
Boulevard Big Band, 2000
Brit Legn Cent Band
Bundeswehr, Die Big Band der
Burtons, The, 1979
Buy As You View Cory Band,
    2003, 2005
Callaway Liz, 2001, 2011
Camacho, Thelma, 1969
Campbell, Glen, 1986, 2001, 2007,
    2012
Carlton, Larry, 1996
Cheeze, 1991
Chicago Metropolitan Jazz
    Orchestra, 1998

Christie, Tony, 1975
Clayderman, Richard, 2002
Peter Collins with Style!, 1977
The Creator, 1997
Cruz, Edgar, 1995
Daly-Wilson Big Band, 1977
Davis, Larry, 2011
Ray Davies Brass, 1998
Davis, Rhett, 1975
Disco Fox Girls, 2005
Dominique, Miss, 2006
Ethereal Architect, 2012
Dave Evans Orchestra
Executives
Fender, Jack, 1979
Ferguson, Maynard, 1990, 2005
Mike Flowers Pops, 1995
Fountainhead, 1970
Four Guys
Four Preps, 1993
Four Tops, The, 1998, 2005, 2007,
    2008
Goober & the Peas, 1992
Greco, Buddy, 1974, 1995, 2007
Grimethorpe Colliery Band, 1989,
    1998, 2008
Haenning, Gitte, 1989
Harkness, Gordon, 1979
Harrington, 2000
Healey, Mikael, 2005
Herman, Woody, 1969, 1999

Hietanen, Pentti, 2009
Hopfenmusig, Die, 2015
Les Humphries Singers, 1975
Mike Hurst Orchestra, 1969
Innocence, 2007, 2008, 2009
Jacott, Ruth, 2012
Waylon Jennings and the
   Kimberlys, 1969
JJB Sports Leyland Band, 1999
Kenton, Stan, 1986
Kerr, Catherine, 2001
Koyanagi, Yuki, 2001
Kramer, Wayne, 1991
Kush, 2007
Københavns Politi Orkester, 1975
Lages, Eduardo, 2006
lang, k.d., 2000
Lass, Martin, 1997
Last, James, 1987, 2004
Byron Lee and the Dragonaires,
   1979
Ray Lefèvre & Orchestra
Lewis, Ramsey, 1968, 2002
Lindroth, Lloyd, 1991
London Pops Orchestra, 1997
Longthorne, Joe, 2001
Lowry, Ron, 2005
Magic Hands, 1996
Magic, 1977
Majestic Wind Ensemble, 1986
Maravella Orchestra, 1988
Marcovicci, Andrea, 2000
Mason & Dixon, 1970
McGovern, Maureen, 2008
McRae, Carmen, 1968
Meco, 2010
Merenbooty Girls, 1988
Merrill, Buddy, 1968
Michaels, Marilyn, 1968
Midler, Bette, 1997
Monopoly, Tony, 1976

Munich Symphonic Sound
   Orchestra, 2007
Neal Morse Band, 2015
Negro Problem, 1997
Nero, Peter, 1994
Nicoletta, 1968
Noelia, 2008
Ohio State University Marching
   Band, 1974
Only Men Aloud, 2008, 2010
Oskar, Juan, 2010
Pipedreams, 19??
Plastic Penny, 2003, 1967
Presley, Elvis, 1968
Prysock, Arthur, 1994
Psychotica, 1998
Queers, The, 1994
Dino Radu & GSO, 1995
Reed, Les, 1976
Reese, Della, 1997
Ricciotti Ensemble, 1991
Diana Ross & the Supremes,
   2008
Royal Philharmonic Orchestra,
   1993
Ryan, Lloyd, 1977
Sarducci, Father Guido, 1980
Sawyer, John, 2008
Sharp, Brian, 1986
Sam Houston State University Jazz
   Ensemble, 2012
South Notts Brass Band, 2006
Stephanie Sheri, 1992
Summer, Donna, 1978
Surprise Package, The, 1969
Sweden, 2004
Syme, David, 1995
Templeton Twins, 1970
Tomlin, Lily (as Tommy Velour),
   1982
Allen Toussaint Orchestra, 1988

Towers, Lee, 1987
Ukulele Orchestra of Great Britain,
The, 2004
Underwood, Carrie, 2005
Valesquez, Regine, 1999
Vocal Majority Chorus, 2003

Williams, Andy, 2017
Woofers on Tour, 2017
Wu-Tang Clan, 1999
Yankovic, Weird Al, 2003
Yorkshire Imperial Metals,
1999

Richard Harris, Karen Machon, and Jimmy Webb. *(Courtesy of Henry Diltz)*

JIMMY WEBB SONG LIST
(Partial List)

2001 and the Killing Ain't Done
A Chance to Be a Hero
A Good Thing for a Bad Man
A Series of Affairs
A Song for My Brother (aka "Wooden Planes")
A Song for the Open Road (aka "Chevrolet")
A Tramp Shining
Acting Alone
Adios
Adoration
Ain't No Romantic Song
Air Is Everywhere (aka "Cloud Man")
All I Know
All My Love's Laughter
All Night Show
Almost Alright Again
Almost Like Dying

Alyce Blue Gown

And If You Want

Angel Heart

Angel of Watergate

Anna

Another Good Woman Goes Down

Another Lullaby

Any Friend of Yours

As Long as Life Goes On (cowrote with son Christiaan Webb)

Asleep on the Winds (aka "Stay Alive")

Baby Come Back

Back to Love

Before There Could Be Me

Beth

Between West and Texas (cowrote with Joanna Jenet)

Between Your Heart and a Hard Place

Beyond Myself (aka "Feeling in the Air")

Bite Somebody's Neck

Black Rain

Block Party

Brand New Eyes

Breakwater Cat

Brown Clothes

By the Time I Get to Phoenix

Caga and Teeny (aka "Kaga and Teeny")

Calvary ("Galveston" with Alan Carlton)

Campo de Encino

Can't Get Back

Can You Die from a Broken Heart?

Careless Weed

Carpet Man

Catharsis (aka "Mr. Shuck 'N Jive")

Cheap Lovin'

Christiaan, No

Christmas Will Return

China (cowrote with Nikki Jean)

Class Clown

Cloudman (aka "Air Is Everywhere")

Clowns Exit Laughing

Come Back Half Way

Common Knowledge

Cottonwood Farm
Cowboy Hall of Fame
Crack Rain
("Crazy") Mixed-Up Girl (aka "Mixed-Up Guy")
Christmasey (cowrote with Brian Wilson)
Crying in My Sleep
Cuando Llegue a Mi Destino ("Phoenix")
Didn't We?
Do Me Like You Told Me
Do the Dirty
Do What You Gotta Do
Don't Settle for Less Than Love
Dorothy Chandler Blues (aka "Big Opening, Mr. Critic")
Dreams / Pax / Nepenthe
Driftwood
Dump Her
Early Morning Song
Earthbound (Prologue & Epilogue)
Easy for you to Say
Echo Mountain
Elvis and Me (aka "Overheard in a Bar")
End Title (Elvis theme)
E/R
Even Though I'm Small
Everybody Gets to Go to the Moon
Everytime We Touch
Evie
Exclusive Right to Hard Times
Fair Weather Lovers
Fame and Fortune in America
Fancy Ladies
Farther Than Eyes Can See
Feeling in the Air (aka "Beyond Myself")
Feet in the Sunshine
Fight for It
Film Noir (cowrote with Carly Simon)
First Hymn from Grand Terrace (Intro)
Five Thirty Plane (aka "5:30 Plane")
Flash of Fire (In a Young Girl's Eyes)
Flesh and Blood
Friends to Burn

Galveston
Gayla
Gettin' Ready Early
Girl's Song
Give Just a Little
Gloryell
Golden Girl
God's Gift
Goin' for It
Gone
Goodness Without Bitterness
Gotta Get out of L.A. (aka "Jerusalem")
Gray Skies Are Better Than Blue (Gray Skies Are Better Than Blue, When
    I'm Underneath Them with You)
Grow Young
Gypsy Moths
Halfway in the Middle
Hannah
Have Fun!
Hello, Dog
Here I Am
Here I'll Stand
Here's a Little Verse
Here's Four More
High Rent Ghetto
Highpockets
(The) Highwayman
Highway of Freedom
Him or Me
Himmler's Ring (aka "Hemler's Ring")
His World
(The) Hive
Hola Soleil (cowrote with Carly Simon)
Home of the Brave (cowrote with Paich, Lukather, Williams)
Honey Come Back
Hot Rod Queen
How Can You Do It, Baby?
How Quickly
Hurt Me Well
(The) Hymn from Grand Terrace
I Can Do It on My Own

I Can't Believe It

I Can't Get It

I Can't Leave You All Alone

I Can't Quit

I Did It All for You (aka "You Did It All For Me") (cowrote with Frank
   Wilson)

I Don't Love You

I Don't Need You

I Keep It Hid

I Keep On Keepin' On

I Liked It

I Married the World (cowrote with Gerry Beckley)

I Miss the Mistakes

I Need You

I See a Bridge

I Should Have Rehearsed

I Still Love You

I Think the Last One Was the One (cowrote with Johnny Rivers)

I Think We're Gonna Make It, Baby

I Understand

I Was Too Busy Loving You (aka "Slippin'`Away")

I Will Arise (Traditional)

I Won't Let You Girl

I'd Rather Be Feared

If I'd Been a Different Man

If Ships Were Made to Sail (aka "Space Hymn")

If These Walls Could Speak

If This Was the Last Song

If You Be Wise (cowrote with Kenny Loggins)

If You Don't Forget

If You Leave Me

If You Must Leave My Life

If You See Me Getting Smaller, I'm Leaving

I'll Be Back

I'll Be Back When the Winter's Gone

I'm a Gunner

I'm Clean, I'm Clean

I'm Gonna Be Free (aka "Once Before I Die")

I'm in Need

I'm Right Here Where You Left Me

In Cars

In My Dreams (cowrote with Peter Calo)
In My Wildest Dreams
In the Final Hours
(The) Interim
Is It All That Bright and Beautiful?
It Still Hurts
It Takes Two to Tango
It Was Love While It Lasted (cowrote with Keith Urban)
It Won't Bring Her Back
It Would Serve You Right
It's a Sin When You Love Somebody
It's Inside Me
It's Not a Bad Dream
It's Someone Else
Jet Lag Rag
John Dean, Angel of Watergate (aka "The Angel of Watergate")
Just a Little Ahead of Your Time
Just a Little While
Just a Moment (aka "Moment in a Shadow")
Just Another Piece of Paper
Just Excuse the Slip
Just Like Always
Just Like Marilyn
Just This One Time
Land's End
Laspitch
Lean On Me Always
Let's Begin
Let's Get This Show on the Road
Life Is Hard
Light Years
Lightning in a Bottle
Little Ol' House of Rock & Roll
Little Stone Angel
Little Tin Soldier
Livin' Doll
Long Lasting Love
Look at the Man You've Made
Lord, I'm Gonna Keep on Pushing Your Way
Lord, You Gave Me a Hard Row to Hoe
Lost Generation

Louisa Blu
Love Lasts Forever
Love Is Just a Meaningless Word (cowrote with Mike Post,
  Waite)
Love Now
Love Song
Love Years Coming
Lovers Such As I
Love's as Good as It Gets
Lucky Me
MacArthur Park
Mad About May
Make It Happen
Man Oh Man Mainliner
Marionette
Marsha Clark
Menage Ballet
Met Her on a Plane
Midnight Mail
Mirror Mind
Mixed-Up Guy (aka "('Crazy') Mixed-Up Girl")
More Than Enough
Moving On
My Christmas Tree
My Daddy Says
My Father Told Me
My Free Song
My Lucky Charm
My Opening Number
(The) Name of My Sorrow
Nasty Love
(I'm) Never Gonna Be the Same
Never Gonna Lose My Dream of Love Again
Never More
Never Say Die
Never Touched by the Fire
No Good Indian (aka "Willie Boy")
No Signs of Age
Nobody Likes to Hear a Rich Boy Sing the Blues
Nocturne for Piano and Orchestra (Nocturne for lefty)
O Cio Da Terra (cowrote with Milton Nacimento, Caetano Veloso)

Ocean in His Eyes
Odyssey Rock Park
Oklahoma Centennial Suite
Oklahoma Nights (cowrote with Vince Gill)
Oklahoma Rising
(The) Old Man at the Fair
Old Wing Mouth
Once and for All
Once Before I Die (aka "I'm Gonna Be Free")
Once in the Morning
One Cal, My Pal
One Lady
One Last Look Back
One of a Kind
One of the Nicer Things
One of These Nights
One Stands Here
Only a Woman in Love
Only in My Dreams
Orange Air
Orchid Lounge
Our Movie
Our Time Is Running Out
P. F. Sloan
Paper Chase
Paper Cup
Parenthesis
Passover Commercial
Pattern People
Patty
Paul Gauguin in the South Seas
Piano
Please Don't Turn the Lights Out
Plow This Ground
Pocketful of Keys
Port of Marseilles
Postcard from Paris (aka "Wish You Were Here")
Problem Child
Prologue and Epilogue (Have You Tried Love?) The Magic Garden
Psalm 150
Psalm for the Semi Living

Red Clay County Line
Remember How to Fly
Requiem: 820 Latham
Rider from Nowhere
Road Games
Romance of the Century
Rose
Rosecrans Boulevard
Run, Run, Run
Sandy Cove
Santa Fe
Save a Little Something for Joe
Sea Odyssey
Scissors Cut
Second Story Man
See You by the Seaside
See You Then
Severine
Shadows of Summer
Shall We Do a Little Business
Shanty Lace
Shattered
She Makes Me Cry
She Moved Through the Fair (Traditional)
She Never Smiles Anymore
Shepherd's Daughter
Shine It on Me (aka "You Might As Well Smile")
Sidewalk Song / 27th Street
Simile
Skycap
Skylark (cowrote with Paul Skylar)
Skywriter
Sleepin' in the Daytime
Slippin' Away (aka "I Was Too Busy Loving You")
Someone Else (1958)
Someone Is Standing Outside
Song Seller
Sonny's Money
Sooner Than You Think
Spanish Radio
Speaking with Your (My) Heart

Spending of the Green
St. Valentine's Day Rap
Stand Back
Stay Alive (aka "Asleep on the Winds")
Stephen, These Children Are Suffering
Stereo (cowrote with Gerry Beckley)
Still Within the Sound of My Voice
Strike Me Where I Stand
Sucre Noir
Sugarbird
Summer Will End
Summer's Daughter
Summer's Hand
Sunshower
Sweet Smiling Children
Sweetheart Banquet
Take It Easy
Take Marion For Example
Taxi Money (cowrote with Paul Simon)
Tennessee Woman
That World of Yours
That's All I've Got to Say
That's the Way It Was
The Best Man for the Job
The Coldest Night of the Year (aka "Incredible Phat")
The Eleventh Song
The Four Horsemen
The Girl Who Needs Me
The Great Wall
The Hideaway
The Lady Fits Her Blue Jeans
The Last Samba
The Lonely One
The Magic Garden
The Man in the Moon
The Moon Is a Harsh Mistress
The Natural Things
The President's Song
The Smartest Fool
The Summer Lovers
Then

There Ain't No Doubt
There He (She) Goes
This I Promise You
This Is Sarah's Song
This Is Where I Came In
This Is Your Life
This Kind of Love (with Peter Calo)
This One Face
This Time Last Summer
Through These Eyes ("Love Theme")
Through These Eyes ("Reprise")
Time Enough for Love
To Beg Me with Your Eyes
To Make It Easier on You
To the Ends of the Earth
Tomorrow Is Another Day
Too Young to Die
Tunesmith
Up, Up and Away
War Against Lovers
Wassail Song
Wasted Talent
Watermark
We're Ok, You're Ok
What a Nice Proper Tiny Little Life You Have Going
What Makes You So Special? (aka "Hero's Heart")
What Was That Song?
What's Wrong With You
Whatever Happened to Christmas?
When Can Brown Begin? (aka "Where Does Brown Begin?")
When Did I Lose Your Love?
When Eddie Comes Home
When I'm Dead
When It Was Done
When Love Has Gone
When This Moment Ends
Where Have You Been All My Life?
Where I Am Going
Where Love Resides
Where the Universes Are
Where Words End

Where's the Playground, Susie?
Which Way to Nowhere?
Whistletown
White Tigers
Who Under Heaven
Who Will Follow
Why Do I Have to Make You Say You Love Me
Wichita Lineman
Winners Tell Jokes and Losers Say "Deal"
Winter Clothes
Wishing Now
Wives
Wooden Planes (aka "A Song for My Brother")
Work for a Dollar
World Made of Windows
(The) Worst That Could Happen
(The) Yard Went on Forever
You Can't Blame a Man for Trying
You Can't Treat the Wrong Man Right
You Have Going
You Look Like a Winner
You Might as Well Smile (aka "Shine It on Me")
You'll Be Back, I Know It
You'll Just Have to do It
You're Leaving What You're Looking For
You're So Young

ANIMALS' CHRISTMAS, THE (Cantata, 1985)
Carol of the Birds (J.W. music)
Herod
Incredible Phat
Just a Simple Little Tune
The Annunciation
The Creatures of the Field
The Decree
The Friendly Beasts (J.W. music)
The Frog
The Song of the Camels (J.W. music)
Wild Geese
Words from An Old Spanish Carol (J.W. music)

BRONX TALE, A (Musical, 2000)
Belmont Avenue

CHILDREN'S CRUSADE, A (Musical, 1980)
Only One Life

CLEAN AND NARROW, THE (Film, 1999)
Right as Rain

DANCING GIRL (San Bernardino Valley College, 1965)
Dancing Girl
Didn't We?
Where's the Playground, Susie?

DANDELION WINE (Musical, 1981)
Alive, Alive, Oh!
Dandelion Wine
Gee, It's Gonna Be Lonely Without the Lonely One
Kangaroo Tennis Shoes
One and the Same
Simpatico
Statistics
Summer 1928, Begin!
The Happiness Machine
There's Something in This Summer
The Sad Machine
Time Flies
Time Traveler
The Thing at the Bottom of the Stairs
Whatta Ya Want for a Dime
You're Gonna Live Forever

DOC (Film, 1971)
Alhambra Mariachi
Interlude
Mariachi Waltz
The Whore and Cisco

E/R (TV, 1984–85)
I've Got a Real Emergency, Here ('Theme Song')
show no. 18, I Raise You

show no. 19, Merry Wives of Sheinfeld pt. 1
show no. 20, Merry Wives of Sheinfeld pt. 2
show no. 21, All Tied Up
show no. 22, A Change in Policy

FERNGULLY (Film, 1992)
A Dream Worth Keeping
I'm Back Medley: Humans Did It All / The Holocaust / Gather
    Everyone
Remember Everything
Spirit of the Trees
The Battle for Old High Rise
The Grotto Song
Genesis

FRENCH CONNECTION, THE (Film, 1971)
Everybody Gets to Go to the Moon

HANOI HILTON, THE (Film, 1987)
Hero's Heart (aka "What Makes You So Special?")
Dance of the Bamboos
Dance of the Bells
My Native Land
Let Us Sew Warm Clothes
When the Ta-Lu Sounds

HIS OWN DARK CITY (Musical, 1960s)
Sunshower
Highpockets
Laspitch

HOW SWEET IT IS! (Film, 1968)
How Sweet It Is!
Montage

INSTANT INTIMACY (Musical, 1992)
Boat People Are Beautiful
Close By ("Love Me, Love My Dog")
Defiance
I Don't Know How to Love You Anymore
Instant Intimacy

Is There Love After You?
It Only Takes One Guy to Tap
Other People's Lives
That's How a Lady Learns to Flirt
Two Women
Wasn't There a Moment?
What Does a Woman See in a Man
Yours for the Taking

LAST UNICORN, THE (Film, 1982)
In the Sea
Man's Road
Now That I'm a Woman
That's All I've Got to Say
The Last Unicorn

LOVE ME, LOVE MY DOG (Musical, 1990s)
Close By (A Duet)
Females
If You Love Me, Love My Dog
Just Us
Mrs. Metternick

LOVE STORY (Film, 1972)
Love Song
Once Before I Die

NAKED APE, THE (Film, 1972)
Fingerpainting (aka "Fingerpaint Me")
Jesus Loves Me
Saturday Suit
Survival Rag
The Elephant Hunt

PETER PAN (Film, 1969 / 70)

ROLLING STONE (TV Anniversary Special, 1977)
Main Theme

SANTA CLAUSE, THE (Film, 1994)
Christmas Will Return

SCANDAL (Musical, 1985)
An American Woman in Paris ("A Ballet Fantasy")
Claudia's Song "Broom Closet")
Chase and Crash
Dyke Fantasy
Eat Your Little Heart Out
Garage ("Car Horns")
Gershwin Ballet
Gotta Make This Flight
Masturbation Fantasy
Menage a Trois ("Second Ballet Fantasy")
Nice Little Piece
Opening Number ("Fire")
Orgy
She Just Lays There
Telephones
Overnight (Theme Song)
The Most Important Thing
They Just Don't Make 'Em Like You Anymore
Wedding

SEVEN BRIDES FOR SEVEN BROTHERS (TV, 1982)
Angelina's Chili
Baby's Breath
Deep Inside
For Sure, for Certain, Forever, for Always
Hannah
Hold On
If I Ever Get to Talk to You
I'm a Ramblin' Ranchin' Man
It's Not a Bad Dream
Let It All Out
Let's Get This Show on the Road
Long Gone Highway
Main Theme
Men, Men, Amen
Now That I Found You
Old Scarback
Saturday Night
Stomp and Holler (aka "My Brother's Keeper")
The Election Song

Theme
You Gotta Treat a Woman Like a Horse

SHANE THE MUSICAL (Musical, 2004)
The Ballad of Shane

TALES FROM THE CRYPT (TV, 1991)
TFTC: Loved to Death

TUXEDO (Musical, 1980s)
Because He's Free
Bend Your Backs
Event of the Season
Going Up to the Autumn Ball
House Without Love
Hurrah
Ice Covered Lake on a Snow Covered Christmas
It's Not What You Do, It's How You Do It
Lorillard's Four Point
Our Little Lady
Overnight Success
She Moves and Eyes Follow
Tarantella
The Old Tuxedo
The Roarin' Steins
These Are All Mine
Tuxedo

VOICES (Film, 1979)
Across the River (Inst.)
Disco If You Want to (Inst.)
Drunk as a Punk
Family Theme (Inst.)
I Will Always Wait for You (Theme from Voices) (Inst.)
Rosemarie and Drew (Inst.)
Rosemarie's Dance (Inst.) / I Will Always Wait for You (Reprise)
Rosemary's Theme (Inst.)
The Children's Song
The Children's Song (Inst.)
On a Stage

WILDFIRE (TV, 1986)
Wildfire

WINTER PEOPLE (Film, 1989)
Lightning in a Bottle

Self portrait of Jimmy Webb *(Courtesy of the author)*

ALBUMS

- *Words and Music* (1970)
- *And So: On* (1971)
- *Letters* (1972)
- *Land's End* (1974)
- *El Mirage* (1977)
- *Angel Heart* (1982)
- *Suspending Disbelief* (1993)
- *Ten Easy Pieces* (1996)
- *Twilight of the Renegades* (2005)
- *Live and at Large* (2007)
- *Just Across the River* (2010)
- *Still Within the Sound of My Voice* (2013)

COLLABORATIVE ALBUMS

- *Up, Up and Away* (1967) by The 5th Dimension
- *The Magic Garden* (1967) by The 5th Dimension
- *Rewind* (1967) by Johnny Rivers
- *A Tramp Shining* (1968) by Richard Harris
- *The Yard Went On Forever* (1968) by Richard Harris
- *Sunshower* (1969) by Thelma Houston
- *The Supremes (Produced and Arranged by Jimmy Webb)* (1972) by The Supremes
- *Reunion: The Songs of Jimmy Webb* (1974) by Glen Campbell
- *Earthbound* (1975) by The 5th Dimension
- *Live at the Royal Festival Hall* (1977) by Glen Campbell
- *Watermark* (1977) by Art Garfunkel
- *Breakwater Cat* (1980) by Thelma Houston
- *The Last Unicorn* (1982) by America
- *The Animals' Christmas* (1986) by Art Garfunkel and Amy Grant
- *Light Years* (1988) by Glen Campbell
- *Cry Like a Rainstorm, Howl Like the Wind* (1989) by Linda Ronstadt
- *Film Noir* (1997) by Carly Simon
- *Only One Life: The Songs of Jimmy Webb* (2003) by Michael Feinstein
- *This Kind of Love* (2008) by Carly Simon
- *Cottonwood Farm* (2009) by Jimmy Webb and The Webb Brothers
- *Glen Campbell and Jimmy Webb: In Session* (2012) by Glen Campbell and Jimmy Webb

COMPILATION ALBUMS

- *Tribute to Burt Bacharach and Jim Webb* (1972)
- *Archive* (1994)
- *And Someone Left the Cake Out in the Rain . . .* (1998)
- *Reunited with Jimmy Webb 1974–1988* (1999)
- *Tunesmith: The Songs of Jimmy Webb* (2003)
- *The Moon's a Harsh Mistress: Jimmy Webb in the Seventies* (2004)
- *Archive & Live* (2005)

SONGS ABOUT AND/OR MENTIONING JIMMY WEBB

"The Songs of Danny Galway"
By Prefab Sprout
Album: *Crimson/Red*

"Jimmy Webb Is God"
By Boo Radleys
Album: *Kingsize*

"Sometime Next Year"
By Clifford T. Ward
Album: *Sometime Next Year*

"Jimmy Webb"
By Paul Bevoir
Album: *Dumb Angel*

"1937 Pre-War Kimball"
By: Nanci Griffith
Album: *The Dust Bowl Symphony*

Jimmy Webb. *(Courtesy of the author)*

ACKNOWLEDGMENTS

I am very fortunate to have a team of music fans who know me better than I know myself. When the home team was stuck and couldn't find a date, or a place or a song or a photo—these music sleuths always came through. They were generous with their time, memorabilia, and Webb archives. Thank you to my unofficial archivist and leader of the fans Erik "the Dane" Christensen; thanks also to Jon Butcher, William O'Reilly, and Hyde Kirby.

You can count on family, and mine was so supportive during this process. My niece Kelly Kraemer was an undaunted researcher and proofreader. She kept me straight when my opinions were sounding too strong. When she left me to become a nurse, cousin Lisa Trainor stepped in and brought an organized calm to the long editing and submission process. My sister Janice Linnens combed through every box of photos and news clippings in her home. She recounted memories over the phone with me many, many times, as did my sister Suzan Webb and stepbrother Garth Sadler. Garth lived this story with me. As did Suzy Horton Ronstadt, who was utterly selfless with her memories, time, and scrapbooks.

Friends generously answered my questions, compared memories, and dug up old—and I mean old—photos including Nancy Sinatra, Johnny Rivers, Thelma Houston, Bill Medley, Fred and Patricia Tackett, Ray Rich, and Henry Diltz. Henry, I am grateful to you for documenting the lives of so many musicians and for your friendly support in the creation of this book.

There were readers along the way who offered their time and honest feedback: my mother-in-law Corinda Savini, librarian Lauraine (Laurie) Farr, the always enthusiastic Winston Simone, and dear friends who won't appear until "book two"—Linda Ronstadt and Michael Feinstein.

Dr. Richard Zenn mystically dropped into my life at the beginning of the writing process and coached me through. When I wavered, he kept the helm in the wind and the sails close hauled. And just as quickly as he entered my life, when the writing was done, he was gone.

The team that gave me the opportunity to write this book—Winston Simone and David Simone, David Vigliano, and she-of-the-velvet-hammer, my editor Elizabeth Beier at St. Martins Press—you each applauded, pushed, prompted, or made calls with spot-on timing.

When the thought of losing half of my stories became too subjective and emotional for Laura and me, Thomas Flannery, Jr., took on that thankless task with tremendous respect and dedication to preserving the feel and flow of the book. Thank you, Tom.

Behind every leap of faith there is a guardian angel and tireless engine of humanity who struggles with every crisis, large and small. Without my fair and gracious wife Laura Savini, these recollections could easily have been cast to the winds. She was the engine and the angel.